Don't Sleep With a Bubba

Also by Susan Reinhardt:

NOT TONIGHT, HONEY:
Wait 'Til I'm a Size 6

Don't Sleep With a Bubba

Unless Your Eggs Are in Wheelchairs

Susan Reinhardt

KENSINGTON BOOKS
http://www.kensingtonbooks.com

KENSINGTON BOOKS are published by

Kensington Publishing Corp.
850 Third Avenue
New York, NY 10022

ISBN-13: 978-0-7582-1708-0
ISBN-10: 0-7582-1708-0

First Kensington Trade Paperback Printing: May 2007
10 9 8 7 6 5 4 3 2 1

Printed in the United States of America

For my family.
No one could ask for more
humor, love and understanding.

Acknowledgments

Nothing would be possible without the help and love of friends and family, as well as my talented agent, Ethan Ellenberg, and the fantastic staff at Kensington.

I'd also like to thank all the writers who supported my work, generously offering to read the manuscript, as well as friends and family who served as early readers.

Special thanks to the Read It or Not: Here We Come Book Club, and all the humor the women in the club provide.

As always, my beloved children bring me the gifts of love, expansion of heart, world, and mind. Nothing is possible without them.

Author's Note

For the record, I once loved a Bubba. A man whose real name I don't know to this day. He was charming, handsome, funny, and had great teeth and a laugh that still rings in my ears and heart. He did not fit the stereotypical Southern-boy Bubba who awakens drunk, terrorizes cats, gets mean on liquor, chews, spits, totes a gun and drives a Ford F-150.

Well, he did have a truck. But that's about all.

When I say, "Don't sleep with a Bubba." I'm referring to men who are bumpkins with bad attitudes. It's nothing against the name, which Mama says is a nickname for "brother."

But we all know that Bubbas, while they can fix things and drink a case of rotgut beer without throwing up, just aren't . . . well . . . marriage material.

And if you sleep with one, and he's good (if sober, chances are he will be), you may get all mixed up emotionally, as women are prone to do, and actually think you love him and end up marrying him.

As for all of you who've married Bubbas and are happy, I'm delighted.

Maybe if my own Bubba hadn't dumped me after the first date, the book would have a different title. Then again, maybe not.

In the words of my wise neighbor, who's African American and a doctor at the Veteran's Administration Medical Center, "Bubbas need love, too."

Richmond, Tee-tee,
and a Can of Lysol and Hollywood

Virginia is for Lovers . . . and fools like me.

My very first national book came out a couple of springs back, and I was to fly to Richmond, Virginia, to promote it, staying at the ultrafancy Jefferson Hotel, a five-star place nothing like the Econo Lodges I have always found pleasant enough or the Motel 6 where I'm almost certain my son was conceived, bless his heart.

Days prior to my departure, I read up on how to give the perfect book signing. When you're new at this type of thing, you want to make sure everything's perfect. This is your chance, your one shot at the big leagues, and if the author of *How to Climb the Bestseller Ladder: The Secret Is Grooming and Hygiene* tells you to chew 60 Tic Tacs before opening your mouth, well then, you'd better damn well do it. If they say body odor will send potential customers flying out the doors, then, by God, you wear out a stick of Secret Solid. Whatever you do, the author warns in giant letters: DON'T BURP OR FART. Well, okay, she says, "DON'T ALLOW BODILY EMISSIONS TO HAVE FREE REIN."

I had a friend who swears on a stack of Bibles she was at her favorite author's signing and the writer continued, quite unabashedly, to fart herself into a cloud of sulfur, sending customers fleeing for the door.

For this first book-signing adventure, I packed two sticks of deodorant, half a dozen boxes of Altoids, those "curiously" strong mints that could kill small animals, and lots of perfumes and lotions. I was going to smell so good, for heaven's sake, that everyone would want my book.

First, though, I had to prepare mentally, remembering the few grouchy-faced people during my public talks over the years, to discuss life as a columnist. I also knew that a tour in various cities, which included air travel or being in the car with Mama, would require medication or else . . . Well, it'd be ER time. I would hit the floor, crack open my skull and never again write another book.

I rushed to the doctor, in need of something to calm my nerves. "They can be so mean, a few of them," I explained as I beseeched the old doc wearing his white coat and stern expression. "The rest are wonderful. You know how it is giving speeches. You try to pretend they're naked and then you wonder how big their willies are and all of a sudden you're getting hot in the face and the old heart does the long jump from its anchored position and death is imminent. It's not easy, so please help me."

He exhaled with that "Oh, no, not another premenopausal, crazy-ass woman," kind of sigh.

"Have you tried therapy?"

"I'm 40-some-odd years old, Doctor. Don't you think I've been in therapy before? Listen, I've got to go on about sixty radio shows in one month because publishers don't have the money to put unknown authors up in fancy hotels but once or twice or pay for national tours. I have to talk live on the air. I have to drive and deliver funny speeches even when I have PMS and Mama wants to come along. You don't understand. She hoops and yells and bangs on the dashboard, thinking my every vehicular move is going to end in death."

He raised his brows and clicked on his computer. I liked it better when docs didn't have computers. I knew what he was typing: *neurotic woman in need of behavioral therapy.*

"What are you wanting?" he asked, smirking.

"Drugs," I said. "Nerve pills. I have a . . . well . . . a heart condition. Just ask the Rotarians. I once passed out and—"

"Heart condition, you say?"

Click, click, clickety-clack. I'm sure he typed in, *Woman is probably wanting Percocet and making all this book shit up. Maybe she's going to cook up some meth in her doublewide. Note to self: do a police background check.*

"Have you tried any of the antidepressants?" he asked.

"All of them."

Peck, peck, tappety-tap. *Woman is candidate for thirty to ninety days in the ward.*

"Look, I wanted to be a writer so I wouldn't have to face the public. In my job, you just sit down, eat a bunch of junk food and type. You don't have to be witty or answer fastballs those morning hosts hurl. You wouldn't believe what happened on this one show that goes to 450 stations across the country."

He attempted a strained grin and squirted antibacterial foam on his hands. I guess he thought I might not only be crazy but infected with tetanus, too.

"I'm on the air, and it's like, 4 AM Eastern time, and this woman gets on with me and starts talking about . . . about . . . Please, Dr. Popper (yes, his real name, poor man), I need some medicine. I'm having palpitations. I can't do this. You don't understand. I passed out once talking to the Lions or Rotarians, I forget which, maybe both, and had to lie down like a dead bug."

Tap, tap, tappety-tap. *Refer woman to mental health facility ASAP.*

He quit typing and faced me with eyes the color of nails. "What happened on the radio?"

I decided to go ahead and tell him so I could get medicine in case of future shocks that could cause a gal's heart to go into a series of preventricular contractions Oprah says could very well be caused from hormones and perimenopause. You gotta believe Oprah.

"Well, I had all my notes spread out on the bed. See, you can do most radio interviews in your pajamas and have bad breath and no one knows, which is great. You don't even have to brush your hair or teeth. But this woman, she . . . she . . . Well, she decided to ask what I thought about the latest in plastic surgery."

"And why's that so bad?"

"She was referring to the beautification of one's . . . you know . . ."

"No, I don't know."

"The . . . well . . . you see . . . umm. Privates. I couldn't do a thing on the show after she said that but hack like a cat with a fur ball. Please, help me."

"What kind of beautification of the privates?" he asked.

Damn Dr. Popper, the Perv.

I decided to shock him. "Anus bleaching. Labia reductions. Possum perfecting. That type thing."

A genuine, though faint smile was forming across his face as he typed in a prescription and told me to come back when May was over. I'm sure by then, he'll have a commitment order for a mandatory stay at the Haven for Mentally Exhausted and Completely Insane Working Moms.

Once I got to Richmond, I began enjoying a few perks of being in a five-star hotel, such things as being called Mrs. Reinhardt as if I was someone special and a driver to cart my fat ass around any time I wanted, plus luxurious sheets with a 5,000 thread count when mine at home were 250 polyester Wamsutta specials.

The woman who'd interviewed me for an online magazine, Libby McNamee, was a doll and fetched me for the signing at Fountain Bookstore in historic downtown Richmond. First, we went to eat Mexican and I was happy I had brought all those Altoids. I went to the restroom and forgot to squat over the toilet but sat smack down on the lid, right into a lake full of piss.

My legs and thighs dripped with someone else's pee-pee and there wasn't a single sheet of toilet tissue in the joint. I started shaking and shimmying like Shakira, that pop star, and had no choice but to hoist up my fine slacks and hope for the best.

By the time we got to the bookstore, I was sweating, and remembered I'd forgotten to put on deodorant. And then the most unmistakable stench rose up I'd ever smelled: tee-tee. Old lady, old man, nursing home, wet baby-diaper PISS. I smelled like the forgotten bedpan. To top it off, my armpits reeked like a basketball player's after two overtimes and my breath was like an old garbage can's. Where was my perfume? Where were the breath mints? Help. Help! I dug and dug in my purse since I suffer from PDD—Purse Digging Disorder—of which there is no known cure.

I had, in my panic to speak in a town where I knew no one but an old boyfriend who had dumped me in college, forgotten Rule Number One in *How to Climb the Bestseller Ladder: The Secret Is Grooming and Hygiene.* I looked around the little bookstore bathroom in search of anything that would make me smell more human and less roadkillish.

In a box in the corner was a spray bottle of Glade and on the counter a can of Lysol. I pulled down my damp pants and undies and sprayed my ass with the stuff, all but yelping the burning was so intense. For good measure, I grabbed the Lysol and used it as deodorant. As for my oniony breath, I squirted Dial antibacterial soap on my tongue and had a flashback to being 6 years old and Mama catching me saying, "Shit, shit, shit" while putting on a pair of socks, then getting out the soap to teach me a lesson.

When it came my time to speak, this first-ever book tour talk in front of a live audience, complete with a radio crew from Public Radio South recording it for stations all over Dixie, I was ready. It didn't matter that people were coughing and wrinkling their noses, plenty of them sneezing and wondering why the room smelled like a nursing home disguised in every spray available.

Poor sweet Libby. After the reading and speech, she told me how swell I did.

"People really seemed to respond," she said. "They were on the edges of their seats sniffing all around like dogs."

"It's my Glade and Lysol perfume," I said. "Would you happen to have a piece of gum? I swallowed some orange Dial and—"

The owner of the bookstore, a sweet woman, came toward me with a gift bag. Inside was a bottle of K-Y Warming Liquid. Jeez. Not only do I smell like a nursing home, she must think my va-gee-gee is as dry as an 80-year-old woman's.

It was the new "warming" kind, too. What a doll. Whew. Glad that one was over. I just wonder why they never aired my talk on the radio, but I think I have a good idea.

Atlanta and the Dumpster

Next big stop: Atlanta, Georgia, with my mama, Lord have mercy. This was where I'd attended college and was booted from my sorority for being so danged wild and nonconforming. I knew all those Tri-Delts would come to my alumni signing to see how fat and ugly I'd gotten while they'd whittled off the college and postpartum fat with Atkins, lipo, tummy tucks paid for by their doctor, banker, tycoon husbands.

Sugar pies, I was right. There they were. Skinny, rich and adorable Atlanta women and I was in a chunky stage with lots of hanging arm fat.

It all started because my last book gig ran up a big ticket, so the publisher gently suggested I might want to pay for this Atlanta University of Georgia Alumni appearance out of pocket and stick it to Uncle Sam next April.

Mama and I were pinching pennies and eating KitKats, her favorite candy bar that she takes everywhere, even to church and funerals. The hotels in Buckhead, Atlanta's ritziest section where I was to speak in a big, fancy tower, were priced in the triple digits and the traffic a nightmare. We tried one hotel, then another, and weren't about to pay $300 for seven hours' sleep, a few tubs of cereal, a pot of weak coffee and turn-down bed service with a single square of chocolate. We could do our own bed turning and stick a giant KitKat on the pillow.

We whipped the car around and decided to try some hotels

along Buckhead's outer edges. Things are always cheaper on the perimeters. "Let's try that place," I said, steering into a darling stucco-style hotel that is part of a huge chain of affordability, comfort and great reputation.

We figured this place would provide shampoo and a hair dryer in the bathroom, a pot of coffee and a continental breakfast in the morning. Instead, we walked directly into a lobby and nearly fainted, inhaling that unmistakable odor of vomit and tee-tee. Croaker's Rest Home smelled better than this.

Mama, eyes like a lizard's, rotating and rolling around and surveying the stinky lobby, reluctantly handed over her Visa and vital information and took a rusting key from the manager.

A bad vibe encircled us, floating over our heads, entering our bloodstreams and causing our poor hearts to pump and palms to sweat. Men began appearing from nowhere, as if they walked like ugly, whiskery Caspers through the walls. I am talking about mean, unkempt, festering men. I decided to tell a lie so we wouldn't be robbed, shot or raped in the middle of the night.

"We're only going to be here two hours," I said, so the old goats wouldn't break into our room and kill us as we slept. The clerk raised his eyebrows, and winked knowingly. Why is he winking that way? I wondered.

He gave us the key to the back of the building where all these burned-up and rusted cars were parked. Every vehicle appeared to have been pulled from flames or a junkyard. We opened the hotel door and, lo and behold, the beds weren't made and lady-of-the-evening paraphernalia was strewn everywhere. Six suitcases lay open, and spent condoms littered the filthy carpet while empty cans of Colt 45s and cigarette butts weighted the fake-wood furniture. There wasn't a soul in sight.

Mama screamed as if someone had stabbed her. Her eyes popped and I saw more white than I knew was humanly possible, while her jaw fell to her collarbone.

"We may not be rich, but this is NOT us. Run! We are hightailing it out of here."

We all but sprinted to the lobby, fumes of that drug- and sex-drenched room still in our noses and clinging to our skin. At the front desk, I was gleefully telling the management we weren't about to stay in such filth, but, "Thanks for your kindness, and we are sure you spread out a great continental breakfast all the same."

Mama whispered in my ear. "The only thing spread out here is legs," and I just prayed no one heard her.

While chatting with staff and his various staph infections, I was trying to get our hot Visa out of his eager hands when Mama snatched the card and dragged me by the forearm and pushed my fanny toward the car. We flew so fast out of the lobby our suitcase wheels sparked as they hit the asphalt.

"They think we're prostitutes," she said, locking the car with the click of a button and a huge sigh, deciding she'd drive this time. "This is what's known as a Hooker Hotel. We just didn't know it because we aren't locals." She stared at me, then fell over laughing, as she is prone to do.

"They think *what*? Did you say *hookers*?" We were both wearing normal, nonhoochie-mama clothing and looked like Sunday School teachers.

"Susan, didn't you see all those men flocking around while we were checking in and asking us where we had dinner appointments? Those were the old geezer johns the hotel sent our way."

I thought about this and realized that, Lawd have mercy, my mama was right: we were presumed to be hos.

"They think we're a kinky mama-daughter act," she said, burning rubber and squealing from the hotel on two wheels. She pulled off the main road a few blocks later and made an announcement. "This is where we'll get ready for your big event." She cut the ignition and I realized we were in one of Buckhead's finest alleys and parked right next to a green Dumpster.

"There's a lot of five o'clock traffic and plenty of people will probably see us, but that is better than the alternative, right?" she asked, unwrapping a KitKat and telling me to go first while she would be the Look-Out person and warn me when to cover up any naughty bits.

Let me tell you, there's something about being buck-naked in Buckhead that is almost as frightening as entering a Hooker Hotel. I stood scared to death, bare-assed and trying to squeeze my front and back fannies into a girdle no bigger than a tube sock while Mama hollered that a BMW full of men in business suits was coming our way.

"HIDE!!!!" she yelled hysterically.

"I can't."

"Open that trash can door and jump in. It's better than them seeing your possum, isn't it?" This was her pet name for vagina. More on that later.

Well, no, it wasn't. I could not face those Tri-Delts if I was both FAT and smelling like two weeks of rotting garbage.

Sometimes, it's best to be naked in broad daylight behind a Dumpster than in a hotel where the geezers assumed we were hookers.

Sometimes, life offers us only two choices. And we'd made ours. This time, I had perfume and Altoids, plus a stick of Secret Solid.

Hollywood and the Mee-Maw Panties

This is not happening. It's not. Really, it can't be.

Oh, no, no, no. I think it is true. I've gone through the scenario dozens of times, and there's no getting around it.

The ONLY pair of Mee-Maw drawers I own—and I borrowed these from Mama—are missing. I'm talking about the world's ugliest and most gigantic pair of once-white, now-gray, great-granny panties are AWOL, which also stands for Absolutely Wickedly Offensive Ladieswear.

Yes, gone. I should NEVER have packed them. This isn't the type of undergarment a dignified though cracked Southern Belle takes on her first trip to Los Angeles to try and impress the VIPs at HBO headquarters in Santa Monica, now is it?

Of course, my only pair of Mee-Maw knickers have long been known to bring nice, smooth lines to the tight fit of a certain pair of khaki pants. And so this is what won the atrocity a spot in my suitcase.

Since my mother is not fond of Mee-Maw panties, I'm wondering how she came to own them in the first place. Maybe, she, too, had an outfit that would work only if such a hideous undergarment was worn to give the body a natural, I'm-not-wearing-a-thong shape. I'm guessing the drawers must have come from my great-great-grandmother who, at 94 was caught in bed with a 32-year-old traveling salesman who didn't seem to mind such britches.

If I wanted to wear the super-snug khaki capris, there was no other choice but the elephantine underwear the size of a nightstand, no elastic left worth mentioning.

This was LA, Bel Air, Beverly Hills, Sherman Oaks, and I was the Hick in the City and on my way to *Sex in the City* headquarters and didn't want panty lines showing. The Mee-Maw drawers were my salvation. They seemed to slenderize, chewing off chunks of upper thigh and disguising inner legs intent on greeting each other in a chafing hello.

The ten square yards of panty were great. They gave me confidence, along with my Prada shoes bought on eBay. I even waved to Olympia Dukakis, feeling the swish of voluminous nylon as I moved across Santa Monica Boulevard on my way to convince HBO to pick up the TV show my friend Robert Tate Miller, a hugely talented screenwriter, and I had worked up from material in my first book.

Someone, I don't remember who it was over there, liked the book so much they called for a meeting. I flew out first chance I could get and sat on the plane next to a woman coughing up damaged lung chunks and sounding as if she had TB. It was my thirty-six hours of Almost Fame.

HBO headquarters was like stepping into an even more modern version of the Jetsons, with space-age furnishings and electrifying color everywhere. I couldn't exactly tell the chairs from the tables and sofas. I'm almost positive, looking back, that I sat on a fuzzy hot pink watercooler by mistake.

After a thirty-minute wait, in which I nearly died of six heart attacks, Rob and I cruised with pretend calmness into the offices of two vice presidents young enough to be our children. They gave us Fiji water and fifteen minutes of their valuable time. I got all nervous and couldn't shut up, but Rob called his agent afterward and said, "It went great. Couldn't have gone better. It's a good thing Susan flew up for this because a phone conference wouldn't have worked nearly as well as them meeting her in person."

Two weeks later we heard the news from Rob's agent.

"They loved your TV treatment and thought Susan was fun and entertaining, but overall felt there wasn't enough sex in the story lines."

Oh, my mother would be so proud.

After less than two days in California, it was time to pack everything up and head back home. My thirty-six-hour trip to LA. Gone in a sneeze.

To think I was a guest in a fairly famous screenwriter's home—a beautiful semipalace with its own basketball court and swimming pool right outside my bedroom window. To think I cleaned every speck of dirt from that room and properly made the bed before I left, extra careful I'd left nothing behind except a KitKat on their pillow, the toilet tissue pressed into a beautiful triangle at the tip.

To think I'd done everything right and then . . . then . . . Oh, no, please let it not be so!

Almost as soon as I returned from my quick little mission, I felt something punch my stomach. I couldn't breathe. No. No. Please, God. I searched the suitcase a hundred times. The Mee-Maw panties had gone missing. I'd better call Nancy Grace. She'd understand. She'd do a segment for six weeks. I know she would. God love her and the time she takes with missing people and maybe even Amber Alerts for lost undergarments.

OK, don't panic. Think, think, think.

Think "spin." Write the hostess a letter. It doesn't matter she's perfect and rich and wears Dolce & Gabbana intimates. Deep breaths. Pen and paper. Good, thick paper, not the cheap kind from the Dollar Mart.

Dear Robert and Lady Tate Miller

I must thank you so much for the warmth extended during my brief visit to your lovely city. The guest quarters were more than any weary traveler could ever hope to enjoy. I thank you for the pleasure of staying in your inviting and tastefully ex-

quisite home and the charming company offered. Please know you are welcome in western North Carolina anytime.

Again, many thanks,

Susan Reinhardt

P.S. I imagine this may sound odd, but as I placed my suitcase under the bed, I did notice a rather large nylon garment somewhat the size of a tablecloth, bunched about near the headboard. I figured it was part of your delightful Great Dane's bedding and left it alone. Again, you guys were the best!

Erma Bombeck Country

I called the airport to confirm the ticket for a flight to Dayton, Ohio, leaving Asheville on a chilly March afternoon. The man on the other line couldn't understand a word I was saying, nor could I figure out most of his native tongue.

OK, for the record, no one swoons over an accent the way I do. For some women, it's men in uniform; for me it's an accent. I don't care if it's drawling Southern, Australian, Jamaican or Brazilian. Talk to me all day, honey pie. That is, unless I'm trying to get my plane ticket confirmed and figure out a friggin' way to get a unicycle on a small Delta carrier.

The gig I was headed for I was afraid I wasn't qualified to handle. Somehow, through too much wine and a crowd of rowdies, I ended up becoming one of the keynote speakers for the semiannual Erma Bombeck National Writers Workshop in Dayton and was leaving on a jet plane, though the ticket man couldn't understand my Southern and I couldn't understand his Burmese.

For those who never knew and loved Erma, she was quite simply the best—my personal columnist hero. Every two years in her city of Dayton, the Writers Workshop bearing her name has a three-day hoopla of activities, sessions and keynote speakers attended by hundreds worldwide.

Dave Barry—The Dave Barry—was to be one of the keynotes. And I somehow got roped into "following" his act the next day. He gets the nighttime tipsy crowd. I get the hung-over or tea-totaling lunchers. How does ANYONE follow a great like Dave Barry?

I knew I couldn't repeat my Malaprop's Bookstore wine-infused performance. My body tolerates alcohol about as well as a vegetarian can swallow a Hardee's Angus Thickburger. A couple guys from the paper were filming my wild, tipsy speech, and I sent in the tapes and was hired.

Oh, my gosh. Here I am headed for the airport and will have to follow Dave's act as well as that of a big-shot columnist at *USA Today*: Craig Wilson.

I was thinking, "How does a girl top Dave Barry?" Well, she doesn't. Then I remembered my unicycle and figured he could-n't ride one while throwing candy and condoms to the crowd.

This is the point at which I called the airline's 1-800 number and I tried for half an hour to converse with the representative of unknown cultural origin.

"May I take a unicycle on the airplane?" I asked, trying to speak slowly, knowing my hick vowels would throw him for a loop.

"Yu wunt do dake whut?"

"Do you know what a unicycle is?"

"No, ma'am. I do not know such wud be called dat."

I thought a moment. "Do you know what a clown is?"

"Shu I do."

"Clowns ride YOON EEE CYCLES. Day have ONE WHEEL."

"I see. Vedy gud."

He put me on hold for twenty-two minutes while I passed the time eating an entire bag of Extra Cheesy Doritos, and re-turned to say I could pack my one wheel and head on to Day-ton.

"Yu gong haff to take off de pedals fust."

"What? How do you take off the pedals?"

He grew silent, processing my Southern language and ques-tion. "I know nutting bout dat. You also gong put yoon-e-cycle in box no bigger dan twenty von by thutie tree."

I politely thanked him and decided I'd let Dave Barry rule the show. After all, he's earned it. I'll just stalk him instead of trying to top him.

My plane, minus the unicycle, arrived late, but I managed to sit in the fancy black car in the exact spot Barry's slender and probably firm ass had sat. I figured that's as close to the man as I'd ever get. I told the driver to "Please hurry," and was able to catch the last half of his act and, boy . . . was he good. No, he was great.

Naturally, I put him on my Stalking List. But so did five hundred others at the conference, so the line to get to him during his book signing was a mile long. I waited, mingling with other writers and then held out my book to him. I had bought *Boogers Are My Beat*, thinking that would be right up my entertainment alley. He must have been exhausted, but he was more than gracious and smelled like Tic Tacs and good cologne, and I just knew he'd read *How to Climb the Bestseller Ladder: The Secret Is Grooming and Hygiene*.

After he signed my copy, pretending to have actually heard of me, I rushed up to my room, excited about what he must have written with his hot little pen. Perhaps it was, "Loved your first book!" Or maybe, "Ditch Tidy Stu and Run Away With Me."

I locked my door and took a deep breath. And there it was. "To Susan Reinhardt: A Goddess. Dave Barry."

Oh, mercy saints alive! Is this REALLY what he wrote? That night I went to sleep happy and dreaming of my future as his replacement, just as other humor columnists have held that very same and impossible dream.

The next day there was quite the commotion during one of the sessions. Women everywhere were talking about what Barry had written in their books. This is when my enormous balloon popped.

"He said I was a goddess," one woman shouted in euphoria. "Me, too . . . me, too . . . me, too," fifty more squealed.

That ended my stalking of Dave Barry.

Later that evening, however, the Bombecks arrived. As in Erma Bombeck's family. I'm crazy about Erma. The conference was premiering a public television documentary about her life, and the entire family was seated onstage for the five hundred of us to gawk at and perhaps question after the film.

First, I'd like to say that her children, Betsy, Andrew and Matthew, are precious and not a bit snooty, nor is her husband, Bill, a kind and quiet man. They stuck around for most of the conference.

On Saturday, Tim Bete, who is supersane and calm and in charge of everything and who did a splendid job, informed me that since I was the lunch keynote I'd be sitting with the Bombeck family. Had he told me that before he hired me, I'd have NEVER had the nerve to do this gig but would be in a ditch somewhere drinking Mad Dog and foaming at the mouth and nostrils.

After recovering from a heart attack the moment his words were out, I excused myself to the ladies' room to either die or pray. I fell on my knees, not caring that a woman muffled a scream when she saw this.

"Dear God," I prayed aloud, but not too loud. "Don't let me mess this up. I'll cut my sin count in half. I'll give more to the poor. I won't complain about having four breasts when some poor women have none. But please, just this once, let things go well, and I won't bug you about personal favors such as less cellulite or an end to bloating. At least not for an entire week will you hear that selfish stuff from me. Amen."

I have to say it couldn't have gone better, save for the statue of Mary covering her ears and blushing when I told the crowd about my friend Brewster's near fatal crotch amputation. Only one lady folded her arms and gave me that mean, "I hate you and plan to kill you" stare. No one threw things or booed.

But I did throw things at them. I had some hot-pink tape measures as a promotional item and hit an attendee so hard in the face she may need a glass eye. I told her how sorry I was and gave her a free book.

My new friend Laverne, who writes funny senior citizen columns, said, "Whine, whine, whine. It's not like she doesn't have an extra eye." God, I love Laverne.

The highlight of the event was when Betsy Bombeck, a fun-loving woman, bought two of my books. In fact, that was the highlight of the entire year promoting this first book.

I guess she bought them because I didn't take out her left eye.

She's smart enough to realize they come in pairs.

Four Teats to the Wind

Here's the problem: I have four tits.

Five if you count the time I had a zit the size of a golf ball on the right boob. If not, then four, just like a cow. Mooooo. Though my father said cows will often have an underdeveloped hind teat or, if you want to get techy, a supernumerary and nonfunctioning hint of a teat.

It didn't used to be that way. After suckling two pigs (children of my own), I was a normal, though quite saggy, regular-breasted mother of two. Those who read my first book know I broke down and purchased myself a set of fake knockers. It was a procedure my husband said was for bimbos and redneck women, so I'm not sure in which category I fit, but I threw him right into the asshole category for even saying such a thing. You can bet he didn't get to see them for quite a long spell.

All I know is that I was glad (at first) I got the old floppers lifted, stuffed, tucked and upgraded. It meant no more trips to Home Depot for duct tape every time I wore a swimsuit.

What was even more frightening than securing the Lost Girls, a pet name for the old pair (since I used to have to fetch them from various locations), was the areola spreading like Oscar Mayer bologna. A lot of people don't know the difference, especially men, between a nipple and an areola. I didn't until I gave birth.

A big sweet nurse came in and said, "You got to put the are-

ola in that child's mouth or his ass gone be starvin' to death."
She was white but had a hip-hop accent and two gold teeth,
one formed with a cutout star.

"It's in there. See? There's my nipple in the baby's mouth."

She reared back her head, those teeth blinding with a setting sun. "Girl, that's yo nipple? That tiny, chewed-off piece a
skin? Can't no baby get a drop of milk lest you stick the whole
wad up in their mouths. With a nipple that size, yo baby's
lucky to get his tongue wet, much less a meal. You need to stuff
the areola up in there wid it."

Nipples. Areolas. I figured it was your basic nipple unit, an
all-in-one package. The nurse bent in for a closer inspection of
my feeding units.

"Yo sweet, sore ass may not have a decent nipple, but, whoa,
check out dem areolas!"

"What?" I stared down at my achingly full, sagging boo-
bies.

"Honey, they big as flapjacks. They looked like satellite
dishes wide enough to pick up the Al Jazeera Network."

And this is exactly why, upon learning I had this problem, I
paid my handsome surgeon an extra thousand bucks to take
my Oscar Mayer–sized discs and snip them around the edges
as one might a Simplicity pattern until they were the perky
size of a cheerleader's, preferably a cheerleader who hadn't
given birth.

My husband was livid upon seeing my itty-bitty areolas,
wanting his satellite dishes back. But I had made a choice, paid
for it and insured the suckers for the next ten years. It wasn't as
if I was planning to get a job as middle-aged stripper at the
local VFW or Croaker's Rest Home. Not any time soon, that
is.

That was three years ago. I figured by now they would have
deflated, popped, leaked or sagged. Naturally, I paid the $100
for the warranty, thinking I'd at least own them as long as I did
my Whirlpools. I thought one round of sex on the stairs would
have done them in for sure. I guess these bags of saline are
much harder to destroy than one may believe.

It's also a big myth that only hussies, divas, rednecks and insecure narcissists go in for hoo-hoo restoration. Plenty of women like me who resemble *National Geographic* pinups ask for the workup. I've had several mommy friends who got Up Grades because their babies had sucked the life and vitality out of their nack-nackers. I remember my own children pecking at my chest night and day as if I was roadkill, and the kinfolk horrified and asking, "When you gonna wean that child?" To which I responded ever so pleasantly:

"When she can put four quarters in the Coke machine."

Those who are wondering what three years can do to a decent boob job, wonder no more.

One morning, after gaining a few pounds from my late-night perimenopausal nacho-platter feasts, I realized my restoration had undergone a few unsavory changes, mainly in size and number. Yes, number. You read this correctly.

First, you've got your base units—the smooth, round Mentors my handsome doc wedged underneath the chest muscle, kind of like cracking a giant oyster with a crowbar and sticking in a huge, inflatable pearl. Seeing it on TV, I was horrified that they use what resembles auto-mechanic tools to get the tit bags up under there. No wonder I was black and blue.

Everything was great for a while until my uterus turned on me once again, deciding it would become my brain and continued ordering me to "eat, eat, eat!" and gain some weight, stimulating my appetite to the point I had nachos nightly and began to see a new set of cleavage atop the implanted and stationary base units.

The problem was that my original set of natural breast tissue was growing from weight gain and the fibroids within as well as swelling from caffeine intake. Seems they decided to give in to gravity and take flight from the base unit. Perhaps they were upset and jealous, or maybe had turned into Earth Mamas wanting nothing but surroundings that were natural and organic, which saline and silicone are not.

As long as I remained in a standing, upright position, everything looked fine, if not slightly lovely. One night as I rolled over in bed, my eyes caught a glimpse of something I can't bear to ever see again as long as I draw air. I screamed a real bloodcurdler. My original boobs, which, as I mentioned, had suddenly grown and gained a good bit of weight and new tissue, had up and slid right off the Mentor 350s anchored to my rib cage.

"Stuart!" I yelled. "Please come up here. Something horrible has happened."

"What now? Another fake heart attack?"

He was referring to the winter I called 911 three times and went by ambulance to the ER swearing like Fred Sanford and saying, "This is it! This is the Big One," convinced my palpitations were a heart attack.

After about thirty minutes of hearing me moan and freak out, he finally trudged upstairs.

"Come here," I said. "You aren't going to believe this."

He shook his head as if to say, *"Great. Here we go again. Brown recluse bite this time? Ebola virus? Giant lumps on scalp indicating exterior brain tumors?"*

"What?" he asked.

"Just wait a sec. I'm going to have to lay down to show you." I climbed in bed and removed my shirt and bra. At first, his eyes lit up and ear tips glowed red with lust. "Get over here. You can't see it until you come over toward this side of the bed."

He was clearly frustrated and wondering what his weird wife had done this time. I leaned over and let my original breasts roll right off the implanted Mentor 350s. Believe me, the saline rounds will stay put forever. I could go to the nursing home and they'd still be right up there even when my nipple and areola package hit my knees.

"See? See this? These, rather?" I pointed to my udders.

"No. I don't see anything but a naked woman laying on her side acting crazy."

"Here. Are you blind? Put on my magnifying glasses."

He reluctantly slid them onto his ears, probably thinking that if he obliged he may get some later, and since I was already half naked . . . "Lean close and tell me what you see."

He bent toward my chest. "I see boobs. Big ones. Redneck titties is what I see."

"See? I told you. Boobs!!! Not a pair, not a set, not a couple . . . but boobs. Boobs galore! How many are you seeing?"

He literally snorted, bull-like, and backed off as if an alien inhabited the Sealy. "And if I twist my body over the other way, same thing. Tell me the truth. HOW MANY DO YOU SEE?"

He shook his head and turned on the TV.

"I'm calling the doctor!" I cried out when he began cussing ESPN and not paying my udders a bit of mind.

"You better call the shrink," he mumbled.

"Are you saying you don't see four?"

"Four *what*?" He turned off the game and came back to the bedside, God love him. I picked at my breasts, lifting and flipping them about like boneless cutlets so he'd be able to count better. "Four. Four tits. Look, fool."

"No. I see what appears to be some form of malfunction, but I am the one who told you not to get that bimbo shit in the first place."

"I never knew they'd multiply with age," I yelled. "I don't only have two fake boobs, but, as you can see, I have grown my originals to the point they're quite migratory and have a mind of their own and left the anchored pads the doctor put in."

He snorted more and yawned. "I'm going to bed. You may want to get some rest. You could be seeing things."

"I'm having a mammogram tomorrow, so I'll just tell them about the multiplication of my teats. They'll have equipment to prove it. I'll just lay down on their dirty old tile floor and show them I have four and not two like most women."

He shook his head and shut the door. I scooped my four breasts back into place in their bra cups and hurried to my laptop, clicking onto my saving grace, www.implantinfo.com, the lovely Nicole's Web site where there's a chat room with tons of support and wonderful ladies (and men with implants, too). They are the ones who helped me get up the courage for the operation to begin with.

"Help!" I typed, using my pen name, Sally. "I've got a problem."

After the other chatters finished up their conversations about how big they'd gone and what kind of bras to buy, someone noticed my plea for help.

"What's up, Sally?"

"Well, they finally dropped, like y'all said they would, but I think they've done more than just drop."

"What do U mean?"

"I have four. I look like the underbelly of a goat or cow when I lay down on my side."

About six chatters started writing things like, "LOL, I'm laughing my ass off." and "Oh, my God." and "You've got to be kidding."

One even wrote, "Wow. Your husband is one lucky man."

"Don't pout," one woman said, "I am growing a set of back tits. I put on a bra and tight sweater and my husband said, 'Hon, you've got bigger tits under your shoulder blades than you do up front. You'd think you could get a four-cup bra for those suckers.'"

"Hey," I wrote. "I'm needing the four-cup bra, too. What can I do? I swear they are OK when I stand up or lay flat on my back, but once I roll over, say, to be sexy and gaze into the eyes of my man, all he does is stare in disbelief and pretend he only sees two tits instead of the four any other human being could see and count."

The chatters had a field day and hissy fits of laughter.

"Sounds like you need a lift," one of them said.

"I got a lift," I said.

"Sounds like you need some Gorilla Glue," another said.

"I already thought of that, too, but when I asked at Lowe's if you could use it on the breast tissue they called Security."

"Is there some sort of procedure the doctor can do where he stitches the real breast tissue onto the round Mentor mounds?"

Oh, mercy.

"Enjoy them," a woman said. "Think about this. You get

older every year and your original models are going to fall farther and farther south. By the time they're at your abdomen, you'll still have the two humps up top and maybe nobody will notice the lumps in your pants. If they fall low enough you can just say you have a set of balls."

I loved that line. I loved all these chatters. "Wait till you get a mammogram," wrote Cindy Big'uns, who'd been silent in the chat room up until now. "I had mine last week, and ain't nothing now where it ought to be."

"What do you mean?" I panicked. "My mammogram's tomorrow."

"You think you got problems with four tits? Wait till you throw them suckers on the Old Smasheroma and that nurse tries to flatten everything out and see if you don't come out screaming and all lopsided. I had one pop right then and there on the table, and it made such a loud noise we thought a gun had gone off. Half the lobby screamed."

I knew that most of the time, mammograms were fine and good screeners for cancer. I also knew that women with fresh nack-nackers were cautious about having them and entered the Squish parlors with much trepidation.

I stayed up half the night worrying about the procedure and its effects. It ended up being no big deal. I truly believe the cell-phone conversation I endured in the office was much more painful than the actual procedure was. There I sat, about to enjoy my first four-tittied mammogram when some stupid jingle ("Roll Out the Barrel")—fitting since she was shaped like a barrel—rang throughout the waiting room and a saucy lady, who'd forgotten to Jolen the left side of her mustache, lifted a teensy phone from her billowing lap.

"Hello . . . Yeah, I'm setting here waitin' to have my yearly Hooter Hammer . . . Uh-huh . . . Well, just put the pork chops in the sink and they'll be thawed out in time for supper . . . There's a box of Shake-n-Bake in the cabinet and you can get it started up while I'm tossing up the goodies in this place, you hear?"

Ma'am, we all hear, I wanted to say. Everyone in public now

hears things meant to be said behind closed doors. And talk about loud? No one ever, *ever* whispers into a cell phone. They yell. They yell about their surgical procedures while others are trying to eat out. They talk about colonoscopies and drainage and goiters and rampant infections while other diners are coaxing their throats to swallow their $50 entrees.

What cell phones have done, since becoming more affordable than a standard wall unit, is open a Pandora's box on private lives. Everywhere Nokias and Samsungs are stapled to eager ears, clipped onto trousers or slipped into purses.

How many times have I been in the Discount Depot, trying to find the carpet cleaner and rawhide bones, maybe a carton of Slim-Fast, when *ring-a-ling-a-ling*—or, worse, an extraloud rendition of "When the Saints Go Marching In," blares from someone's belt loop? Talk about eavesdropping and blushing. It's like a party line we're not sure we want to be privy to. Conversations such as the following:

"Hey there, Barbara Beelicious, now what chu up to? . . . Oh, lawsy, I'm here in Jabba the Bargain Hutt buying Vienna Sausages for Roy Dale's third birthday. Little Devil, we're going to have his party at the Twist and Tryst . . . Huh? I can't hear you. Did you say what's the Twist and Tryst? Uh-huh . . . Why, of course I realize it's an adult bar not based on biblical teachings, but they do have that wonderful video game room and—Yes, I know that . . . but Roy Dale's uncle has connections and the price is good."

About fifteen years ago—during pre-cell phone affordability—the gadgets were the novel toys of upstarts or those who wanted to play like they were celebrities. Then the price dropped and everybody got hooked up, giving rise to a boom of irritating, ceaseless chatter that follows one from the birthing room to doctors' offices to shopping centers. And even a burial.

Yes, a burial, for heaven's sake. I was at a funeral service several years ago when someone's cell phone blasted out, echoing throughout the church sanctuary.

My friend Randy T. Ford, a former Chippendale's dancer who is considering a business called Make Your Funerals Merrier, topped that one. "I was at a funeral home and a phone went off right in the coffin, the 'Farewell March.' I figure they forgot to remove it from the deceased's coat pocket or did it on purpose, which gave me the idea to make funerals more fun. I think I'll find a strong market in need of such a service. I'm dreaming of all the melodies I could crank out . . . Maybe even voice mail messages for those in attendance, like, 'I'm so glad you all turned out for the service. Don't cry. I'm going to be in a much better place than this stink hole.'"

And I figure the woman in this Mammogram Parlor talking about pork chops and goiters while I'm about to have the remaining vestiges of my four tits steamrolled into Pringles, is not about to shut up until the nurse calls her name.

"By the way," she said, loud enough for the Lord to hear, "I read a story the other day . . . I think it was some kind of contest in Ohio for people who wanted to take a stab at writing like Erma Bombeck . . . Anyhow, this woman was talking about her first mammogram and how the machine caught fire while she was all hooked up . . . Uh-huh, that's right. No, she's fine. They doused the flames with a fire extinguisher."

As soon as her words were out for all to hear, a nurse appeared in the doorway, clipboard in hand.

"Mrs. Reinhardt?" she asked. "Come this way, please."

I strode passed the gabbing lady with half a mustache and hissed. She and her dumb phone had up and ruined my first multitittied mammogram. Just up and ruined it.

The entire experience wasn't as bad as I thought, pain-wise. But once it was over, for at least five days, I had six breasts instead of four when I would lie in certain positions. I decided not to tell my husband about that. Thank goodness we're back down to two on most days, four on other days. I can handle that.

What I can't handle is the fact that he said tummy tucks are also for redneck bimbos and pole dancers. Why, my sweet Aunt Essie who went in for a hysterectomy—lucky dog—ended up leaving sans uterus (this is why she's the NICEST member of the family) but with a complimentary tummy tuck.

I've always wanted one, but realize the family budget can't support such vanity. I'll just have to settle for multiple breasts and four tummy rolls to match. Maybe if I go to Lowe's and get the Gorilla Glue without asking questions, they won't call Security. I could pull up my stomach skin and glue it beneath my bra-top swimwear.

Not Junior League Material

Some girls just aren't Junior League material. We aren't quite hussies and we aren't quite saints. Our hearts are pure and loving, but our minds and actions can take quite a few unexpected turns.

We weren't born with great chances of turning out normal enough to conform to society's ways and rules, the code of living and wage-earning, the coat of arms and breeding to get us into such circles.

The fact a sorority or two wanted, even requested, my admittance into their Greek system and circles of exclusivity was shocking enough. The fact mine kicked me out three years later for not acting "the part" and being a wild child, was to be expected when you mix girls like me—those with their own ideas about how to behave in college—with a bunch of Izod-wearing, espadrille-footed coeds with bobbed hairdos and clear skin and the Clinique trio of cleanser, toner and moisturizer.

Girls like me had regular old Nozema.

These future Junior Leaguers of America, God love them, and I swear I do, were girls who mainly went to prep schools and finishing schools and whose mothers and fathers were well heeled and, for the most part, either intelligent or boring or both.

I was fortunate enough to have oddball parents: smart, loveable, crazy and selfless. Nothing normal about them.

Both grew up dirt poor but fairly happy. Mama had a kind-hearted, but part-time drunken father who one time, on a bender, bought his daughters a pet mule. The three girls rode the mule to death. They came home from school one day and it was lying in the yard on its back, all fours in the air stiff as trees. They also had a goat that ate the clothes drying on the line and anything else it could get hold of.

My daddy had chickens, cows, sheep and a fairly public circumcision at age eight that was the talk of the town. I'm not sure why he didn't get snipped at birth.

It's no wonder I turned out crazy—from the time I began shaving off my eyebrows when I was four and wearing wigs in first grade, courtesy of my mother's odd beautician experimentations, to the times in high school when I'd pull stunts no one else had the nerve to try.

No one will ever forget my swinging the skinned cat from biology lab in front of the teachers' picture window in the cafeteria as they ate lunch. Or getting tipsy and driving a boyfriend's black Trans-Am through the practice fields and into the marching band's formations without so much as denting a tuba.

If one was to pinpoint the moment of genetic differentials, of who gets what and goes where in this world, I believe a big part occurs when sperm meets the egg of two unusual people and thus have no hopes of giving birth to anything other than mutant, though quite precious progeny.

It all began when Mama was 22 and went into labor on November 12, 1961. The doctors knocked her out cold because she was hollering up a storm and scaring the other laboring women and genteel moanings emanating on the ward.

A few hours later they woke Mama up and said, "Here's your baby girl."

She was coherent enough to notice that something about the doctor's face wasn't right. He wasn't smiling and seemed chalky. "Looked like Elmer's was coming out of his pores," Mama said many years later.

He haltingly handed her the baby (me) in a pink blanket,

doing his best to hide my temporarily disfigured and frighteningly ugly face. Mama gasped as if she'd been shown an alien or was a character in one of those sci-fi movies where the mother opens forth and delivers something lizardous.

"Sh-sh-she won't look like th-this forever," the doctor stammered. "It's just a matter of, well . . . Your p-pelvic bones wouldn't . . . you know, and we had to use the forceps and when that didn't work we resorted to our su-suction method, but unfortunately that failed so we had to call maintenance and b-borrow their Industrial Strength Hoover Mega Vac, but don't worry, we sterilized all the major attachments and brushes."

Mama's mouth opened as if she was going to scream, but being so young, she couldn't find the words and after wiggling her tongue around and bulging her eyeballs at the doctor in what she hoped was a threatening gesture, told him to get his no-good butt out of there and that if her baby didn't present any better the next day, she would be Hoovering his own head.

"This isn't our baby," she told my dad. "There's been a big mistake."

She never told me this story until I was fifteen when she had decided that there was a chance I may not end up tragically unattractive after all.

"Your nose was all the way on the other side of your face, lopped over like it was trying to scoot off your cheek and climb into your ear," she said, showing me the pictures. "Your head had all these humps and rings around it. Kind of like Saturn but shaped awfully funny, plus you had all this black hair covering your body, and I just wanted the floor to open up and swallow me whole. I'd never seen such an ugly and hairy baby, oh, but we loved you and just prayed you'd get prettier. With your ears being what they were."

I didn't say a word as she reached for my hand with her own and squeezed it. "You realize they were the exact size at birth they are right now? A full-grown set of sticky-out Farmer in the Dell ears on an infant. Lord have mercy you were a sight. I thought I'd given birth to a part chimp, and you had one ear that tried to migrate toward the nose and was sort of curling inward, you know, like how a sunflower will tilt its head and lean in toward the sun."

I instinctively reached up to feel my features, hoping they had settled into their proper place after forty-four years of living.

"Thank the dear Lord they handed you over in that pretty blanket and showing the good side of your face, the side that had a nose on it. Plus, of course, they had the cap on you and must have worked on that ear to get it up under there so we wouldn't have to see it curling toward your bent nose. Thank goodness the doctor said we could mold your face, so every night your sweet daddy would go to the crib and work on your nose and ears, kneading them like Play-Doh."

This is exactly how the world began for me.

As for my sister, born two years later, she started out in life being hailed the most beautiful baby to EVER come into the world at Spartanburg General. She had the perfect head, not a mark on her.

When Mama went into labor with Sandy, she wore a beautiful aqua gown and robe set—like something Eva Gabor from *Green Acres* would wear—and gave birth to the most breathtaking baby girl anyone had ever seen. The doctors and nurses couldn't take their eyes off this perfect specimen of brand-new human life.

"She is so angelic," the nurse told Mama as she held her daughter in a pink teddy bear blanket. "Nothing like your first, is she?"

Mama didn't know what to say. "You remember her?"

The nurse sort of blushed and stared at the floor. "Hard to forget her, but I hear she's much better or I wouldn't have brought it up."

"Oh, yes, she's gotten so much cuter since you saw her in here. Lots of the fur has rubbed off and her nose is starting to inch over more toward the center of her face, thanks to my husband's handiwork. He's a true sculptor, that man."

The nurse had no manners. "What about those ears she had? Biggest things we've ever seen in this hospital. I am not supposed to tell you this. Shhh, our little secret, but we had some plaster and made molds of them because we were absolutely certain no one would believe it when Dr. Milner wrote it up for the *American Journal of Abnormalities*. We didn't do photos, knowing you could have sued us. One of her ears was much larger, you know."

Mama was getting mad and her pain meds were wearing off. "We figure her head will grow and everything will eventually balance out," she snapped. "I measure them once a week to make sure they're stabilized and not enlarging, and when we go out, until she gets more hair to cover them, I have handmade bonnets with flaps that do the job. She's really a cutie-pie nowadays, so go on and give an enema or two and let me be unless you have more pain meds on you. My bottom is throbbing like it's grown its own heart."

"I'm sure your firstborn is now pretty as a picture," the nurse said with a quivering voice. "Oh, but look at this little piece of heaven's finest you have now. The good Lord sprinkled beauty dust all over her precious features. Those ears are flawless and so cute and tiny."

Yes, it was true, my newborn sister's ears lay flat against that lovely round head that needed neither forceps nor the hospital janitor's Ultra Hoover to pull her 8-pound body from Mama, since I had seasoned her passageway with my brutal birth and donkey ears.

Sister Sandy stayed pretty for the whole week until Mama checked out of the hospital, the entire staff still marveling and cooing. The very next morning, during an afternoon feeding in our little bungalow near the duck-filled lake, Mama walked into the nursery and screamed. Baby Sandy's genetically perfect ears had sprung from their resting position plastered against her head and shot out like two slices of bologna, huge and perpendicular to her skull. They also grew four inches apiece over the next three weeks, scaring everyone who saw them as they glowed red and were hot to the touch.

To this day we aren't sure what caused our ear malfunctions, but, needless to say, Sandy had a plastic surgeon correct

and beautify her pair. I left mine alone, targets for years of bullying and teasing.

We had no hope for turning out to be anything but crazy.
Birth sets the stage, parts the curtains and gives a new human
life its first audience. If I tried to pinpoint the exact age that
any chance of turning out a regular kid was nipped in the bud,
I'd have to say around four years old, when Mama and Daddy
signed me up for Kiddie Ranch private kindergarten in Thomson, Georgia, a little Peyton Place town just outside of Augusta where the Masters Tournament is held each year and it
meant something if you could get tickets so my daddy got on
the list and always had them.

Here's one big mystery: If your daddy can get tickets to the
Masters, why isn't his daughter asked to join the Junior
League? Not that I care. Not that I'm still sore, mind you.
Twenty years of therapy and I'm fine, you hear?

Throughout my entire life I've both loved and feared and
tried daily to please my daddy. I think he was mystified by
being the father of a nervous, jittery little child with tics and
annoying behaviors that linger to this day.

David Sedaris, one of my author heroes, also suffers from
OCD—Obsessive-Compulsive Disorder—and tics. I read it in
his book *Naked* that he licked things: lightbulbs, fixtures, furnishings, and he jerked his head around and rolled his eyeballs
up into his skull.

My disorders were checking things a million times and pee-
ing every three to five minutes. This is when the Kiddie Ranch
teacher tattled on me and told Mama I tee-teed more than I
breathed.

"We went in there with her forty-two times in a single day
and, sure enough, I hear it trickling out plain as day," the teacher
said. "Where she's getting this water I have no idea because all
we give them is a Dixie Cup of Kool-Aid. She must be like a
camel and store it all in her humps."

The teacher smiled at her witty remarks, but Mama was all
in a tizzy as any mother would be whose kid was a human PVC
toilet pipe.

She carted me to a kidney doctor in Augusta, who saw my bare possum (vagina) and I died a thousand humiliated 4-year-old-girl deaths. He prescribed the teensy Valium I took every morning before kindergarten to stop the tics and pee-peeing. I guess it worked. I fell asleep by 10 AM and never awakened until Mama pulled up in her aqua Plymouth, cigarette smoke curling from the windows like kite tails.

There was no way of turning into debutante material with a mama and daddy like ours. I'm not saying that as a bad thing. I love my mama and her sacrifices and selflessness, but her infamous spankings with flyswatters, some of which still had giant Georgia-fly remnants in the webbing, and her constant fears her daughters would become hussies and not get husbands, were terrorizing.

So was her insistence on calling our vaginas "possums." I know of zero women whose parents refer to their privates as a possum, but ever since I can remember, that's what my parents have nicknamed my sister's and my you know whats.

We'd hear things like this throughout our childhoods: *"Did you wash your possum?"* and *"Cover up that possum."* and *"I need to take you to Dr. Grayson and see why you keep picking at your possum."*

My parents explained that they chose that euphemism so no one else would catch on.

"It's not like we can say 'vagina' in public, Susan," Mama said. "Everyone would know exactly what we were talking about, and I'm sure not about to call it a vulgar term. I've never cared for the word. It sounds like an emotionally needy body part. It's too engulfing a term, like a giant maw ready to swallow up the world and cause all kinds of chaos."

How right she was about that.

So I asked my daddy, who shrugged his shoulders and said, "Your mama names the body parts."

What else could he say? He's the poor boy who had a public circumcision at age eight after being told he was going in for a tonsillectomy, and still recalls the embarrassment of all the aunts and his own mother standing over his bed and peeling back the bandages so each could get a good view of the new and improved tallywhacker.

"Looks like he's going to heal nicely," an aunt would say, sipping her sweet iced tea as she gazed at daddy's scabbing penis.

"He'll have a much easier time with the women when he gets older," another said, as if my poor daddy's third-grade self wasn't even conscious. Fact was, he lay in the bed mortified.

"Women don't like a smelly region," one of them whispered loud enough that my dad and his giant ears could hear. "My first husband wasn't circumcised so you can bet he didn't get much attention to his needs, shall we say. No one wants to play the ice cream cone game with one of those doggy danglers."

Lunacy, the sticking-like-a-barnacle kind, is usually handed down many generations. It's hard to shake it from the DNA and often mutates and regroups into other odd familial behaviors.

Mama, for instance, tended to take everything to the extreme. She meant well and everyone loved her and still does, but that's her nature and she can't help it. She was convinced we'd catch diseases and germs, and fall victim to kidnappers, carjackings, knifings, maimings and murder.

"Get sand in your hair and you'll go bald," she shouted because she didn't want to wash our hair every night as we played in the sandbox back when we were living in a house built on a former landfill. "Let a boy stick his fat, wet tongue in your mouth and the next step will take you directly to unwanted pregnancy, teen motherhood and men with El Caminos."

When my younger sister and I were little, she'd drive us by the county jail and say, "See up there on the second floor where those bars are? That's where you'll be if you don't act nice. They don't feed prisoners either. Nothing but rutabagas (she knew we hated them) and raw oysters" (another food we abhorred).

About once a month when we were naughty, she'd crank up the green Plymouth wagon with the fake-wood-paneled sides and off we'd go to view the county jail and endure her comments about their diets and lack of food. "Beans and water. On good days."

The saving grace for most who have mothers on the histrionic side is that they tend to have fathers who balance the equation, daddies who go with the flow, read their newspapers after work, drink a few highballs and ignore most domestic situations.

On Saturdays, when not golfing or grilling, they'll throw their children a few confidence-boosting bones and play with them outdoors or tell them how great they did during the cheerleading routines on Friday nights.

My daddy was hilarious and crazier than we were. He'd compete with his daughters as if we were his peers, setting up croquet in the yard and getting upset if he didn't whip our scrawny butts. He once took an old curtain rod, painted it yellow and invented a game called Rolly Bat, which he just HAD to win or he'd sulk a bit. He was the kind of daddy that while quite demanding at times and punitive, was loads of fun, especially when half-loaded.

We grew up on a lake and had a boat parked at the marina where we'd stock the cooler with Millers and take my friends waterskiing when we were teenagers. He told off-color jokes and Mama would say, "They are going to need finishing school, Sam, the things you say to them!"

Maybe this is one reason I didn't get into the Junior League, though I'm beginning to get over it after two decades' of affirmations to ward off ghosts of past rejections. With all this in mind, it's no wonder the Gambrell girls turned out the way we did.

"Remember that time we were in the movies, Susan," my sister said, "and you whipped around to that bunch of boys we didn't know and said, 'Go get us a Coke and box of popcorn'— and they got up and did it?"

Oh, we had our charms and our ways, but normalcy wasn't

one of them. We drew from the DNA Deck and got a couple of jokers, good parents but ones who had their own creative and very different ideas about raising children, daughters in particular.

It all boils down to one thing: some of us are just not Junior League material. I thank the dear Lord every day I'm not nor ever was.

A DWI on Horseback and a Showdown with a Snapping Turtle

I can't say this booze-drenched fellow's real name because he'll flat-out try to kill me. He's the craziest son of a bitch I ever met. Make that sumbitch.

I'm going to call him Brewster, on account of how much he loves beer, especially Old Milwaukee, one of the cheaper kinds he drinks from cans while standing in his yard turning reddish purple from the sheer force of all that sauce abuse on his heart and organs. When I met him he was all belly, a not-bad-looking man (from 100 yards) straining to stand on his thin, wobbling legs in cut-off shorts. It appeared as if any minute he'd collapse from the heat of summer and the cases of beer over the years.

I had the pleasure of his acquaintance one day while strolling my then baby girl.

"Hey," he slurred, waving his water hose. "Aren't you that old Nancy woman who writes for the paper?"

I wanted to be friendly and neighborly, but could smell him from two houses away. He walked toward me on those drinking straw–like legs, round gut shaped just like a Nike basketball blown to the point of popping. He had a nice smile and friendly face, and even though it was eggplant purple, there was a certain kindness and humor etched in his semitoothless smile and pretty blue eyes. He had some sort of aura that forces one to stop in her tracks, even when her better sense and Mama's strict raising says *"Keep moving."*

It was as if a cloud of fairy dust floated from the sky for the sole purpose of mesmerizing and caused me to stop what I was doing and introduce myself. He had cast a spell with that Old Milwaukee in one hand and wriggling garden hose in the other. He didn't seem to be watering anything but his gravel driveway.

I should have waved and kept walking, but sometimes I just can't help myself. It is the weirdo magnet. Once activated, I have no control and slide smack into these creatures most normal people wouldn't give the time of day.

I'm attracted to kooks because they are natural-born storytellers, who I could listen to for hours. They are far more interesting than are most men and women in suits and who wear Banana Republic on weekends. That's not to say I'd be attracted to or date this man . . . I was only planning to stop for a friendly neighborly chat. He was so different from what my husband refers to as the "Patty White Crowd," meaning the country clubers, Junior Leaguers (God love them) and other social climbers, who for the most part act as if cut from the same bolt of khaki cloth—all alike they are—forming a well-oiled machine of excruciatingly boring pretense.

Naturally, there are exceptions and I have friends, along with a mother-in-law, who frequent the country club, and quite a few friends (make that one) in the Junior League, to which I was never invited. Well, Sugahs, no wonder. None of them would be caught dead talking out in full public view with Brewster, yet, in my mind, people are people and if someone's entertaining, I don't care if he's half orangutan.

Give me the weirdoes and kooks. Forget the Junior Leaguers, bless their hearts, for not inviting me to join. Why, I could have brought color and zest and energy into that organization. I could have taught them how to find Kate Spade bags at Goodwill and how to let their hair down and go wild. I might even give them verbal lessons like that Jenna Jameson Mega Huss, who wrote *How to Make Love like a Porn Star*, only mine would be called, *How to Give Old Faithful the Ride of His Life: Even If It's Only on His Birthday or Christmas*.

Which brings me exactly to what Brewster enjoyed—the ride of his life. And, no, it wasn't provided by me.

For the record, in case he's still kicking around and comes searching for me, as he did the time the snapping turtle nearly bit off his 11-inch trouser serpent (he says 11 inches, but believe you me, I would NOT know), I'm not living in this country anymore. I'm in Guam. Not really but that's the information I want Brewster to have in his reddish purple head.

He got mad when I wrote the story about the turtle going after his jibblybob. Guess he was afraid the snapper would prevent him from ever entertaining another girl with his wondrous willy.

But let's not put the turtle before the horse. First, Brewster's horse-capades. Later, I'll tell you about his tango, which led to near bloodshed and dismemberment with the massive-jawed snapping turtle.

Brewster's not particularly proud of what he did, and it took six months of stopping by his trailer, begging and cajoling to get the full story. He knew that if he told it in bits and pieces, one scene at a time, I'd keep stopping by, being the kind of journalist I was and wanting the full story.

One summer evening as he watered his tomatoes and gravel driveway and doused his brain with beer, it all flowed out like the keg he wished was on his porch instead of the old Sony TV with the picture tube shattered from what appeared to be a man's booted foot.

Brewster was a former army veteran who likes to tinker with cars and grow his own fruits and marijuana, and that day, while slurring his words, his clouded blue eyes going their separate ways in his cranberry-red head, he uttered, "Ain't nobody gonna ever forget my ass. I'll go down in history, just like Rudolph the red-fucking-nose reindeer."

I was glad my baby girl wasn't yet two and prayed she'd forget his bad language. It may be a stretch, though, since she seems to pick up bad words faster than a bird can snap up worms.

I'll never forget how I learned this little lesson. It was after my husband had come home from a late-night gig and our baby girl was up in the middle of the night as usual.

"How's Daddy's little darlin'?" Tidy Stu asked, getting smack dab in her face.

"ASS!" she said. "ASS! ASS! ASS!" (What a smart baby I had.) "I'm gonna whup yo ass."

That's what Tidy gets for letting a toddler watch Eddie Murphy movies all day instead of *Blue's Clues*.

"Try to watch your language, Brewster," I said, cocking my head toward my child. "She's like a Pest Strip about catching cuss words and retaining them."

Brewster grinned, a few dark holes in his mouth where most of the molars had evacuated, and then he started telling the whole story about what had happened in the mid-1980s when he made North Carolina history—on horseback.

"I'll get to that in a minute," he said, knowing I was waiting on that full story like a starved animal staring at a caged bowl of raw hamburger. He wanted to tease me with his other tales first. Wanted to tell me his entire life's story.

I sat on a large rock, ready for his long and winding string of escapades. The conversation turned to his past. Seems he had lots of careers, and before he'd tell me about what happened on that horse he beat around the bush and stalled to keep me hanging on.

"I was an orderly in the army," he said. "And it was my job to shave up all the vaginas before we'd take out the uteruses." Oh, my Lord. Here was a MAN talking about va-gee-gees and uteri, if that would be the plural of uterus, but probably not.

I was stunned. "Orderlies can't take out uteruses."

"They sure can if there aren't enough doctors. We were in a war here. Vietnam. It was rough and women wanted them out for this and that reason or another. It was my job to soap them up real good and squirt Betadine all over them and shave them beavers bald. Then, if a doctor could be found, he'd use the salad tongs and pull the thing out."

I was transfixed, watching him drink, smoke and turn redder by the minute.

"Did you know"— he asked with more seriousness than I'd ever seen him exhibit—"that the uterus is a pear-shaped organ?"

Oh, me. Why couldn't he just talk about his own organs like all other men fixated on their swelling, bothersome prostates and PSA levels?

After he spoke of yanking uteruses out of suffering women, he bragged about going to Jamaica and working as a naked dancer. He also told me he passed out in the middle of the ocean after scuba diving and lay on top of the water for eleven hours without drowning, even while surrounded by sharks. He'd been hitting the tequila that day.

I didn't know what to believe, but once he got onto the story about the horse, I checked it out with the police and arresting officer and it all panned out as the gospel truth.

On that famous day in North Carolina history, Brewster woke up hungover as usual and made a breakfast of eggs and Old Milwaukee. Maybe a bit of toast. As the day progressed so did his drinking, and by nightfall this colorful character was ready to go rebel-rousing. Only his mother, who lies and says she's 42, which is younger by ten years than Brewster is, stood in the road in her housecoat and wouldn't let him drive one of the many half-broken-down cars scattered about his property.

"You ain't a'goin nowhere, buddy," she said, spitting a wad onto the ground. "You's drunk as a drowned rat and I'll lay in this road like a suicidal possum, and you'll have to kill me if you think you're hitting up the dives and pool halls tonight."

It all stemmed from beer and loneliness as he sat home that fateful night, clock ticking toward the hour when most brush their teeth and slip on their jammies. Instead of going to bed, where he definitely belonged, he'd gotten a notion to visit a Patton Avenue watering hole, which is real close to downtown Asheville.

"Rather than driving the truck," he said, "I thought it would be better to saddle up my stallion than drink and drive."

He saddled up Ol' Smokey, all right, but it was more of a mule-looking thing than a stallion, though you have to realize all men love to use the word "stallion" every chance they get.

"Hey, hon, wanna check out my stallion tonight?" "Oh, baby, my stallion's been thinking of your sexy body all day." And so on.

Somehow, a very drunk and staggering Brewster managed to guide the horse down Hooper's Creek Road. But even in the darkness, he recognized a familiar face coming toward him, moon flowing through her white nightgown and giving her the appearance of an apparition, one of Heaven's more menacing angels.

"You better get home with that horse before I break me off a switch," his mother growled, her moonlit face set in that Lord-help-me look mothers of wild boys often wear. I tried to imagine her switching a 52-year-old man.

Brewster ignored his mama, and waved good-bye like the Lone Ranger with a full tank. He figured Ol' Smokey would be a decent designated driver; plus, the horse had a good, sober brain and knew the way back home. "He's just like a human being but smarter," Brewster always said of the stallion that, truthfully, looked like a mutant and gigantic brown goat. "He used to help me with my math when I was calculating costs to lay tile and build rock walls. He knew good tile from bad, too, and would pick up a piece that was flawed in his big old teeth and whinny until I got it from him."

They trotted down the two-lane, horse clomping and tapping like a clogger onstage. When he made it without incident to the bar, some three miles from his house, he tossed the reins of his fine goat/steed to the doorman, also known as the bouncer. "Make sure no one dents my Jag," he said, winking and going in to wet his brain with draft beer.

"While I was inside drinking and having a good time," Brewster said, "the doorman was letting different girls get on Smokey and walk him around the parking lot, and all over the neighborhood behind the bar. Some asshole up yonder ways spotted the horse churning up his lawn and musta called the police.

"I had no idea of this," he said, face beginning to explode in sweat bubbles instead of just rolling down his cheeks and neck.

He continued with the story that made history, as he was the first, and maybe ONLY man in North Carolina to get a DWI on horseback.

He keeps saying he's not proud, but I could tell he was getting a huge kick out of telling this wild incident. A few beers later and the rest poured out of him like his hose on the gravel drive.

"It was closing time," he continued, "and I was ready to go home and so was Smokey. We left the bar, and both of us were hungry so we went right on through the McDonald's drive-thru window and I ordered a Big Mac with fries and Smokey had a Happy Meal because he likes the toys, especially them Beanie Babies. I sure as hell wish you could have seen the look on that woman's face when she saw me and Smokey and I told her, 'Go 'head and put the handles of that there Happy Meal directly in his mouth. He'll know what to do with it.'

"We galloped on out of there and a few minutes later I seen the flashing blue lights all around and my ears rang with pain the siren was so loud. I wasn't about to stop, but was trying to find a quiet place for Smokey and me to have our picnic."

The blue lights spooked the calm out of Ol' Smokey, and Brewster held on for dear life as the horse let loose and tore through town as if he was in the Kentucky Derby and its rider a drunken jockey. They fled through the ritzy and sleeping neighborhoods of Asheville, both not wanting to drop their burgers because if Ol' Smokey could keep his Happy Meal in his teeth during all of this, then Brewster could hold on to his food too.

"It was a wild chase that lasted over an hour," he recalled, popping the aluminum tab on another can of beer.

Brewster thought he'd lost them at one point when he hid in the woods near the Holiday Inn Golf Course. For thirty minutes he and Smokey laid low, dipping their fries in ketchup, eating their burgers and catching a breather before taking off again into the kind of night when the moon is too full to stay up high and sort of sinks low and yellow, like it could hit the ground at any minute.

"Another mile and I'll be home free," Brewster thought.

But as soon as he got back on his road leading home, the lights of five patrol cars bathed him in troublesome blue. Behind the wheel of one of those cars was Lt. Leroy Barnes, a sour-faced sheriff's deputy.

"How the hell you gonna stop that there horse?" boomed the voice of a fellow officer over Barnes's police radio.

Barnes couldn't resist being funny. He picked up the microphone and said, "I guess I'll just have to yell WHOA!"

Using the public address system built into the patrol car, the officer took himself seriously and hollered, "Whoa!" loud as he could. But Brewster and Smokey kept going until they came to a dead end, where their journey was over. They were trapped, ketchup on their lips, cheese stuck between Ol' Smokey's chompers.

"I kind of got cornered by a house, fence and all the cars," Brewster said. "Smokey was hysterical and his stomach hurt from the cheeseburger, I could tell. He was pretty upset the prize was the duck-billed platypus and not the zebra or pink flamingo because he just loves them there pink birds. He was on his hind legs with his front ones in the air, and I was having a time hanging on. I saw several guys get out and I thought we were both going to be shot."

Instead of taking a bullet, they took Brewster to jail, where he was fingerprinted, photographed and arrested for driving while impaired and failing to heed the blue lights and siren. Lt. Barnes hauled the tired but otherwise healthy horse to a safe place for a little R&R.

"It was a very expensive night," Brewster said. "It cost $90 to get out of jail, $100 for Smokey the horse, and $800 for a lawyer, who lost the case."

"Whatever happened to Ol' Smokey?" I asked as he handed me a brown paper sack filled with tomatoes, a very neighborly thing to do, I might add. He explained that Barnes, being a good lawman, brought Smokey home a few days after the arrest.

"He knew he was home," Brewster said. "He started whinnying, and when we got him out of the trailer, I've never seen such a happy horse. He ran to the other horses, so glad to see them. He stood on his hind legs, going 'Whee-oooo, Whee-ooo' and then ran around and cut a few flips. He's the only horse I know that can do gymnastics better than some of them girls on the Olympics and a lot better than the one who's now selling sanitary napkins on TV since her career is over."

I tried to form a mental picture of the horse but couldn't see it.

"My sweet Smokey laid down on his back, all four legs pawing the air. After he calmed down, I went and hugged his neck and gave him a new Beanie Baby and told him I was glad he was home. With those big eyes, he looked at me and I swear he said something very close to *Meeeeee, tooooooo*."

I left with my tomatoes and a pretty good story, thanked him, and it was a while before I heard from him again. Then, late one afternoon he called the newsroom breathless and seemingly sober. Of course with him, it's always hard to tell.

"Well, Susan," he said, "I finally met my match and it weren't no woman."

I knew to get a fresh blank screen and let him dictate his oral jewels. He was one heck of a storyteller, especially after sixteen beers. "I met my match in a shell," he said. "Meanest snapping bastard of a turtle ever lived, and that reptile's ass nearly took away the very thing I love most."

That would be one of two or three things. His horse, his claims to an 11-inch jibblybob or his Old Milwaukee beers.

"If it weren't for me," he said, "that screaming lady and her carful of booger-faced children might have been killed. All them stupid idiots were out in the road trying to call that turtle out from under the car like it was some kind of damned pussycat."

I typed at the keyboard and he could tell I was taking notes. "You gonna write this up?

"I might."

He seemed pleased. "I was driving down Milk Cove Road on the way to get me some refreshing beverages at the BP when I seen this lady and her young'uns flagging me down near the STOP sign. I was in my truck, took the screwdriver out of the ignition and was on my feet ready to help within seconds.

"Like all the ladies," Brewster said, "she ran toward me fast as she could. 'What's the matter, woman? You been shot?' I asked, looking for blood and bruises."

"'No . . . There's . . . th . . . th . . . There's a m-m-monster under my car,' she says.

"And I say, 'No need to be getting all hysterical.'"

He patted her on the shaking shoulder, probably wishing he could drop his hands lower.

"Let me just have a quick look after I swallow the rest of my lunch."

"It appears to be some form of prehistoric dinosaur!" the woman screeched.

Brewster had spring fever and knew this was his chance to show off a bit of blooming testosterone, all stored up from winter and undiluted. She wasn't bad looking, especially after his morning six-pack and lunchtime 40-ouncer. Ditch the kids and she was good to go.

He got back to telling the story, not talking until he heard my fingers clickety-clacking, him wanting it all written down for posterity.

"I got out like Crocodile Dundee and caught the fucker by the tail," he said. "I pulled and pulled. It was mad and gave me the evil red eye. I finally pulled it out from under her car and held it up like I was one of them big-fish-catching fellers. You know, you see them all pumped up and grinning on them piers? I held that killer turtle and them children scattered through the hills screaming and crying. That woman looked at me with pure lust in her eyes.

"'Listen up,' I told her. 'This here's a mud turtle, a snapping turtle, and if they bite you they won't let go until it thunders or until you beat on your grandma's washpan.'"

He also told them that such turtles were delicious and packed with seven different and succulent kinds of meat.

"It may look like only one creature," he said, still holding the 80-pounder by the spiny tail, "but it has all them varieties of meat on it. They got a bit of turkey, chicken, beef, lamb, fish . . . everything you'd want all under one shell. You just gotta make sure it don't get your meat 'for you get his."

Brewster said his good-byes, tried to get the woman's phone number, to no avail, and hoisted the seething and hissing turtle in the back of his truck, toting it home, where he immediately placed it in a huge garbage can and fed it canned salmon and rice.

"I'd go out and talk to it now and then," he said. "I could tell it was listening, too, 'cause it'd look at me with those soulful eyes, them ancient eyes that have seen millions of years on this here Earth. It would open its mouth trying to talk, but I told it, 'Shhhh. You ain't gotta say nothing. Not unless you a damn woman.'"

The next day, after a twelve-pack and Cheetos, he called a bunch of his friends, who came by to see his new plaything and pose for photographs. "I used to catch all kinds of turtles when I was younger," he said, tossing the snapper a few Cheetos. "We'd write our names on their backs with fingernail polish. Thata way we could find the same turtles every year and see how much they'd grown."

On day two of his snapping turtle's captivity, the merriment went flat and the newness sank like a day-old balloon. With the turtle still in the trash can and sending him menacing glances, Brewster reckoned he'd best set it free. He called a few friends over again to take final photos of their last days as a team—him and Snapper. As he lifted the minibeast from the trash can and was grinning for the camera, the aggressive reptile did the unthinkable.

"I was holding it up by the tail and it whipped around its head, bigger than a fist and, quicker than a flash of lightning, it opened its giant jaws and grabbed hold of me right in the crotch," Brewster said, then started laughing. "I hollered like a man on fire, but it wouldn't let go. I beat on its back and it would just clamp down harder. It was hanging there and I was looking for anything to hit it with. It had me crushed in its jaws and I knew I'd never get to pole dance in Jamaica again if I didn't act fast. I poured my beer all over it and it finally took a few swigs and let go, then tore off through the woods like a jackrabbit. It ran just like a tipsy baby dinosaur."

While Brewster says he's a little sore and won't be chasing women for a couple of weeks, he's thankful he was wearing jeans. "I was wearing my 501 Levi's and the only thing that saved my . . . er . . . stallion was my zipper. I wouldn't have had nothing left of my Caped Crusader. It'd be in some incinerator and I'd have a wooden dick or one of those prosthetic metal claw dicks, if anything at all. Thank God for that zipper. I'm fixin' to call the Levi's company and ask if I can do a commercial for them jeans like Crocodile Dundee did for all them cars and whatnot."

I thought about this carefully.

"You know, while you're at it, you should also call the Budweiser people and see if you wouldn't make a perfect Super Bowl commercial with your beers and riding your stallion up to a drive-thru window. You could have a Bud in one hand and a Big Mac in the other."

He got all excited and I hung up and wondered if I should tell his turtle story or not. A few years later, we moved off the mountain and I haven't seen him since.

People tell me he's still kicking, drinking, waiting on spring and home-grown tomatoes, and some girl to come along and admire his chivalry—be it on horseback or hauling mauling reptiles.

Wherever he is or whatever he's doing, I'm certain there's an interesting story waiting to emerge. All it will take is a case of cheap beer and a lady's smile.

Give Me a Tag and I'll Give You My Uterus

If someone gave me a choice of a trip to the DMV or the gynecologist—boy, what a toss-up.

At the DMV, also known as the Department of Motor Vehicles, or, in my mind, the Den of Madness and Venom, the poor and underpaid workers don't give out tags and other legal must-haves unless you have more documents than can be stashed in a four-drawer filing cabinet.

Used to be a driver's license and insurance card would do it. Now, you best come in with a steamer trunk full of everything from proof of life to promises of organ donation.

I stood in line for an hour, my hands shaking and feet perspiring, knowing it would take me three to four trips to get legal on the roads, and this was just my first try. I thought about how much less nervous I was hours earlier, seeing a brand-new gynecologist whose nurse gave me a paper gown made out of that cheap toweling—probably Marcal or Scott—and ask me to "strip down to skin and grin." At least, I thought, she has a sense of humor.

Maybe the doctor would, too.

Seemed like I was waiting an hour in that scritchety-scratchey giant picnic napkin that covers nothing like the linen gowns they give pregnant women. You remember those beautiful pink robelike garments those with fetuses are given before the doctor examines their hooches?

Well, for a regular-old puss peep, you aren't going to get the linen treatment. You get the paper napkin, and thus I lay there naked and rustling in that paper towel for at least thirty minutes, sweating, and thinking, I'll bet my freshly washed region has suddenly begun to lose its freshness. Even though on gyno days, I spend the morning cleaning my body cavities as if I was walking naked through a high-powered car wash or that within an hour I'd be in a car wreck and the ER staff would first remove my undies.

This insecurity about our private bidness, the things "down there," is due to all those sick TV commercials that make women feel like their va-gee-gees are festering crotch mackerels. I'm sure some men turn gay when they are around 12 and the commercials come on TV about feminine odors and sprays. I say if you smell that bad, get thee to the Squeal & Wheel Car Wash down on Tunnel Road and don't bring the car.

On gyno days, I always choose underwear that are A-grade, but not thongs—except for that oft-mentioned nightmarish occasion when I had no choice but to wear one during my daughter's birth, which my mother has yet to forget or forgive.

Never wear C- or D-grade lingerie to the gyno because, chances are, when you wad up your clothes and place them on the chair, they'll fall to the ground and the nurse will tell everyone in the office how hideous they were. Same goes for bras. It's best to wear a good one, not the kind I have where the underwires poke through the material.

A crazy nurse friend of mine told me, "We don't want the women to think we're staring at their Coochie Snorchers so we kind of gaze around the room and often our eyes fall on their undergarments wadded up in a chair or on the floor. It's flat-out scary what some of them dare to wear. Nasty, girl. Pure-T nasty."

I knew this was what happened in some doctors' offices, so that is why one should always go for broke and wear the good stuff on Pap smear, Anal Jab, Drape-'n-Scrape days.

When this brand-new doctor finally came in to examine me, he didn't even bother to start off with a warm-up question . . . such as, "Nice weather we're having, isn't it?" No, sirree. He just dove right in, so to speak. "How's your health been? Anything unusual? Any pain with intercourse?"

Intercourse! Now that's a word for you. Why do they all say intercourse? It's as gross as calling my love contraption a VAGINA. Intercourse could mean a number of things ranging from communication to talking and disclosing information.

I was lying upside down as he cranked the chair so my possum was getting closer and closer to his bifocaled eyeballs. Hard to answer questions when one's vagomatic is rising and legs are spreading.

"Pain with what, did you say?"

"Intercourse. Sexual intercourse."

"Oh," I said, trying to press my knees together so he couldn't see my snorchie cooter or whatever that nurse friend of mine calls it. "I don't have that. I'd much rather just blow the man's whistle from time to time. Doesn't take near as long and frees me up for all my shows like *Grey's Anatomy* and *American Idol*."

I felt really PMSy and have been begging a doctor in another practice to yank out my uterus for years, but she said there's nothing but trouble ahead if she did such a thing, and my mama, of course, had to agree and say what she always says, "You'll grow a beard and a bumper crop of testicles . . . maybe a starter penis, too."

She thinks whiskers and a deep voice will lead the way to the rudimentary penis should I have my lady parts tossed in the incinerator, where I'm convinced they belong and I'm hoping this doctor will agree.

"I've had four periods in six weeks," I say, trying to let him know things have gone to seed. He said nothing. "That's a lot of money for Tampax I could be spending on alphahydroxy creams with grapeseed extract, you hear?"

He continued with his exam as I lay there wondering how to tell him I needed the surgery.

"How often would you say you are enjoying relations with

your husband?" the doctor asked again as I suddenly felt his fingers dive in for the kill.

"Ouch! Don't you think you could have at least bought me a drink first?" I asked, trying to be funny. He did NOT laugh, just poked harder, probably noticing dust bunnies, cobwebs and a few brown recluses. I hear they like dark, undisturbed places.

"Sex? Are you referring to sex when you say 'relations' and 'intercourse'?"

"Yes, that is the terminology we use here."

"I entertain him on occasion, but, truth is, it hurts. Painful it is, indeed. It hurts especially on the nights he forgets to thank me for the fine dinner I made or the days when all he does is grouch and complain. And that, my dear doctor, is why the man isn't getting any. You know what 'getting any' means?"

"I assume it—"

"That's right. He isn't enjoying this fine source of inter-course. No nookie. No hump-de-dump. No—"

He shut me up with the noise of instrument preparation and was silent for a while, then said he was going to insert this and that and hoped it was warm because they sure try hard to heat things up a bit before going spelunking. He didn't say spelunking, of course, because he had the wit of a nit, which is the egg of a louse, which would be singular for lice.

"There are new products and creams, even hormones that will help increase your—"

"No thanks. Once a year is fine. Christmas wouldn't be as special without our annual Sealy celebration. We're just at that age and stage in a marriage."

The doctor was silent and probing. Then the most embar-rassing thing of all happened, just when I thought I'd escaped it. He must have used his digging and scraping of cervical walls as think time, rolling my name around in his head, finding it familiar and wondering where he'd heard it. I've been around for twenty years in this town writing several columns a week. I knew it was coming. It always does while their heads are halfway in the birth canal fighting spiders, fallen bladders and whatnots.

"You wouldn't happen to be the Susan Reinhardt who writes those stories in the paper, would you?"

Oh, no. What does one do? Admit that, yes, as you are viewing my cornucopia of feminine charms and noticing it hasn't been waxed or groomed for summer activity, I am indeed the writer at the paper. Or I could say, "No, but I know her. She's really nice and lots of fun."

"You look just like that woman in the paper." His head was still in my hoo-ha. Great, my face looks like a Coochie Snorcher.

"WHAT!!!!!" I screamed as his index finger the size of a bratwurst enters my virgin Arschlach (anus) and I cannot help the evil that froths from my mouth.

"I sure hope THIS isn't the picture you're referring to," I said, trying to cross my legs so he'd get the idea, though, in truth, it might be better looking than the one the paper is currently running.

I wondered if the man had even seen my face. He'd done nothing north of the border since he entered the room. "I like your hair," he says, and I am wondering if he's talking about the many new and controversial hairdos the paper has run or the hair he's currently viewing? I wanted to get out of there. FAST.

With gadgets and digits occupying nearly every orifice, he proceeded to tell me how much he enjoyed the piece I wrote about the woman who was using a Porta-John when the forklift came by and scooped the booth into the air and carted her down the road a few miles.

"I loved the part how you described her trying to open the door and seeing all the cars whizzing by, no pun intended." Great, suddenly he gets a personality. I preferred him as a louse egg. There's nothing worse than a gynecologist who talks ONLY when he's down THERE and not directly to your face. I just want them to examine parts I'd rather not know I have, proclaim them healthy, write up prescriptions for Wellbutrin and tranquilizers and send me home all squishy from the K-Y jelly. Or, in this case, I wanted him to say my uterus was not functioning properly and needed immediate removal and incineration.

My mother, prim and proper and very Baptist, always gloats after her annual visit with her gynecologist. She has never let any man but my father view her snorchie, and I'm highly doubtful he's ever come as close to that view as her gyno.

"Dr. Whiteside said I have a youthful and healthy vagina," Mama beamed. "Says it's one of the best he's ever seen for a 68-year-old woman, or any woman, for that matter. I'm not going to tell your daddy."

I want to throw up when she says this, but she's not being gross, she's completely elated at her vaginal perfection.

Toward the end of my own exam, just before I was about to slide off the tissue paper–lined table, feeling as greasy as a Wesson-oiled turkey cavity, this doctor managed more questions without looking into my eyes.

"Are you using birth control?" he asked, removing his gloves. "I assume a smart woman like you would certainly—"

"Well, no, not exactly. I am fairly abstinent, like I told you. We are holiday humpers. Not much in between 'cept the—"

He wrote in his computer and made a strange face. "Don't worry," I said. "He's fine with it. Makes him look forward to Christmas that much more. He'll even hang lights in our bushes if he thinks he'll also get to hang something in my bush." Hee hee hee. The doctor didn't laugh at all.

"Aren't you concerned about birth control?"

"Doctor, I'm 44 years old. The only thing I'm concerned about is being able to survive this perimenopause without killing the man. Do you realize I planted an oleander bush at my house? What does THAT tell you? I ride by pawn shops and twitch at the gun displays. I really came here so that you'd tell me I needed to get my uterus and its sidekicks out ASAP. This is the main source of all my misery and misdeeds, I assure you."

"No, it's healthy and normal from what I could see," he said, and I wanted to swat him. "You have a couple of small cysts, which are quite common. It's probably all in your head from the many decades women over a certain age were all but guaranteed hysterectomies. A good number of those surgeries were never needed."

"Four periods in six weeks?" This is not in my head.

But this is what all men say. That everything we complain about is all in our heads. I wanted to take his off. "I know y'all give out samples of Lexapro and Prozac," I said, "but I was wondering if you had some extra boxes of Elephant Lady–sized tampons and pads as I'm certain to have another period in five to seven days?"

He left with one of those perplexed, "I'm-a-doctor-minus-a-personality" expressions, and I left with my K-Y'd parts puddling.

Then, to make matters worse, my next errand was to get my car tag renewed. Only fools will schedule a Pussyectomy and DMV visit on the same day. I'm that kind of fool.

I stood in line wondering if in a week the boring old doctor would call and say I had a reattached hymen from lack of intercourse. The line here wasn't moving so there was lots of time to think irrational thoughts, my number-one hobby.

The man in front of me was picking his nose, checking the contents out and even chatting with them before putting it all into his hanky and saying, "Bye for now." I kid you not. And the woman with the six kids behind me was yakking on her cell phone to a man I presumed was her husband or live-in about how the line hasn't moved since breakfast and her hemorrhoids were giving her fits.

"You get your ass up here you no good sumbitch and stand here with these six young'uns. It's *your* restored Gremlin. Not mine. I'll give it one more hour, then I'm taking my sore ass home and soaking in some Epsom salts."

She reminded me of my poor friend, a beautiful pharmacist, who was walking around in labor begging the doctors to administer the epidural to her giant hemorrhoid instead of her spine. "I'd been in labor 44 hours and the thing was huge," she said, sipping red wine and discussing its size while all of us fell over laughing. "I can't figure out why they didn't just go ahead and give me what I wanted."

A few minutes later at the DMV, the lady who was working the counter alone was helped by a man who looked as if he'd been tortured by the government and recently released. He was such a sad sack he made Eeyore seem manic.

Every single person who finally inched up to the counter was sent away. None had proper documentation. No one ever does.

Here's what I heard from these government-paid public slaves:

"YOU NEED A NOTARY TO SIGN THIS BEFORE YOU CAN GET A TAG, MA'AM."

"SIR, WE'VE CHANGED THE REQUIREMENTS SINCE YOU WERE LAST HERE FOR TITLE WORK. YOU'RE GOING TO HAVE TO PAY CASH AND SHOW DENTAL RECORDS. YOU COULD BE ANY-BODY OFF THE STREETS."

"But I wear dentures," the man said, taking them out and setting them on the counter.

At that point I was ready to run.

Then it was my turn.

"Oh, what have we here? I remember you. You're the little bitch that pitched that fit four years ago when it took you seven tries to get a tag. Welcome back," she said and scrunched up every feature on her face until she resembled something from *Lord of the Rings.*

"I'm going to need to see a current license, birth certificate, proof of insurance, PROOF OF LIFE, proof you own that damn car, and we'll also prick your finger to make sure you are really who you say you are. Standard policy now with all the car theft going on."

I was stunned. K-Y jelly was running down my left thigh. I wanted to go home.

"I'm not leaving without a tag," I said. "My temporary blew off in the car wash and I have nothing on my back bumper but a fresh coat of paint. It needs some letters and numbers or I'll be wearing them on my jumpsuit as I clean liquor bottles from I-240. Please, Madame DMV."

She clicked and typed and came back with a secret manila envelope.

"You wanna make this trip shorter?"

"Please. Yes."

"I see you got 'organ donor' listed here on your license."

"Yes, I am a great believer in donating anything you—"

She made that creepy-crawler bug face again. "Shhhhh! This is between you and me, Miss Priss. Now you and me both know you wouldn't have proper documentation if it jumped outta your ass. You know that. I know that." She leaned in closer. "It's not offered to all our customers, but if you're willing to be a living donor, that is one who'll give body parts prior to receiving your personal toe tag in the morgue, you get a renewal plate pronto and don't have to pay the taxes on the vehicle for a year."

"Do what?"

"That sweet little Lexus your ass is driving around town? You know how much you're going to owe on that baby? Here's the deal, sign this paper that you'll be a LIVING donor and we'll stamp you clear, give you a tag and set you loose."

"Living donor?"

"Means we'll call if we need half your liver, a kidney, some skin for grafting, maybe a fallopian tube, cornea, thumb or shin bone, that sort of thing. Parts you don't really need to live a normal life."

I was speechless but definitely interested. I thought about the visit to the gyno and the parts down south I sure didn't need. "You can have my uterus," I said. "I was going to sell it on eBay or send it to a hide tanner and turn it into a change purse, but I figure someone might need one."

She mumbled and gave it some thought. "What else you got to give? A uterus is just a start."

"I'll sign over the entire bitch patrol: ovaries, tubes, any eggs that are viable. Just let me have my basic unit 'cause come Christmastime my husband will be wanting it."

She handed me a tag and let me go. The lady with 'rhoids and six kids was up next. Madame DMV eyeballed those children like prime rib on a buffet table. She must have been mentally tabulating all the potential organs from that one client.

"Want a tag?" I heard her whisper, going into the live-donor speech. "Sign the papers promising us parts such as a bile duct or portal vein, and it's all yours."

The woman rubbed her ass and gasped.

"Shhhh!" Madame DMV said. "If you are simply too attached to your portal vein, we'll also take lung lobes and extra ears, healthy liver sections and other parts you don't really need to live the good life." She eyeballed the woman's large and dragging boobs, seeing the dampened spots on her blouse. "We'll take a wet nurse, too."

The poor bedraggled, hemorrhoid-angst woman signed.

"Here's your tag. Have a nice day."

That night I went home exhausted and defeated and decided it would be one of those evenings where I'd just lie in the bed with a row of Ritz and channel surf—my mechanism for coping after a bad day. As soon as my Lifetime movie about a born-again teen bulimic cheerleader on crack ended, I flipped to an infomercial and nearly jumped out of my pajamas.

There before me was the most frightening hawker I'd ever seen.

THE JUICE MAN.

He sported tufts of white hair and eyebrows that looked like two bearded caterpillars pulled upward by an invisible string. He kept staring at me through the TV, grimacing and grinning, telling all of us that we were on our way to Coffin Central if we don't snap up his juicer and start downing all those liquid, straight-from-the-plant vitamins.

The man was in sheer fruit-and-veggie heaven as he plunged whole carrots, beets, apples and anything he could find into his pulverizing juice machine. He'd take a sip and just literally have a happy fit. I'm quite certain the freak had an erection to match his eyebrows.

I may have been tired and my bottom still squishy . . . I may be facing a future with one lung and a missing cornea, but I swannee that man had a bulge in his pants. Could have been something he was planning on "juicing" later.

He kept yelling through the TV and I continued watching and listening, completely horrified to the point of fascination.

"Order the Juiceman and get a free bread machine!" he shouted.

I just don't trust a man that high on juice. Even so, within twenty minutes, the Juice Man almost snagged me. He peered close to the camera and I felt the tug, the Visa whispering, "Come get me" from my purse. What juicing magnificence! What a pair of brows!

I could call and tell the ladies working the phones that I'd order one only if he'd throw in his eyebrows. I could use them to clean up under the toilet rims or the burners on the stove. They'd be perfect for digging down in the hollow valves of my son's trumpet to get all the spit and crud out. I'd never have to buy another box of Brillo pads.

In the end I resisted, turned off the tube and decided to call it a day. First the gynecologist who said I looked just like my photo in the paper while his face was one inch from my cervix. Then the DMV lady who gave me a tag only after I signed over any and all body parts that wouldn't kill me if excised.

Maybe I'll go soak in the tub and eat a carton of Milk Duds. If the candy yanks out my teeth, I can always save the good molars for the DMV lady in order to be certain of getting a new tag next time it came due.

Hooking Up With David Sedaris

One day my fairy godmother arrived in the form of a publicist.

She waved her magic wand and set up a meeting with a famous writer I've long admired and loved and had naughty fantasies about. No matter that he's gay.

I turned into Cinderella in a dress from the Goodwill on the day I met this literary genius the world knows as David Sedaris at a hotel, spending at least ninety minutes awed and enraptured. I couldn't think a clear thought or form a complete sentence as I felt my dark hair turning platinum blonde and my IQ dropping from its normal 50-to-70 range to around 35 points.

I couldn't take my eyes off of him. I wanted to invite him to sit in my lap, the cute little thing that he was. Being a big girl, 5 feet, 8 inches on a flat-heeled day, he could have nestled against my motherly tummy and I could have petted his brilliant little head.

He looked at me expectantly. I knew what he was wanting. He was like most men and wanted to get in and get out, quickly. I wanted it to last. Foreplay, lots of foreplay, even if it was in the form of staring and saying nothing. So that's what I did. It's all I could do. Stare speechless for quite some time.

"Sooooo," he said, and his famous and distinctive voice, one heard by millions on National Public Radio and his audio books, made my knees weak. It was that utterly unmatched blend of North Carolina, New York, European nasal delight. The man was nominated for two Grammy Awards for Best Spoken Word Album. His voice was his meal ticket.

"Any questions?" he asked, probably wondering why I was sitting there in a trance.

Questions. Shit. I was supposed to think up some sharp and extraordinarily original questions. I'm a reporter, a columnist, a foolish woman who, upon seeing this man, went from my mid-40s to being 17 and acting as if I was staring at Peter Frampton.

I mumbled and felt my hands shaking as I took out a pen that turned out to be a tampon attached to a panty liner that had escaped its plastic shield. Shit. Shit. Shit. He raised his cute little eyebrows, lit a cigarette and allowed one of those completely charming half smiles as I switched for a better pen. This time, an eyebrow pencil.

Mercy, things were going poorly. I knew he must have thought, "Wow, they sent a real winner to my hotel this time."

"Sorry," I said. "Let's see now . . ."

I was imagining we'd have intelligent conversation, exchange witticisms and then declare our soul mate status. Then reality hit. I'm married. He's gay. This is not a match made in Heaven or a match by any means. This was simply a famous gay man I was in love with cerebrally. One who would NEVER love me back.

But in my wild fantasy he would tell me what I longed to hear beautiful or smart gay men say. "I will no longer ever want another man in my life. You have changed me forever. I'm as straight as plywood."

Regardless, here he was, sitting directly across from me in a wrinkled shirt, shadowy stubble and that quirky face that reminds me of a gnome's only cuter.

Now, getting this once-in-a-lifetime chance to meet him at a motel, which the high class call hotels, was the highlight of my year, considering I hadn't given birth or done anything major in quite some time.

I wanted to enjoy cranial gymnastics with Sedaris, and then by the end of our interview, have him declare he was in love and that he'd have to drop poor Hugh, his boyfriend of one hundred years.

Of course at some point in a fantasy, one must face reality. Sedaris will never love me, and after our ninety minutes together I will probably never hear from him again unless I turn on my CD player and listen as his delightful voice chitters on about hitchhiking, youth in Asia or my favorite story about Santa and the six to eight black men.

While this first interview may well be our last, I must still consider myself blessed as both a journalist and a woman. Not a lot of gay-loving heteros get to meet David Sedaris in a hotel—especially one as opulently masculine and volcanically inspired as the Grove Park Inn, located in Asheville, North Carolina.

Here's how it all went down.

Thunder cracked and the sky emptied as I pulled into the swanky hotel parking lot with my notepad, nerves and audio recording device. I adjusted my bosoms, two unless I lie down (as you may recall), which are now approaching their third birthday and beginning a frightful descent that might require action should they not quit falling and multiplying.

I approached the concierge's desk. "I'm here to see Mr. David Sedaris," I said with great jubilance and measured control. The gracious and dignified hotel employee raised one brow, as if I was a loony fan trying to pull a stalking. Perhaps that much was true, but I didn't want to let on. Plus, I had Little, Brown's permission to meet the huge star of radio and stage, a major player on the *New York Times* Best-sellers List, the man who single-handedly turned a job as a Macy's elf into one of the funniest stories ever written.

My heart tripped as if I was 17 and meeting Frampton, which I never got to do because as I raced the stage during one of his concerts, the security guards grabbed me and put me in the "jail" at the Omni in Atlanta until the concert was over.

The concierge rang David's room.

"Yes, Mr. Sedaris. There is a reporter here who SAYS she has an appointment with you, but I wasn't sure this could possibly be the case . . . Yes . . . so you say. Well, then." The suspicious concierge, surprise on his face, grimaced and cleared his throat. "Mr. Sedaris will meet you here at my station momentarily." I gulped the humid air and listened as the rain pounded the hotel's tiled roof, rolling off in sheets as guests enjoyed the storm while sitting snug in giant rocking chairs under the covered porches.

I thought I would pass out and felt the palpitations coming on. Not now, I told my heart. I can't go to the ER now. I coughed and beat on my chest like a mad gorilla to get my heart back into proper rhythm.

Things kept dropping from my clumsy grip. First the notebook. Then the recording device. His people had said no camera, so I obeyed, thinking, "He's as a bad as a woman. Still, I love him so!"

I inhaled some yoga breaths and exhaled mightily, blowing the leaves off a small plant. I did some more breathing and chest beating and was gathering a bit of a crowd.

"Are you all right, ma'am?" the concierge asked.

"No. Do you have some defibrillator paddles like those they have on airplanes to keep people from dying of heart attacks and various and sundry arrhythmias?"

Just when I thought the room was going black and the heart attack had arrived, there he was. Precious David. Walking toward me in a wrinkled, striped yellow shirt and beautiful beard stubble. Was he smiling? Could he possible be smiling at ME????

I dropped my purse and blushed. "Sorry. I'm Susan . . . uh . . . Hi. Umm . . . I be with the . . . What I meant to say is, I'm *with* the paper. Not I *be* with the paper . . . Anyway . . . Oh, never mind." I couldn't remember the name of the paper or my last name. "I'm just here, well, to talk to you about stuff."

Stuff. Who says "stuff" to David Sedaris? He is accustomed to scholars analyzing and interviewing him, not country bumpkins who can't even remember their names and occupations.

We shook hands, though mine was already shaking on its own. We were about the same height. Should I hug him? Should I ask if he'd like a piggyback ride around the hotel just for fun? He couldn't weigh that much—maybe 110, 120. We could go up and down the great hallways giddy-upping and just forget the whole interview thing since I had no idea what in the world I was going to talk to him about.

"Hello," he said in an almost childlike voice and I moved forward to hug him, but it's a good thing I didn't, and you'll hear more about that later.

He didn't introduce himself. I figured it was because he is shy, and saying, "Hi, I'm David Sedaris" would be like a big movie star playing demure and saying, "Hello, I'm George Clooney." No need for introductions on his part. We decided to go someplace where he could smoke his Kool cigarette. I'd never known a white man to smoke Kools. Seemed like Kools were the top cig choice for hip African Americans and Marlboro Lights were for white folks.

We chose a small table in the main room where the fireplaces are big enough to engulf most of my living room. Dulcimers dueled, and I could barely hear the soft-spoken writer. I kept imagining him leaning over and saying, "Forget this. I think I love you. Isn't that what life is made of? Though it worries me to say that I've never felt this way."

He had probably watched *The Partridge Family*. I'll bet he liked David Cassidy, too. And Bobby Sherman and Peter Frampton.

He lit his cigarette, and I just sat there drinking in the smell as if it was aromatherapy and not carcinogenic. I panted and palpitated and wondered if maybe he would get upset if I did the gorilla defibrillator thing on my chest since I was again beginning to black out from nervousness. I had read in one of his books where he used to lick things like doorknobs and lightbulbs and that he suffered from an assortment of obsessive-compulsive behaviors and neuroses. Surely he would understand a girl trying to beat her heart back into a steady pump-pumping.

I was still wet with rain, rustling my papers and parcels like a dog trying to get comfortable. He smoked and stared and didn't seem to mind he was there for an interview and I was doing nothing but daydreaming and thinking of love songs.

I'd better ask something . . . anything. "Have you been here before, to Asheville?" My voice came out squeaky, twangy and very Loretta Lynnish.

He smiled and relaxed with his legs crossed and his arms loose. "About four or five times. Lisa's here with me," he said.

Oh, I guess he meant to throw that in so I'd know his "bodyguard" sister was on call in case I had any ideas of sinking my heterosexual fangs into his sweet gay neck meat.

This would be Lisa, his older sister, and one of his personal assistants of sorts. Other siblings also play starring roles in his books, which include *Barrel Fever*, *Holidays on Ice*, *Naked* and *Me Talk Pretty One Day*, the latter two becoming immediate best sellers. His latest that I owned, *Dress Your Family in Corduroy and Denim*, is also a best seller and I've read them all at least twice.

What could I ask next? Hmm. I just sat with the cat holding my tongue hostage and a recording device by my side. He stared at it several times. "It's not a camera," I said, laughing nervously. "I was thinking maybe later, we could have you do a little reading, a minireading into this microphone."

At this point he could have laughed hysterically at the preposterousness of my plan. Here was a man with a golden voice and here was a hicky, though I prefer drawling, Southern Belle with a cerebral crush on a very gay man trying to coax that voice onto her recording device.

His face registered utter kindness. Or maybe I was misreading things. Perhaps he was humming a Frampton tune. Maybe he was thinking how refreshingly small my pores were. I'll admit my skin was looking rather good since I burned it off with some acid ordered from eBay.

OK . . . What to ask? Other reviewers and interviewers always talk about his political satire and genius ways of describing the human race and condition with just the right blend of humor.

"I'm not the sort of journalist who's going to ask you those kinds of questions," I said.

He nodded and produced a "Mercy, what-did-my-publicist-get-me-into?" smile.

Instead, I asked about his wrinkled shirt. Turns out his plane arrived, but his luggage did not. We talked about his clothes, and I said to the most famous writer I'd ever met, "Why don't you go to the Goodwill and pick something up? I could drive you there. I bought a great Kate Spade with only a small flaw on the handle, kind of looked like a rat or dog had maybe chewed."

More of that look. He sort of cocked his head. Ah, he's cute. So small and fine-boned and adorable. I wanted to take him home and have him bronzed like a pair of baby shoes. Or maybe set him on the shelf. Or maybe just have him sign a few books I could set on the shelf.

"I love the Goodwill," I said. "Do you?"

Shit. I just asked David Freakin' Sedaris if he loved the Goodwill. I'm so fired. My career is over.

"I've been to the Goodwill before," he said and I knew then we were meant to be. If only it wasn't for that minor problem of me being married. And him being gay.

It's not like he was a snob. Lots of stories in his books talk about him working rather gross jobs including cleaning apartments in New York's rich section for a living.

"I won't buy pants there, though," he said, blowing curls of his Kool into the air.

"Really? Why not?" Oh, good, our conversation was finally off to a start.

He sucked his cig. "The last time I did, I got the crabs."

Saints alive, David Sedaris is talking about a sexually transmitted disease! This was going to be a great interview after all. "Oh, I got those one time, too," I said, wishing the hell I hadn't. "I was dating this gorgeous man, cute, even with a horse-shaped head and horsy teeth, and he passed them along claiming he picked them up off a workout bench at the Y. I know he cheated."

David seemed entranced and even leaned forward, closer to my face. I decided to divulge more. "I got rid of mine easily, since I couldn't find but two, but he was such a wooly booger he had to shave himself. Then guess what happened?"

"I can't imagine," David said.

"When all that fur grew back, the crabs—I call them crotch crickets—well, they came back, too. Do you know what he ended up doing?"

"I can't imagine," David said again, and I could tell he was bemused and enchanted and this subject was far more interesting than some fancy *New York Times* reporter picking and analyzing his brain.

"See, he was just planning on scaring them with his Bic lighter, but instead, he caught his whole pubic area on fire and had to go to the emergency room. His region blew up like that because he'd put Polo cologne down there for some odd reason and it sort of didn't mix with the Bic's flame."

Why am I saying this shit?

By now we had decided the dulcimers were too loud and moved to one of the long corridors of the inn. We faced the inner courtyard. Here, it was quiet. No music to compete with. No smoke. Nothing but sheets of rain and a wrinkled and stubbled famous author biding his time with a little-known reporter and doing so with grace. He didn't glance at his watch but once.

As we talked, his sister Lisa appeared and politely interrupted. She had a list of spa treatments she presented to her famous brother.

"There's the custom-blend facial or a hand-and-foot massage," she said. She also suggested he might enjoy the gentleman's wax, a paraffin for the hands and feet.

"You know I hate being touched," he said, drawing in his arms and getting twitchety about the face.

I thought about how I'd wanted to hug him. "I'm glad I didn't hug you," I said, and he agreed it wouldn't have been a good idea. "Southern women like to hug, you know?"

He pulled his arms in like a kangaroo's and smirked, that trademark grin, a smile without teeth.

He decided against the spa and planned to get to his Malaprop's gig two hours early. He knew the crowds would be thick; his performances sell out and the multitudes would run into the hundreds and thousands. That's a lot of books to sign. And he'll stay hours—sometimes until early morning—until every book is autographed. He's that nice of a guy, and I was surprised he was so low-key and quiet one-on-one, as opposed to his typical effervescent audience performances.

He even enjoys the book tours, something other authors dread but know comes with the territory. The airplane rides, the hotel stays, lack of sleep, countless media interviews—it's exhausting, yet Sedaris seems to thrive on the pace.

Typically, he converses with everyone who has come to see him, and has something witty to say or write in their books. The only thing that seems to irk him is the age-old question that haunts most humor writers—"Is this stuff for real? How much is exaggerated?"

That's like asking David Copperfield to reveal the secrets to his disappearing acts. He won't do it. Another drawback to fame and writing about his family is that Sedaris had no idea people would decide they knew them personally. It never occurred to him, either, that he'd become so popular—gaining in notoriety and building a bigger following with each book.

The fame has rather stunned him. He figured people know him through his National Public Radio readings, but recently, in Toronto, where there's no NPR, six hundred fans showed up at a bookstore.

By this point in our interview I'd given up talking about the Goodwill and fiery pubic mounds and asked him to reveal the secrets of his successful book signings.

"I had only eleven people come to mine in Charlotte," I said, "and nine were relatives."

What he usually does during these touring events is read stories for twenty-five minutes. "After that I run my mouth," he said, "and answer questions." His new way of signing is to draw a stick of dynamite and write "TNT" within the sphere, and then "You're Dynamite" on the book's page.

It was time for our interview to end and him to prepare for this evening. I shook his hand, wanting a hug, but knowing better. He accepted a copy of my book and said he looked forward to reading it. I doubted he ever would. But that's OK.

Later that night, amid the huge crowd bursting to get in the doors at Malaprop's, many pressing eager faces against the outside windows hoping for but a glimpse, Sedaris worked the room as a waiter might take drink orders.

He gets as many books signed this way as possible—to avoid dragging back to his hotel at 3 AM and keeping bookstore employees up into the wee hours.

Because his luggage never arrived, he told the crowd he was lacking in his typical gift-bearing routine for the young people.

"I figure they'd rather be doing drugs or having sex, so I like to give them a prize for coming to a book signing," he said.

And with that, he handed out dollar bills, shampoos and lotions from various hotels, and other trinkets. This is the Sedaris way of saying, "Thank you."

Two days after our interview, he sent me a humorous postcard, thanking me for interviewing him. On it were two bimbos with huge tits.

"I think your new breasts look terrific," he wrote. This means he at least read part of my book.

It's a card I'll save forever.

Fishing for a Date

For quite a few years now, more than I care to admit, men have all but quit glancing my way. That's fine, I don't look their way too much either due to my wild estrogen swings and wayward hormones, which, long ago, could have been called whore moans as I was a tigress on the prowl.

These days, even the bald-headed fellas tend to "ma'am" me as if I'm old enough to be their mothers. They may look my direction with a modicum of interest, and as soon as they're close enough to see the years of living etching my forehead and the upper arms waddling like a pelican's pouch with a fresh fish, they glance elsewhere. Usually at my enhanced chest, which is entirely another story with an ending that sends people either reeling or peeling with laughter.

A friend of mine lined up for a host of cosmetic procedures shortly after her divorce, saying she had to get "shelf ready" or "market fresh" as if she was an Arby's sandwich or something. Another friend looked at her as if she was crazy. We middle-aged women tend to travel in packs and it helps to talk about our wrinkles, which tag along with zits, bloating and wiggling body parts.

"I'm having a major overhaul," this friend, who looked great to me, said. "It's like being a car with 50,000 miles. The engine may be good but my paint's dulling, my belts (skin) are loose, I need new tires (titties) and my muffler fell," meaning her butt dropped.

"Why would you want to do all that?" I asked. "Sounds painful and expensive."

"How else will I find another husband?"

"My mama always said personality and a sense of humor goes a long way."

"Well, I have no personality. But I'll have the flattest stomach in North Carolina and the firmest thighs after my dual lipo and thigh lift."

"Good Lord, girl. I'd much rather have good furniture at this stage in life or travel to Europe and the Caribbean. You know what happened after I gave myself that chemical peel I bought off eBay? I forgot the most important step, that part where you neutralized the acid so you don't burn to bone, and swear to God I saw a piece of skull. Don't mess with yourself. Just get some Crest Whitestrips and a decent girdle. If you find the right man, make him buy the procedures, sugar pie. They will, believe me. Men like pretty things hanging off their arms. It all goes back to the days when they carried carcasses over their shoulders."

She harrumphed and sipped her coffee.

"A push-up bra is a good idea along with a fine-fitting pair of jeans," I said. "Go to the Gap. They size pants all wrong, in a good way. I wear a 10 but can get away with a 6 at the Gap. They have good mirrors and lighting and know a thing or two about marketing to our crowd."

Women, as we all know, have a need to feel attractive and be told this OFTEN by the men we are with. If they fail to do so, I can all but guarantee we will dump them like cantaloupe rinds in the compost of our past melons. Men, I'm told, at least the metrosexual ones, have the same needs. Wimps. Seems to me the mirrors or reflecting storefronts they're always peacocking in would do it for them.

One of the measures by which we as men and women gauge our appeal is by how many eyes move to meet our gaze. What few single friends I have are beautiful young creatures with bodies unscathed by breeding and Big Macs, and yet these lovelies have the gumption to complain about the slim pickings and how only creeps have the nerve to approach them.

"Well, count your blessings you at least get a nibble," I tell them. "My bait's so old even the bottom dwellers won't bite. All I get are men who want green cards or I'll get long, hand-written letters that come to my office from lonely prisoners convinced we are soul mates and if I would just read their 1,200-page book, I'd for sure realize they don't belong on death row for killing their wives, which, naturally, they didn't do or so they all say. Whew. That kind of mail will sure make a gal swoon."

"I'm a magnet for the grossest of creatures," one of my dearest middle-aged, twice-divorced, once-widowed and newly single friend said.

"Aren't we all?" I ask. "The unsavories are the only ones with guts."

I then began explaining to her how to get a man, the advice coming from a woman who has been out of the dating pool for seventeen years. However, prior to my marriage, dear Single-tons, I had my share of toads, warts and the occasional semidecent human being. But when you're young, my pretties, there is a sad tendency to toss out the good ones, thinking—actually, knowing—schools of these fine fish will be swimming by constantly and you can choose whichever one you want at any time. Provided, of course, you don't weigh 200 pounds and are terribly unattractive, bless your hearts.

Well, let me tell you cute girls something. Eventually, time runs out and the schools of fish swim in other waters. When you reach a CERTAIN age, the only thing swimming by are fatso hairy men crowding the lanes at the YMCA indoor pool in their Speedos, with swollen balls and perverted grins.

Fear not, though. There is always hope, which can arrive and occur in the strangest of places.

A couple of years ago, during a family vacation, I learned how to catch a man even if you have fat sacks, rolls of sidemeat, and a face that could benefit a hoisting by wooden clothespins or some serious shrink-wrap. All you have to do is put on a decent, décolletage-enhancing swimsuit, a sarong to hide anything lumpy or mottled, and cart around a fairly nice fishing rod. Yes, you read correctly: a fishing rod!

Skip the ones with Mickey Mouse on them. The other fisher-
men won't take you seriously and you'll be called a Poser, which
is a middle-school term meaning some sort of faker or pre-
tender.

Go to Wal-Mart or anywhere else that sells sporting goods.
I like to go to Dick's because just saying the word gives me a
sickish pleasure. While there, invest in an adult fishing rod. A
$15.99 special will do and don't forget the tackle box—even if
it's really your makeup kit. He'll never know. Make sure you've
got a Ziploc bag of bait. I like the dead shrimp and squid, personally.

Here's what happened one fine sunny day on the great
sparkling Atlantic coast in Hilton Head, the ritzy beach in
South Carolina. I set out to fish during one of my marital-discord
(PMS) days and squeezed all extra flesh into a purple rhinestone
swimsuit, paired with a lavender sarong appliquéd in taffeta-
like butterflies. Add to this fishing getup some pink lipstick and
a single strand of pearls and designer sunglasses, and, I must
say, you've got yourself the perfect Southern Belle fishing attire.

The whole getup might shock some people at first, but they
will get over it. Take my son, for example, upon seeing his
mother in her Ready-to-Fish Wear, which should be hitting
Vogue magazine any day, once one of their editors reads this
piece.

"You're wearing THAT fishing?" he yelped as we headed to
the beach and proceeded to spear shrimp and rank squid parts
onto a rusted hook and cast the line, my arm fat waving at the
sea, even with my thick golden bangle acting as a decorative
triceps' girdle.

My first cast soared about two feet. The second and third,
not much farther. I heard laughter. Male giggling. I saw to my
right an attractive man shaking his head.

"What's so funny?" I asked as I professionally recast, this
time my line going a good ten yards while I carefully and very
prolike, took out the slack.

"I've never seen someone like you fishing."

"What's that supposed to mean?"

He seemed taken aback.

"I'll have you know I grew up on a lake and have been fishing since I was 7," I said. "I even take them off the hook with my bare hands, gut 'em and roll them in cornmeal."

"Did you dress like that back then?"

He grinned and had the prettiest smile with all teeth in place. I knew he was using his Crest Whitestrips on a regular basis.

"Don't go letting a few fake pearls and gold bracelets fool you. Soon enough I'll have a hammerhead on this hook, so you best body surf a few hundreds yards south of us." He was adorable, like the plumber on *Desperate Housewives*.

I gave him a flirtatious side tilt of the head. "You're too cute and I'm too married," I said, though at this moment, I'd like to use parts of him as bait and see what sinks its jaws into my hooks. Had I been single, I'd have asked him to come on over and watch, and I'd show him some pointers, other than my fairly new hooters.

Being still married at the moment, I decided not to pursue this line of flirting, having been raised by a proper mother who scared us to death when it came to sin and the flames of Hell sure to cremate us daily. I didn't want to reel in another man when the first was still on my line. There's no sense catching one yacht till the other's tied to the dock, so to speak.

The cutie-pie fisherman took off when he saw he wasn't making progress, in or out of the water, but my point is this: I could have had him. He was cute, had ALL of his teeth, a two or three-pack set of abs, most of his hair and only a slight case of that puffy-face syndrome older men who like beer will get. And you could have had him, too.

Fishing, my dears, is a great way to meet men. Not swamp, creek, river or bridge fishing, but classy fishing in the finest bodies of waters, wherever one can find those.

If a fishing pole isn't feasible, try browsing in Dick's Sporting Goods anyway for an hour or two, or one of the hip bookstores that also serves beverages. I see swarms of fellows drinking their Mocha Lattes while reading in bookstore/coffee shops. If he is reading a *Penthouse* or *Hot Rod* magazine, run the other way.

I do not advise Laundromats as fertile grounds for meeting potential sweethearts. If he can't afford his own damn washer and dryer, you best move on unless you notice he's washing a barffed-on comforter or giant dog bed, which means he doesn't want to spoil his own set of sparkling Maytags.

Another excellent place to meet men is Home Depot or Lowe's. Go in and say the following to either the help (although even if he's cute his wages can't be too high) or a handsome shopper:

"Sir, I'm so sorry to bother you. I'm just not feeling at home here as I do at Tiffany on Fifth Avenue where I know my way around every locked and sealed counter. Would you mind showing me where the nails and screws are located?"

Why, they'll drop everything if you're fixed up a bit and don't resemble a giant lesbian getting ready to tar a roof. You might want to smile at this point and say, "Me being here would be similar to you trying to buy eyeliner at the Estée Lauder counter."

He'll either run or ask you out.

As far as that old line about finding men in the frozen-food section of your local grocer, that may work, unless it's a store called It's Old But Won't Kill Ya, Animal Organ Central or Dented and Dated. Only the high-dollar grocery stores, even health-food stores, will sometimes net a decent catch.

As for Internet dating, the wave of the current trends, I have witnessed plenty of men and women catching fish this way, then later either marrying them or throwing them back into cyberwaters. It may be the foam of the future, but those representing themselves can and DO lie. Dating sites on the Internet might end up being no more than electronic negligees, so watch out is all I'm saying.

For those who already have a man and need a boost in the commitment department, I'm here to help. Remember, I'm the sister of a woman who once had seven diamond engagement rings and I can reveal her secrets now that she's joyfully wed Husband Number Two she met off the Internet while wearing her cyberlingerie.

Remember, timing is everything, and men's horny-mones start cranking up around the first cold snap and continue through Valentine's Day when merchants and TV commercials remind them that they can get laid if they buy chocolate and diamonds and say gushy stuff and act like they mean it.

This is open season on mate snagging. Whip out those arrows and give Cupid a run for his sharp-shooting aim. The months between Thanksgiving and mid-February are the busiest time of year for engagements, according to somebody I can't remember at WeddingChannel.com.

The woman is known as one of the busiest wedding planners in the world, advising more than 720,000 brides each year. She's penned a Top Ten list of "Signs Your Boyfriend Is Going to Propose This Valentine's Day."

Some of those clues are obvious. Let's say, for instance, he starts talking about platinum rings and princess cuts. These aren't topics most men gab about. If you say princess cut to a regular ESPN-watching man, he'll think one of the Royals had been stabbed. Mention marquise and he'll think of the sign lit up at the All Night Nudie Den.

Another clue is if you catch him suddenly pressing his face in the windows of jewelry stores. He's either looking at rings or pulling the old Peacocking routine.

Still another clue is a ring missing from your jewelry box. If he's not on crack or a major thief, chances are he's trying to match up your size. It's also a positive sign that you'll be treated to a dazzling diamond if he tells you not to make plans for a certain evening but won't say what his intentions are. If after saying this, he takes you bowling, dump him. Unless of course there is a giant, flawless princess-cut diamond in one of the bowling balls and he's also springing for the beer and hot dogs.

Watch out, too, for the more subtle hints, experts say. What if he starts making his own coffee instead of plunking down cash at Starbucks, along with brown-bagging his lunches? Maybe, just maybe, he's saving for a ring. Either that or he's a secret gambler and lost big at poker or at the races. Or maybe his Internet porno bill came in the mail and he didn't realize just how long he'd sat there last month dirty-chatting and tugging his man meat.

Please dump all Internet porn viewers. Unless you enjoy the same habit. In that case you are a True and Unreformed Hussy.

Another way to find out his mission, without breaking and entering his private plans, is to sit at his computer for a spell. Nothing like forgetting to erase one's history to know where he's been in cyberland. If wedding sites pop up like frogs after a heavy rain, you can be sure the question will pop as well. If porno ads pop up like . . . Skip that simile . . . It's best to ditch and flee.

Lots of these suggestions, some from the experts and some from my own and my sister's experiences, are all good signs you've got a man who's not scared of marriage. Yet it can be fairly hard with some men—this convincing him you're the best thing since Sam Adams, and that a platinum band with at least a full carat or two flashing isn't going to kill him but merely gouge his bank account. Nothing a tourniquet won't cure.

If you're worried that the man you've invested all your best years in will never make an honest woman out of you, I'm sorry. Cut that fish from the line and let him sink to the muck below. He's nothing more than a bottom dweller and will never rise to decent levels.

All that out of the way, let's discuss what's out there in terms of heterosexual men.

First, the kind we love: those who adore marriage or at least tolerate the notion. No problem pulling these babies in. It's like fishing in a stocked pond.

Next, you have the Lothario who considers himself something of a Hugh Hefner and likes being encircled by the estrogen variety pack. He'd never consider settling down to a home-cooked meal with a permanent Little Missus. This fellow isn't going anywhere near a jewelry store but has probably made plenty of trips to the STD clinic.

The third and by far most popular category, in my opinion, is the man who can take marriage or leave it. He will continue dating you until every tooth falls out and Croaker's Rest Home has you both on its waiting list. This lazy paramour is going to need hints and coaxing and, I daresay, maybe a cattle prod to get him moving. Fear not. Here are a few tips. Some are from me, just a middle-aged woman with years of experience in dating duds, creeps, commitment-phobes, and an array of normal and ultrafine fellows I stupidly rejected in my youth, thinking schools of fish would always be swimming by.

First of all, if he's in the category of men who would rather be carted to an anesthesia-free vasectomy den than down any matrimonial aisle, cut him faster than you would a snapping turtle and let him swim off to ruin someone else's life.

Second, if he's the type who's begging you to marry him, check his temperature and his police record, and interview all friends and former neighbors. Extreme eagerness is a warning sign no matter how cute and darling you might be.

Finally, there's the lazy and blissfully blasé group of men, You may want to come right out and drop hints—huge, heavy, in-their-face hints. My favorite is talking very loud on the telephone to your best friend so that he can hear it when you say, "Julie Ann, I'm telling ya, girl. If he doesn't have a ring on my finger by February 14, I'm going to go ahead and put myself back on the shelf. Know any nice single men? Oh, right. You were telling me about him. Hmmmm."

Be sure at this stage of the conversation that your slacker is listening. "Uh-huh. Of course it doesn't bother me a bit that he quit his medical practice to become a senator and goes to Africa to feed the hungry every summer. Yes, I'm not one to care about money, but it is good he has that ongoing trust fund . . . Oh, my! You are KIDDING? Sounds great . . . He can't possibly have said I was THAT cute . . . You just set it all up and call me . . . WHAT? Did you say nine inches!!! You are a naughty girl, Julie Ann, and I love ya for it . . . OK, then, I'll talk to you later. Love ya. Bye now."

Games in relationships are taboo so they say. But they are also like voodoo. Sometimes, it's the only thing that jabs a man where it counts—in his commitment zones. Even though I'm in the relationship camp that the delightful *Bridget Jones* character calls "Smug Marrieds," I like to dip my pen from time to time into the dating pool and see what's new out there for my wonderful singleton friends. Many of them, both the young and not-so-young, are back in the game. Some have found love on the Internet, which we've addressed and undressed earlier.

Others have hooked up with beaus from the past. This hot trend is not my cup of tea, as my feeling is, "Why resurrect something you buried for good reason years ago?" Still, some find it quite fulfilling to excavate the heart and pump up old treasures. Good for them. May the joy be with them.

I received a list the other day about first dates and given that supposedly about half the U.S. adults are single, duty says pass this on. I've narrowed it down and call it the "Seven Rules for Successful Firsts." I've also included my own tried-and-true no-no's for those debut dates.

1. Order food you like. Sending it back is obnoxious.
   My rule: Don't say, "I'm not hungry," or tell the server you'll just have a house salad and Diet Coke. This sends a message you have issues with food or are borderline neurotic.

2. Don't brag about how great you are. Don't ask how much he/she makes or what he weighs or anything about their ex's.
   My rule: It's not a good idea to talk about how fat both your front and back fannies were before Jenny Craig, or how your ex did time while you were in detox and met the man of your dreams down the hall. That said, if you're in this for an Anna Nicole deal, it's OK to ask how much the person brings home after taxes.

3. Don't chew gum. It's trashy and annoying. Pop a mint instead.
   My rule: If your breath is bad, don't even go on the date. Reschedule after a session with a tartar-removal specialist.

4. Turn off your cell phone. The date came to talk to you, not hear you chat up someone else.
   My rule: If a guy answers a call during a date and he's not the president or the father of sickly children needing tending, you can bet he's self-absorbed or a crack dealer. You might want to say, "Excuse me," then leave and don't return unless you are super desperate, which you are NOT.

5. Ailments and current health issues should be saved for later dates.
   My rule: Nothing scrapes the romance from a date's potential sheen like talking about your latest Pap smear results. I once had a first date who told me he almost had to cancel because of a bout of what I call "Die Rear." It was my first and LAST date with this human toilet.

6. Leave work at work.
   My rule: I think this one is a bit harsh. Some people like to hear about other's jobs. If he's closing his eyes or yawning, you may want to make up a career. If you're desperate—which you're NOT—you could always tell him you had to give up your evening job at Bubba's Nudie Den because of shin splints. If his eyes don't open, run for the door. If they do open, run anyway.

7. Be a good listener. If you're doing all the talking, you're not on a date; you're giving a speech.
   My rule: If you are out with a political candidate, you can bet your last dollar he's going to campaign his little heart out on your date. Tell him/her you need to powder your nose, then hightail it out of there as quickly as possible. I

once had this happen and ended up buying two tickets to a political pig pickin' just to shut him up.

I realize it's not easy out there in the dating world. But with these tidbits of unconventional wisdom in mind, I know you'll net the fish of your dreams.

Cast on, Sugahs. Just don't forget the pearls and sarong, the lipstick and bangles.

Ode to Bald Men, Precious Thangs

I used to glance right past bald men, a shallow woman I was before I encountered gray hair and sagging skin mottling my own middle-aging body, a condition of muscle atrophy I call the "Crock Pot" effect.

I may not be terribly fat, but since I gave up exercise, my meat's falling off the bone like a Crock-Pot chicken I tell my friends who have personal trainers and muscle definition. I guess they have time for such frivolities as good health.

Being in my forties, I've learned time will teach a girl a thing or two. And one is that if a man is bald, he's usually not as vain as those with full heads of hair and is less likely to plunge as Narcissus did into a pool upon falling in love with his own reflection.

I have never taken a formal poll, but my guess would be they are less likely to cheat. Also, if they have all their teeth in good to excellent shape, to hell with their hair or lack thereof. There is one exception to the baldies. This would be that unfortunate condition I like to call the "potbellied pig" male-pattern baldness.

This is when the poor man has one hair here and another there, some of which is spaced a good half inch apart and stiff as a bore's, just like pig hair. Bless their oinking hearts.

Regardless, I've personally come to love bald men, especially the partially bald ones that have the fringe around the edges and no hope in hell for a comb-over. While not at all proven, my theory is that this clownlike pattern of male baldness generally occurs in your more jovial and intellectual men. I'd like to do a study on this, but am too busy worrying about my children growing up decent and not going to jail or marrying Bubbas who drive and/or restore El Caminos.

I don't care how many full-fluffy-haired men are out there. If a girl can get past her fear of the shining egg, she'll learn there are not enough great things to be said for Bald Men.

Truth is, Bald Men are a Win-Win. Maybe someone will see my idea (it was here first) and make up some bumper stickers and I can get rich enough to buy retail and the real Crest Whitestrips instead of the store brands that all but pull out my teeth.

You don't need to read the above paragraphs again. You have read correctly. If a fellow has good teeth, there's nothing wrong with a head minus hair. My personal motto is: Teeth are the Foundation. Hair is but a Shingle.

All this bald talk stemmed from a column I wrote in which a certain reader got all riled up, as my readers will do from time to time, particularly on the days when their Vicodin prescriptions run out. The man had taken offense to my column about "fishing to catch a man," in particular the part where I mentioned attracting only bald men who "ma'am me." He was so angry he canceled his newspaper subscription. It wasn't funny, he noted, and e-mailed me wondering how I'd feel if a man wrote an article saying, "Even the flat-chested ones quit looking his way" in describing women.

I replied:

Dear Sir,

My husband's going bald and I'm four-chested, much like a milking cow. Also, as a side note, I've been going bald for two years but have learned the great art of the Female Rooster Comb-over Puff-and-Spray, a new look for women who are receding.

I continued in this euphoric type-fest:

Look in the mirror, dear smooth top.

Be proud that you are hair-free and that when you cook, no one can accuse you of dropping a hair into their Quiche Lorraine. I praise bald men. Purely love them.

He picked up the phone about an hour after our e-mail exchange, slurring, "You old snooty witch. Who do you think you is? I lost my hair in a turkey-frying accident and how dare you insult follically challenged men in your sorry-ass col-yume?"

"I apologize, sir," I said, "I have grown to love, admire and respect the bald men of—"

I'll have you know," he said, "that turkey-frying incident on Thanksgiving took my eyebrows and lashes along with it, along with part of my bottom lip, and since I was out there nekkid, it being 4 AM and all, it singed away my pubic area.

Oh, damn. What does one say to that? Should I tell him about my boyfriend who lit his own genny-tale-ya fur afire on purpose to kill a bad case of crotch crickets? Should I hang up?

Before I could answer, he continued. "Women like it if you ain't got no hair down there to get caught in their teeth, if you'uns know what I mean. Looky, here. All's I'm saying is be nicer in your col-yumes about bald men. You never know how they got that way, you'uns hear me?"

"Yes. I'm sorry. Now what was your name again?"

"Bubba. Bubba the Bald Wonder."

Since a humor columnist can hardly write a single paragraph without setting off a blazing fire of anger from the ultra-sensitive or the special interests groups, here are my true and purest thoughts on why it's lovely—even preferred, to a degree—to be bald:

1. You will save at least $8 a month on shampoos, $10 on electricity from the lack of blow-drying, and $15 because only the ear and nose hairs need a trim and you

can do that yourself. (Unless you're like Bubba the Bald Wonder and burned those during a manly grill out or turkey-frying inferno.)

2. Don't forget all those savings on conditioners, gels and sprays. Enough to buy you a case of Bud Light.

3. The only toiletry bald men need for the head department is sunscreen with an SPF of 30 in order to protect the Great Hairless One's tender top.

4. Bald men are less likely to crash into a storefront window while peacocking.

5. They are less likely to cheat, unless addicted to the Web site www.womengoingintoheatoversmoothtops.com. I made that up, but may start one and charge a hefty fee to go along with my bumper sticker business.

6. With bald men, you won't have to wash the pillowcases as often, like other women whose husbands shed profusely, unleashing dandruff and the odors of the day trapped in all those crevices.

7. If you forget your compact, you can just tell him you'll need a full head tilt.

8. You won't have to wash his combs nor will he require an extra towel every time he showers. Men with too much hair typically use multiple towels.

9. You'll be able to get out the door much quicker in the wintertime. Cap him and shoo him into the vehicle. No need to wait on him to festoon a 'do.

10. But best of all, and the number one reason to love a bald man is . . . drumroll, please . . . If all that blood isn't circulating on top of his head, it's got to be going somewhere else!

If It's Not in His Kiss, Could It Be in His Boxers?

Most junk mail that comes across my computer gets trashed. But when the headline screams, HOW TO TELL IF SHE'S READY TO BE KISSED, well, curiosity gets the best of me.

Especially when it's a guy telling us these things.

The author of the Kiss Test, at www.datingsecretsonline. com, said just thinking a woman's lips look luscious isn't indicative of her interest. Well, duh, dude. He says a guy first has to touch a fair maiden's hair and comment on it being soft as he feels and smells her tresses. If she smiles and seems to enjoy it, then she probably won't mind if he up and plants one on her. So says he.

If I was with a guy who started messing with my 'do, I'd have to knock out his teeth then and there. You don't fool with just any woman's hairdo, I don't care where she's from. Certainly not if it's been sprayed and lacquered, maybe even put in a kiln, glazed and fired.

We take our hair seriously. I remember Tidy Stu saying, long after we got married, "The first time I felt your hair it was like grasping old hay that a mule had upchucked." Wow, glad he kept that to himself back then.

Look here. I may be out of the dating pool, but I sure remember plenty of times when I wanted to be kissed and got nothing. Or when I didn't want to be kissed and got clobbered or slobbered. The Web site author, who I'm sure is a precious and peachy thing, also claims he knows top-secret body language to keep a woman's attention, things like: how to approach a new woman you'd like to meet and what to say to start a conversation without resorting to pickup lines. He also knows of fun places to take women that are free, thus no paying for expensive dates.

Personally, I don't like cheap dates. I don't mind poor dates, but if they are tightwads with money, they can hightail it elsewhere, preferably the nursing home, Croaker's being my personal favorite. Mr. Cheapy Pie can entertain the ladies with his guitar and cheesy smiles. Maybe if he opens the case, someone will throw in a few pennies. Or dentures. Or a wad of tissues, maybe a walking stick or prosthesis.

Not to be shallow, but if on a first date a man takes me to a church event, that's fine and impressive. But he'll score more points and chances for smooching behind the pews if he plunks down a fistful of cash in the collection plate when it passes amongst the crowd. A good woman doesn't mind a poor fellow as long as he knows where to direct moolah when it does come toward his pockets, and that would be to us or the man upstairs.

What's really bad is when you go out on a date and he forgets his wallet or credit cards and then swoops in like some rabid bat and plants a toothy kiss somewhere between your lips and chin, maybe even causing an open and bleeding wound if he has hyena choppers or fangs a dentist failed to file.

There is nothing to ruin a kissing mood like a set of hyena teeth. Sugar pies, there are men (and women) out there with teeth like the Ugliest Dog Alive's, though he's now dead, God rest poor Sam, the Chinese Crested's soul. You wanna see him? Go to www.samugliestdog.com.

My beautiful friend Myrtle who is making me call her Emma in this book because she's always wanted to be an Emma, says many a date or potential suitor ended up ruining, flat-out destroying the mood, when he opened his mouth and flashed some Ugly Dog hyena teef. Not teeth, my dears, but *teef*.

She's been surfing Match.com and is suddenly learning why

some of the men don't smile in their photos. She found one who had great possibility as a prospect and decided to meet him in person, getting the fright of her life when he accidentally smiled and his hideous (we pronounce it hid-yus) set of Billy-Bob teeth caused her to swallow her Ultra-Whitening Tic Tacs and began hacking uncontrollably. It was a shame, she said, because he had so much going for him, things like a job and 401(K) plan and a fairly decent and restored Pacer.

"I broke down in an e-mail and told Houston he needed his teeth bleached," she said, laughing and wailing. "They're crooked, and I don't mind that as long as there're enough in the gums so it's not like looking down a dark hole, but, damn, they are brown. BROWN! Not just yellow but dark brown. Shit brown, Susan!"

Being charming and Southern, she said in her gentle e-mail to this man, "Nicely bleached teeth would show off your beautiful dimples and gorgeous blue eyes." She knew how to get another date with him and slap the Crest Whitestrips or Zoom machine his way.

"You gotta be honest," she said. "There's no pussyfootin' around when it comes to teeth."

Hear that, ladies and gents? Get thee to a bleaching den ASAP. You can have a brighter smile for as little as ten to thirty bucks if you buy over-the-counter, which sure beats not getting another date. Also, it's a great idea to use dental floss for more than holding up bad socks or strangling insects.

Brushing once a day, as one of my dearest friends does, isn't going to cut it either. If you don't have hair, that's not your fault, however, if you don't have teeth, then you are a lazy SOB or, bless your heart, have a gum disease that's NOT your fault.

I had to tell as much to my dear friend who grinds and is dangerously close to having himself a set of Green Giant Niblets corn teeth.

"But I brush them long and hard," he said.

"Your butt will be at Affordable Clackers if you don't floss, get to a dentist and use something besides that toothbrush from 1986 to scrub those tartared teef."

Bless their molars. The latest research shows gum disease as a result of tooth neglect can cause heart problems, even death. It's all a matter of that old jingle: the hip bone's connected to the leg bone . . ."

Regardless of oral care or lack thereof, let's jump back to the part where that dating guy says he knows when a woman wants to be kissed. I think I know more than he does, as my information stems from the mind and experiences of a reformed Hussy Queen who's had plenty of practice, too much, by my double-virgin mother's standards.

First, the woman who wants to be kissed will casually lick her lips (I'm not talking about a slutty motion or a dog about to get a steak). She may even stare at your face and lips. Then again, if she's not a Recovering Hussy and is in full huss mode, she'll just do all sorts of vile things with her mouth and tongue to get your attention.

Second, she'll subconsciously pucker. Third, she will be wearing perfume and nice clothes, not a muumuu with orthopedic slippers and a steel-belted radial bra or ugly old Mee-Maw drawers with crotches the same color as bad teeth.

For starters, a kiss is like the salad, and if it's bitter, wilted or made entirely of iceberg, well, the entree can't be much better. It goes without saying the teeth must be tip-top, as should the man's breath.

An astute editor at my paper approached my desk with another one of those Harlequin Romance reports featuring the topic of kissing—best kisses, most kissable men and women, and best movie kisses.

First, let me preface this by saying I've lived long enough to have survived some horrendous kisses, and no doubt delivered a few myself before proper training. As a young girl, I practiced on my own hand, windowpanes, even trees if the bark wasn't too bulky or rough, pine trees being the worst.

Before we drumroll to Harlequin's top kiss picks—who, I'll go ahead and tell you, are all the usual suspects: George Clooney, Julia Roberts, Halle Berry, Brad Pitt, Jennifer Aniston, Will

Smith, Jennifer Lopez and Michelin Tire lips, aka Angelina Jolie—let's return to those early kisses of youth.

I'd like to share with readers some of the notables on the Buzzard Fleet, that pet name chosen for my ex-boyfriends. I share this fleet because these are the types most of us will have run-ins and lip-locks with rather than the Mel Gibsons and Pierce Brosnans of the Harlequin Calendar world. Here they are, my pretties . . .

THE PECKER: This male is like a hen in a coop, stabbing the female face with painful, jabbing pecks at lips, cheeks, chin and anything else he finds worthy of the craw. Never go out on a second date with a Pecker unless you like scars and wounds. Those with hamster and hyena teeth are notorious peckers.

THE SWOOPER: Here's a guy who'll come diving in at all the wrong angles, craning his neck and plummeting like a blind, fanged bat, never meeting with lips but instead crashing into various other parts of the face. Tragic sense of landing, the poor fellow. One nearly bit off my nose.

THE WRITHING MISSILE: What this muscular wonder loves to do is show his dates he's got a mean tonguing machine ready to burst out of its own enameled gate and enter yours. Warning: Clamp down hard to prevent a damaging onslaught. His tongue is lizardlike, rough as a cat's, and like some sort of hardened piece of mobile liver. He is of the wrong notion that the farther he can cram his missile down your throat, the happier you'll be. Get a clue: if your tongue's not dark chocolate, don't stick it in so freakin' far.

THE STEAMROLLER: When he decides to kiss, he lays one on so crushing it could all but suffocate a girl. What's typically left of a woman once he's peeled back the passion is a set of flattened lips and loose teeth. Steer clear from this Kissing Battering Ram.

MR. OVERMOISTURE: You can see him from a mile away, licking and relicking his lips, greasing them up with an assortment of balms and fruity ChapSticks. This, my darlings, is a condition known as OCD: Obsessive Compulsive Disorder. Remember? I had it back in kindergarten when I peed every three minutes. This buzzard is one with an unhealthy fear of dry mouth. Same holds true for the constant gum chewer. Makes you wonder what he's been gnawing all day or if he's never met up with an Oral-B in his lifetime.

THE SALIVATOR: Oooooh, heavens. This may be the worst. This fountain of fluids produces an overabundance of saliva that has caused many a woman to seek higher ground. The Salivator should put his liquid gifts to good use watering a few plants before picking up his dates.

THE BRICK OVEN: Should we even go here? Men who smoke pot (I only know from what my friends report!) have mouths like parched and cracked fields. It's like kissing a bag of dry dirt. The antidrug campaign could use this truth in its TV spots: Pot Ruins the Perfect Kiss.

With the kissing part addressed, we can now turn to the area where this dating expert, mentioned earlier, says he knows all the secret body language to attract women. Again, I think a recuperating Huss would know much more than he would. No offense, fellow.

Let me give you a few pointers on what WON'T attract girls but will send them fleeing faster than fair maidens being chased by hyena-toothed men. Here are some no-no's I've put together if you want to show your menfolk these major turn-offs for us women:

1. Flexing one's muscles in front of mirrors while working out at a gym.

2. Gazing at one's self in store windows while walking with a date downtown, a condition also known as Peacocking. Also known as a condition occurring more frequently in men with Littlecocking.

3. Sashaying around like some kind of superstud let loose (perhaps from the penitentiary) for the first time in a decade.

4. If a guy struts and moves like he's on the prowl, cut him free and send him packing.

5. If he plunks down lots of money in the offering plate and tips well at dinner, you may just let him touch the tips of your hair.

6. Also, for those paying attention, pickup lines are very 70s. A friend of mine's sister invented a game called 52-card Pick Up that's a much better gimmick for snagging interest than coming out and uttering idiotic phrases like, "Baby, you're like a fine grand piano and I'd love to pluck your keys."

This friend's sister created a deck of conversation-starting cards designed to get the ball rolling. One of my favorite cards says a plain and simple, ¡*Hola!* What guy could resist a girl who sends over not only a cold beer, but an *Hola* card and, maybe, a shot of Cuervo?

I'm also partial to the card that says, "Oh, Behave!" and one asking, "Sushi on Saturday?" Well, fine, buster, if you got the teef to chew through the seaweed in the center.

With these tips in mind, go forward confidently. Choose wisely, and remember, a kiss is more than just a kiss. It takes skill, practice, timing, tenderness and TEETH!!!!!

If there's not one you can kiss at this moment, maybe a bit of digging and circulating in the real world or even the cyber-world can remedy that situation. There's nothing like digging up past flames, according to yet another recent Harlequin Romance survey.

The big discovery in one report revealed quite a bit about the human heart; in particular, how a good many of us long for that special someone from our past. One in four of us, Harlequin says, still carries flaming torches for lost loves, even to the point of making it hard for us to find Mr. or Ms. Right.

The thought of rummaging about and recycling some castoff from my past sends cold shivers up my spine. Others were fine catches but I was stupid and didn't see it at the time. If I was to try to dig up the good ones, they'd probably tell me to stick it.

As for the Buzzards, how could I not have foreseen the icky or twisted paths a few of these former suitors would take? On the flip side, they are probably relieved as well they didn't end up with me or my lovely sister, God love them. In our day, my sister and I used to drag home some real doozies for my mother and father to all but hit the floor upon meeting.

Allow me, if you will, a trip down Memory Lane, doused with the rejects (both those we tossed and those who tossed us):

LIFE'S A PILE MAN: This monotoned beast belonged to my sister for about half a summer. He would show up in his Burger Chef uniform, smelling of a deep fryer and loll about moaning, "Life's a Pile," every time one of us said a word, no matter the subject. For example, during dinner at my parents' house one night—a nice grilled rib eye, baked potato and salad—Mama was talking about one of her bridge biddies having cancer.

"Life's a pile," he said, cutting into his meat.

Later during the meal, my sister said she'd love to go see *Jaws 2*, and this man forked his buttery tater and said, "Life's a pile."

I never heard him say anything else and decided to perform a mean test on him.

"I'm the LaGrange High Homecoming Queen from 1979," I said, grinning as wide as I could, as if this news would certainly elicit other verbal phrases to utter. "I won because I carried the black vote hands down. I get along much better with black people than whites for some weird reason."

"You know," he said, and I was getting hopeful. "I'm telling you one thing."

"Yessss?" I just knew he was going to say something brilliant.

"Life's a pile. That's all there is to it, man."

THE DUKE OF HABIT MAN: It was unto this twitching semigeriatric I was engaged twice. Once for two hours. The second time for about three minutes. He was double my age, rich as cream cheese frosting and crazier than a rabid baboon. He had a routine that could not under any circumstances be broken, including the habitual act of swallowing hundreds of vitamins, standing on his head, eating cafeteria lunches and, most annoyingly, making to-do lists all day long and scratching off each of these activities with giant moans of glee as he sat on the toilet and would not leave the house until he'd had four bowel movements. Talk about romance!

RACCOON MAN: He, too, belonged to me. A true delight in tony restaurants, this creature refused to order a drop of food until the waitress had brought him ice water. As soon as the glass arrived, he dipped his paws into the ice and bathed his face, leaving it gleaming with water beads. If his face dried, he would rebead with more pawing and water splashing throughout the meal. My mother suggested he be tested for rabies.

DIE REAR MAN: He was charming at first as he took me to Six Flags Over Georgia and won the stuffed lion that took up half the room. Charms fell fast after Mom's homemade spaghetti dinner and his continual trips to our guest bathroom, where he must have missed that silver knob on the side known as the flusher.

My sister rushed up to my room after I kissed my doting, lion-winning date good night at the door, so happy he was a SMOOTHER—that breed of kisser not listed previously but who is just right. Soft at first, no tongue until things warm up, and then just enough so as not to hit the uvula or bring about asphyxiation.

"Your new boyfriend left you a big present," said Sister Sandy, slowly delivering an evil grin.

"You're just jealous of my big stuffed lion."

"Oh, how wrong you are, my precious big sis. He left you something much more special and personal, and it sure will make that lion pale in comparison."

She yanked me from bed and forced me to follow her downstairs to the bathroom where Mr. Six Flags Over Georgia had deposited what seemed to be a week's worth of intestinal storage. I refused to EVER take his calls after that and brushed my teeth fourteen times after having kissed his crapping self at my door.

THE FROG MAN: This one belonged to my sister. He was her true love, the stealer of innocence, the man with a chunky class ring and ugly Kermit-green letter jacket she wore every day. He had a head shaped just like Mr. Ribbit's and big old wet amphibian eyes. His nose looked exactly like a frog's body minus the hind legs. I once saw his tongue flick out and catch an insect, though my sister swears it was an M&M. I still say it was either a horsefly or mosquito because, and I'm not one to lie, it had wings. Big, veiny wings.

FEMININE HYGIENE KING: Oh, all right. This odd bird was also mine for a spell. So sensitive, so understanding, so in touch with all things girlie. Every month (and how he knew exact dates is a mystery to me, unless he noticed all the oleander and rat poisoning on my person during "that time"), he'd send in the mail a huge supply of possum products and chocolates, even a lovely new lipstick to carry me peacefully through PMS. I've heard of penis envy, but I swear this oddball had Va-hee-na envy.

After reading what we had to choose from, it makes me grateful on occasion that I married Tidy Stu, a man who genuinely gets a buzz from spraying Tilex or steam-vaccing the home turf. The sound of the washer rumbling is music to his dear, thoroughly clean ears.

Nothing makes him happier than a new tube of Crest Whitening toothpaste and a little white box of waxed Oral-B dental floss, which he actually uses between his teeth and not to strangle palmetto bugs or hang jalapeno lights.

My Eggs Are in Wheelchairs

Those who read my first book know that I blame all my mean and irrational behaviors on my useless and utterly evil Uterus I've named BIB, which stands for Bitch in a Bag. Anything from hissy fits and conniptions to going crazier than a shot cat. It's all my uterus's fault.

If any of you have read *A Confederacy of Dunces*, my all-time favorite humor book, you'll know about Ignatius and his "valve." Anything that went wrong, and plenty did in walloping Ignatius J. Reilly's crazed life, he blamed on his valve closing.

Valve, uterus, prostate . . . We all have a menacing body part or two. I'll wake up with a semiflat stomach and for no other reason than to be pure mean, it'll start to swell up and cause me to wish for elastic stirrup pants by noon. The damn ute has a mind of its own, and now that my kids are born, it doesn't do me a bit of good, though Mama swears if I didn't have one all the other organs would fall right out of my possum.

She loves to tell me about her spayed friends and the body parts that have slipped from their vaginas, pronounced "Va-hee-nas" by my friend John Boyle who thinks he's speaking Spanish.

"I've got this one friend who lost her bladder that way and another whose doctor confirmed the bottom third of her esophagus shot straight out of her possum," Mama swears. "I also told you one thousand times, you'll grow a beard and maybe even a small starter penis if you don't keep the parts God intended unless they are damaged or cancerous."

What if these parts just make you mean? Why won't HMOs and PPOs and all the Os insure women who are veering toward Velma Barfield's way of life—she was the North Carolina "black widow" executed for doing in a few men and husbands. Don't cheap-ass insurance companies know unmedicated women are like assault weapons in the wrong hands? Wouldn't it just be cheaper and safer for all parties concerned to yank out all potentially murder-inducing parts?

My friend Kelly, a book club member who suffers from hormone shifts and fallopian madness, said she gave her doctor the What For. In the South, that means he's in deep sheeeeiiiit if he doesn't comply with the raging woman's wishes for something, anything, to prevent disaster on the home or public front. He put her on birth control pills, said the hormones in them should "level you out."

Oh, but it did not, my pretties. She went crazier than a drunk coming off Mad Dog. Three days later she was back in his office, smoke curling from her ears, saliva dripping from her incisors. "You either take me off this, or I'll personally see to it you are fully responsible for the murder I'm liable to commit." He stared at her and raised his gray eyebrows. "Surely you don't want a murder bloodying your hands?" Kelly more or less spewed. "If not, I suggest you take me off these pills and get me on something new, some sort of homicide-prevention plan."

He began to tremble and with a twitching eye, wrote her two prescriptions. One for Lexapro, a high-powered mood elevator, and one for a tranquilizer—my all-time favorite group of drugs I call my "heart pills," and "The Good Mommy tablets." Without them, I'm a squealing mess.

And so are a bunch of other women in their forties who are going through some bizarre physical and mental changes. Poor Kelly is so much more tolerable now that she's medicated. "I'm just a pure and plain-old regular-ass bitch now," she says. "I at least don't want to kill anyone. Not today, anyway."

I confessed to her the time I tried to poison my own beloved. It was during one of my rare drinking episodes when I got fairly schnockered in Myrtle Beach, S.C., and was so mad at Tidy Stu I plucked an oleander leaf from one of the many poisonous bushes surrounding the hotel, having just read the book *White Oleander*. I realized he'd have to chew and swallow the plant to die, so the leaf was just what I like to call my "warning garnish."

I had horrible PMS and so did he, so I slipped one of the long leaves in his bottled Foster's Lager. It was so long the tip rose from the hole where one drinks so I KNEW he'd see it. Who wouldn't see a green leaf jutting from his beer bottle? Well, he didn't!

I watched from the hotel balcony as he sipped his Foster's while the sun set, him probably thinking how grand life is and me all mad that when we go to the beach he does nothing but lollygags and expects me to do all the cooking, cleaning and childcare and then "service" his parts at night.

I didn't want to kill him—he's really a decent husband and great father. I just wanted him to suffer a warning message or nasty case of Die Rear for a day or two. Thank the dear Lord the leaf turned out to be as benign as parsley, which I knew it would be, but I warn all others not to tamper with oleander, as it can be, in the wrong hands, deadly. When he finished his beer, he pulled out the leaf without so much as a thought and tossed it on the ground.

Point is simple, sweeties. Women who drink right before their periods are dangerous. Remember that. We are potential murderesses and the gynecologists and therapists worth a pinch of their hourly salaries know this. Kelly and I both, along with thousands of you, my friends, are showing them this.

The doctors now prescribe meds and plenty of them. To fail to do so would mean an astronomical rate of . . . well . . .

unpleasantries one's beloved(s) might suffer. Thus the pawn-shops and rat-poisoning establishments would zoom in business should all the docs tell us to breathe deeply and go to yoga classes, down some soynuts, and all would be well in this world. We know better.

It's a good thing most of us were raised in decent, moral-abiding homes and the Ten Commandments were drilled into us like lug nuts in a wobbly tire. It also helps to bounce off these Do-My-Husband-In thoughts with other female friends who are married and harried and have visions of escaping the shackles of its duties. We are the women with secret longings of poisonings, potentially followed by prisons where they serve three squares a day as long as you do a bit of ironing and keep the dykes on your good side.

I knew that buying a gun at Al's Pawn & Lawn wasn't an option. Too many from my state knock off their mates, and I don't look good in orange or on a gurney receiving lethal injections. Plus, my children need a mommy and a daddy.

Like Kelly, I've been on the guinea pig pill wagon so much my brain doesn't register when a mood lifter hits. I thought, and still do, that removing the entire kit and caboodle down there would make me sweet as Mother Teresa or a nice mommy like June Cleaver who spreads a table with a tender roast beef, homemade whipped potatoes and peas instead of a box of Fruity Pebbles and a vitamin tablet for good measure.

I'm 100 percent certain it was cobwebbed old eggs, rusty tubes and the BIB that were purely responsible for a big old fight with Tidy Stu the night he forgot to thank me for a fine fish supper. Husbands with wives going through the change or the pre-change (which can last ten years!) should never forget to mind their manners. Ever. It can get you kilt. Just ask Velma.

So there we all were, a family of four dining on salmon, and I am sophisticated enough to realize you're supposed to pronounce it Sa-mon, without the *L*. I blackened it on my George Foreman Lean Mean Fat-Reducing Grilling Machine so the sa-mon had stripes and everything—including lemon butter and dill sauce. I prepared Uncle Ben's five-minute wild rice and some asparagus with a hollandaise sauce, and set the table quite beautifully with dishes his mother had given us as a wedding present.

It was springtime and my husband was obsessed with the yard and doing mysterious manly things in it and to it. Machinery was always growling, whining and disturbing the peace. He loves to weed whack and mow and blow, snip, plant and prune.

"Dinner's ready," I said, rather yelled from our deck overlooking the gorgeous Blue Ridge Mountains. At least I didn't shout, "Come and get it, you nasty-ass heathen!"

It took a while, but finally everyone was seated and enjoying the meal, my children pretending to eat the fish when I knew they were giving it to our fat gay Pomeranian. After 2.5 minutes, Tidy Stu, who eats like a high-suctioning Rainbow vac, had inhaled his meal, jumped up from the table and was outside massacring leaves with one of his Rambo-like yard tools.

He had forgotten to say the most important thing a woman needs to hear after she's worked all day and cooked her butt off. I was waiting for him to purr, "That was delicious, my sweet beloved," or at the very least, "Good eatin', hon. Maybe I'll grab yo ass later."

My mama always taught us to say, "I enjoyed it," even if the food sucked. I had PMS and was fed up. Two doctors had put me on antidepressants and said, "We are sorry to inform you but your insurance company has denied our Uterus Removal and Incinerator Services."

Stingy HMOs. Thus I gripped Stu's plate, still half-full of fine fish, and walked onto the deck, leaning over the railing where the asphalt driveway is located and where Tidy was blowing everything the earth had ever coughed up.

"STUART!!!!!" I screamed. "YOU FORGOT SOMETHING!"

He pulled out his earplugs, and shot over a look he always gives me, the *What's wrong with you, woman?* one.

"What? What is it?"

I felt the pulse in my neck throb and smelled salmon on my hands. "I worked two hours on this meal and you didn't say you enjoyed it. You just hopped up from the table after 2.5 minutes and said nothing."

He huffed and made a hand gesture, a naughty one that redneck motorists or El Camino drivers are prone to give. As a result, I did what felt natural, since the dishes I had were the everyday and not the good china, bless my sweet mother-in-law's heart.

"Here you go," I said. "A little souvenir so you'll remember the wife you ONCE had and who ONCE cooked SA-MON dinners. Enjoy!" I let the plate with his leftovers sail to the ground, shattering all over the driveway, rice and fish juices, pieces of ceramic flying everywhere and sounding as if a mini-bomb had exploded. Whew, that felt good. The sound of the crash released more tension than going to a kickboxing class or playing Whack-a-Mole at Chuck E. Cheese, a great stress reliever, my dears.

As I brushed off my hands and walked back across the deck, I noticed my elderly neighbors leaning from their pristine gazebo, watching in horror the entire affair. I smiled and waved, then patted my belly as if they could read my mind. *"Just another problem with my uterus, you see."*

Not long after that episode, the moods started to get more unpredictable and continued as the months and years went by. My dear friend Kelly keeps telling me to eat yams and soynuts but all I want to eat are dark chocolate bars and fight the cattle for their salt licks.

Part of this whole, *I'm-40-You-Better-Watch-Out Syndrome* is a cocktail of swarming, screeching hormones reminding a woman she is at an awkward stage in her life. That juncture called Child Bearing or Child Barren? Possibly Fertile. Possibly Out of Order.

Sugahs, it's not a pretty creek to straddle. This is where thousands of dollars in therapy and medications or a few good feature films will straighten out that perimenopausal portion of our lives. "Pills and Skills" is what my dear psychiatrist friend says as he opens his prescription pad and tries this and that.

For me, the turning point, the moment of facing up to halfway curing this new estrogen-swinging nature, arrived soon after watching *Fried Green Tomatoes* following a twelve-year hiatus from the movie. I can't watch movies like men do, who can see the same flick forty-eight times a year and don't mind one bit.

Of course, my own personal Alpha Male wouldn't watch it with me. "That's a chick flick," he said, eyes and ears aimed at the squeaks and pounding shoes of the Lakers whipping the Spurs. Meanwhile, I was glued to Evelyn Couch, the meek and portly housewife in *Fried Green Tomatoes* who transforms into Towanda the Avenger, the woman who rams her car six times into the red VW of a pair of big-haired bimbos who'd earlier mocked her.

Y'all remember the movie?

It's worth renting for a bit of reacquainting. It had been too long since I'd seen a sapped housewife switch gears and tap into her pool of dancing hormones and emerge a sweet yet sassy symbol of assertive goodness. It was time for me to become Towanda. To hell with Lexapro and oleander. My personal Alpha Male had banished everything I'd known and loved, including bath mats and bed skirts, and had laid down the law concerning our woodsy backyard.

"No play set and no basketball goal," he boomed out every week. "There's a nice playground in our neighborhood. I don't want to ruin the views looking at plastic, trailer-park shit all over our nice yard."

I listened with a breaking heart as my children begged for outdoor joy and apparatuses. Finally, after viewing *Fried Green Tomatoes*, again, I invited Towanda into my soul and took her with me as I hit Lowe's, Target and Home Depot.

The result is a backyard populated with swings, a climbing wall, hand rings and a basketball goal I put together with sweat, caffeine, cussing and a teenaged neighbor who encouraged and cheered my inner Towanda as long as I plied him with cappuccinos and Krispy Kremes.

When my Alpha Male saw it, he was livid. He steamed and snorted like a bull. Then I started laughing, falling to the ground and rolling around in the leaves and shouting, "Whew, baby. Look at the white-trash yard getups I have thrown together for the pleasure of our sweet children. Get a load of the climbing wall I nailed into that hideous, good-for-nothing white pine.

"It was Towanda, hon, not me, who decided the kids needed some backyard recreational devices. You told me to get off my meds so I'd want more sex, so it's not my fault Towanda's inhabiting my body and there's nothing I can do about it but say, 'Heck, I'm awfully sorry. The kids worked hard all year in school and did well on those end-of-grade tests that had all the teachers brewing ulcers and guzzling wine coolers.'"

He wasn't about to relinquish control of his Kingdom of Unmarred Acreage. "I told you I didn't want any plastic in the yard. I'm the man. I'm in control."

"Hon," I said as nice as possible. "No one's in control but my parts gone to seed. Until I sell my uterus on eBay or see it swilling in a jug of formaldehyde, I expect it to keep sending signals that will scramble the sane out of any woman. You know the kids needed something to do out there besides light matches and pee in the poison ivy, and that I have a strong urge to hack and hammer things. You understand? Whack-A-Mole was no longer cuttin' it."

He squinted and wrinkled up his nose. "I need your car keys," he smirked. "From now on, you'll drive the '71 El Camino and I'll drive the Lamborghini."

"What Lamborghini? What El Camino?"

"The cars I'm getting today on a trade-in since you decided to ruin my mountain view with a few pieces of plywood, trashy plastic and more of your insanity."

"Great. I love Lamborghinis. I'm sure you and the El Camino will be a perfect match. You can even fit it with a camper top and have a grand ol' time." I gave a little smile and wave before jumping on the new swing as if a kid at the park. You gotta let a man win sometimes. Even Towanda knows that.

For about a week, Towanda laid low, and I briefly became the meek and sweet woman I can sometimes, albeit rarely, become. Towanda didn't stay hidden for long and returned during the pool incident where the neighborhood slut, a mother who likes to walk around prancing and with her nose straight up in the air, gave me a run for my hormones.

This is a time in life when a bit of assertiveness is needed. When another person simply MUST be "taken down a peg or two," as my own mama used to say. The tricky part is balance. A fine line, like a thread of worm silk, separates assertiveness from aggressiveness. I didn't want to be a bitch, just a deliverer of a sweet and well-deserved comeuppance for this middle-aged Britney Spears wanna-be.

I'd begun tiptoeing along that line, holding my tongue to the point of nearly biting it in half due to a couple of bullies who'd decided to make one of my cherubs their target. My son, unfortunately, inherited two separate genetic codes, one for each ear. Since mine stick straight out like the doors of a taxicab, one of his ears is also like a turn signal. While the other, inherited from his dad, is as flat as a Doberman's. People tease him a lot about those odd ears that I, as his mother, adore and want to smooch and flick.

This taking-up-for-our-kids is a hard area for us mama lionesses desiring to sink our fangs into Pit-Bullish children and parents who rip into our youngsters' spirits and suck the goodness from their hearts. We want to attack, but then we remember the Golden Rule: Do unto others as they have done to you. I think that's how I've come to interpret it.

I've sat around listening to so many horror stories from moms and dads who endure the Bully Syndrome—whether at school or in their neighborhoods. If a kid is different in any way, it's as if he or she is wearing a sign: COME AND GET ME. I'M RIPE FOR YOUR PICKINGS. It's hideous and cruel and shouldn't be tolerated.

Here is where I'd like to share my own way of handling

these baby devils and their living-in-denial parents. These methods are not approved by any pediatrician or therapist. All I know is that at times, it feels right to execute parental business in this manner.

I developed these guidelines after an MOB (Mother of a Bully), also previously referred to as the neighborhood slut, was lounging poolside and greasing her body with oil.

She decided it was time to hurl expletives at a group of kids frolicking in the water. Granted the kids *were* acting up. She actually thought they were checking out her 7-year-old daughter's butt. Excuse me? Boys under 11 or 12 are only interested in themselves, Xbox games and nearly drowning each other.

I tried deep breathing but couldn't settle my nerves. Had this woman ordered them to sit out, or called upon their mamas, maybe even sprayed them with a cold hose, that would be one thing. But to cuss the clouds gray? And in the presence of little innocent ears? Ears that at least on my little boy were a set of mismatched body parts.

For her to think they were lusting after her second-grader's behind? No, Sugahs. That tea's not sweet. With that in mind, and if you have bullies in your present or future, here are my Rules for Assertive Southern, Northern, Midwestern, Yankee Or Any Frustrated Mothers to try when shunning the Golden Rule is warranted.

1. Approach the MOB in a calm voice. Choose words sharp enough to cut butter but not so sharp they could fell trees.

2. Dress in something pink and refreshing, such as a huge hat, and big Audrey Hepburn sunglasses. If this confrontation is taking place poolside, the Mama Lion will always want to have her head looming twice its regular size, and the pink straw gardening hat is perfect for minimizing and overpowering the mean slut mama's ego.

3. Lipstick is a must to complete the Assertive Woman ensemble. It's always a plus if it matches the color of the hat

unless the hat is straw colored, which I DO NOT recommend.

4. Delivering your words in a regular speaking voice, even coated with syrup, can't hurt. Instead of cussing—favored by the trashier MOBs—use snappy phrases such as "You possess an intolerably egregious lack of respect for America's youth," for extra punch.

5. Smile the whole time. This is the hard part, especially when you are shaking and about to pass out from sheer anger.

6. If the Trashy MOB hurls an ugly barb, explain to her that her conscience should bother her and if not she will go straight to hell where she will surely fry turkeys in malfunctioning units with evil men on a daily basis and light grills with high-octane unleaded gas.

    "Either that," you can tell the MOB, "or you'll lose all your teeth because it says in the Bible that those who use their mouths for uttering vulgarities will one day wake up toothless." If she asks, "What book of the Bible did THAT come from?" just be prepared to make up something, preferably Proverbs or Tootherotemy Chapter 4, Verse 7.

7. When dealing with the bully directly and not the MOB, it's a good idea to whisper the following words near his or her face: "You can go ahead and call my kid mean names till your tongue forks, but hear me now. I shall twist your ear until your head resembles Van Gogh's but is much bloodier. You remember Van Gogh or does your bullying rectum need an art lesson?" By this point, the kid is usually about to vomit with fear, and this is good. Real good. "Van Gogh, you nincompoop, is the artist who cut off his ear and mailed it to somebody who'd pissed him off. So with that, either leave my kid alone or it's Van Gogh city and your ear is mine, buster. Got it?"

    Works like a charm. Better than yams, soy and perhaps even Uterus Removal Services. Point is simple: When our eggs are in wheelchairs, our possums cobwebbed and our uteruses useless BIBs, Towanda has a place in all our lives. It's just up to us to invite her in for tea. Sweet is always preferable. And a slice of lemon couldn't hurt one bit.

You Can't Clone Decency

This is the story I didn't want to write but felt I had to. I'm doing it for me, to expunge the guilt and the shame I've carried for more than twenty-five years. And I'm doing it for mothers of girls going to college and those young women themselves.

The wood floor smells of spilled beer, dirty shoe leather and sweat mixed with Lauren perfume in the blood-red bottle. Young men, still boys inside their yearning bodies, see the approaching evening as one soaked in alcohol and promise.

I'm at the Kappa Alpha fraternity house of a small Christian college with a boy who's technically a man.

He is 22. I'm 17. And scared. My tiny town life didn't prepare me for this, and Mama had never gone to college and couldn't warn me of what may come. Daddy, an honors student, didn't head out to frat parties after classes. He worked at Sears to help pay tuition while Mama cut hair for a stingy man who stole her tips and paid her a fraction of her worth. She came home with red, chemically burned hands and the smell of ammonia deep in her raw skin. They lived in a cardboard apartment, known as Married Student Housing on most campuses. They weren't familiar with the Greek system and its mostly rich kids who are overindulged, drive cars that still carry that new smell, and vacation in spots where stars and jet-setters tend to congregate.

The only fraternity parties I'd ever seen were in the movies, and I figured *Animal House* had certainly exaggerated them. I never thought getting laid was the goal of these guys whose other mission appeared to be cloning each other in both behavior and attire, all wearing khakis and button-downs, pink short-sleeved Izods, and Docksides or Topsiders with no socks.

I came unprepared, packing Gloria Vanderbilt jeans and Candie's, Clairol hot rollers, Final Net hairspray, inexpensive tops, a pair of purple fake-leather pants, a couple of pairs of Levi's jeans and cords. I had never owned chinos or Izods. All my shoes had chunky heels except the Adidas leftover from cheerleading. White with royal blue stripes, the color of the mighty Grangers, my alma mater's state championship football team in LaGrange, Georgia, just an hour southwest of Atlanta.

I knew about Grangers and Candie's and Bonnie Bell lip gloss and boys who lived to glide from base to base but had the courtesy not to push it if a girl said no. I knew about riding in cars with friends and splitting eight-packs of bottled pony Millers or six-packs of Schlitz and letting it wear off before we went home.

We were in control, even if we didn't want to be. We had parents who waited up at night and would have coronaries and cerebral hemorrhages if they caught us drinking. We were in church every Sunday morning, evening, and even on Wednesdays if Baptist, which we were. Mama taught the Girls in Action classes and we ate the fried chicken or roast beef and gravy on Wednesday nights before the services led by the oldest and most boring reverend I've ever encountered.

Now I am 17 and free to drink as much as I want, and I will. It's been my plan all summer and I can't figure out why I'm so in love with the notion of drinking excessively unless it's because I've been kept on a tight leash for all this time and, finally, I can untie all ropes and curfews and let loose, go wild.

It feels wonderful, as if I am a pigeon suddenly taking flight from the top of someone's encapsulated roof with an open escape hatch. That alcoholism could possibly be brewing in my blood was of no concern or thought. That my grandfather had been an alcoholic who blew his brains out all over the bed-room floor and walls gave me no reason to think I had his genes lurking in my DNA.

I was young and free. Nothing could hurt me. Nothing. Not this preppy man-boy smiling and reminding me of some-one who'd soon graduate and begin a life of shaking a lot of hands, feeding a lot of bullshit to those eating from the buffets of gullibility, probably the type of guy to kiss a lot of ass and end up a senator.

The heat is sticky, the kind that clings to a person's skin, even when she's not sweating. It is the kind of early-September day in South Carolina when you wish you could tear off your clothes and run through a sprinkler for hours like we did as children. Relief appears nowhere because this part of the world quit breathing in August. No wind. No breeze. Just the fevered yawn of a day that won't relent and give over to an evening offering mercy.

The overworked sun begins its descent, streaking the sky in hot passion: purples, swirling pinks and oranges, like Day-Glo colors and neon crayons. I stare at those shades and think they can't possibly be real, almost as if they're in one of those cheap paintings they sell in beach gift shops.

My date is inside chilling beer and cloning himself, proba-bly planning his attack on my innocence as I sit unleashed from a home life that kept me tethered to good morals and choices, all out of parental fear and a conscience instilled from church camps and Sunday mornings. Bad girls don't earn real love. They get boys who lust and, later, reputations clinging like black tar for life.

I am drinking a Tab but waiting on something more potent, something to transport me from the sheltered, small-town Georgia girl to this college coed in South Carolina.

I am part teen, part adult, but not old enough to vote or drink legally. I have been a college freshman for two days, and already snagged a date with a senior who is president of this fraternity where the beach music blares and the beer cools in ice-packed metal tubs. I notice it's a cheap canned beer, one I'd never heard of. My date is supposed to be the campus catch, but I eye him from the front porch with suspicion as he spins the cans, hurrying their chill for the thirsty crowd cramming the small frat house that's really a ranch-style brick home, the kind with three bedrooms and two baths where families of four begin their lives and sit around the dinner table over mashed potatoes and English peas.

I'm leery of these people who all walk the same, talk the same, dance the same, drink too much and, mostly, pursue a campus lifestyle driven by the needy release of what's inside their boxers.

Only I don't know this yet. But I will . . . by morning.

This small Christian college is known for its tough academics, curfews and the outrageous parties thrown on fraternity row—a cul-de-sac of newly built ranchers with Greek letters glued to the bricks and the potential for just about anything once the front doors open, the music blasting and the beer flowing into throats and bloodstreams that will send messages to the brain that it's OK to take advantage of a drunk girl.

This is the late seventies and no one has ever gone to jail for raping an intoxicated coed. Who cares that she's passed out and has no brain function—save for the ability to produce respirations? This is enough for consent in their twisted minds. *She's breathing. Her skin is warm. She's alive. I'll just fuck her.*

I am really still a girl, and the youngest freshman here due to a kink in the Georgia school system years ago that allowed a 5-year-old to enter first grade. My experiences with boys are limited to a handful of encounters, mostly in a silver Toyota wagon with the one skinny guy I dated my senior year and a fleeting meeting beneath a weeping willow with a bowlegged lifeguard a month before coming here.

My date is considered by others as handsome, but I'm swallowing lukewarm Tab and thinking his are the kind of good looks with ulterior motives. There's not much kindness in his eyes, or the hungry smiles he throws my way as he tends the bar, a job he seems born to do. His teeth are too straight and white, his posture too perfect. Boys with his breeding tend to mimic thoroughbred dogs: feisty and aggressive, pumped with way too much confidence and cockiness.

He's not about to move from the huge tin tub on the counter packed with ice and beer. He's trying hard to get them cold, rotating them as if plates on sticks and simultaneously spinning on his Docksides as Chairman of the Board sings, "Give Me Just A Little More Time," and he mouths the words.

I instantly feel the goose bumps of disgust rise upon my flesh, and don't like him but think I should try since he's so beloved on this campus. He must have something going for him, something redeeming.

He asked me out the first day of school. I was in the cafeteria and had arrived on campus with a bad home perm, a killer tan from spending the summer as a lifeguard, and long, thin legs from a devotion to jogging and a fear of fat. I was pretty from a distance, but up close one could see a nose on the large side, and skin still broken out in places, traces of adolescence lingering. I lined my eyes in brown eye shadow, double-coated them with Maybelline's Great Lash in the pink and green tube, and wore Sally Hansen's frosted pink lipstick twelve to eighteen hours a day.

At the end of the first day at this college of under a thousand students, an older girl came into our dorm where we were all watching TV and eating air-popped Orville Redenbacher and made an announcement.

"Susan Gambrell," she said, "you have been voted by the entire Greek system the second-cutest freshman on campus. First place goes to Katie Graham." She was a petite blonde, adorable.

It seems they took a poll in the cafeteria that day, and by evening, I had a date with this man working the beer and singing, "What Kind Of Fool (Do You Think I Am)," while giving me looks that made me want to go home to Georgia and sit in our green living room while Mama fried chicken and

Daddy mowed the lawn. Why hadn't he asked out Katie Graham instead?

I suddenly don't want to be here. This is all too fast. Emotionally, I am still a girl, but this is the course expected of middle- and upper-middle-class kids all over America. You went to college.

No matter that I wanted to be on *All My Children* with Erica Kane, playing her long-lost sister (my idea) because people said I favored Susan Lucci. I knew I could act and perhaps be a Courtland or a long-lost member of the Martin family if the writers didn't go for the Erica Kane connection. Maybe, the Wallingfords would adopt me.

Mom and Dad said I'd end up on the streets, most likely a prostitute on drugs if I went to New York or Hollywood. They always thought the worst of anything that veered from the norm. A French kiss meant teen pregnancy. A few beers meant a sullied reputation. A trip to the big city most likely led to falling into the porn industry or prey for murder.

So here I am at this frat house instead of on the set of *All My Children*, watching this scene unfold, sun setting but not cooling, doors opening on all the family-style ranchers and each fraternity trying to out-blast the other with their stereos playing beach music, the brothers tapping kegs and testosterone.

"Aren't you coming in?" my date hollers from his post at the bar, which is really a Formica kitchen counter. "I got a cold one with your name all over it." He grins and I can tell he is way too in love with himself. He's the kind who thinks the world exists for his eyes only, and that when his senior year winds down all sorts of offers will come his way. He's probably right. He will run for political office for sure. On the Republican ticket.

"Be there in a minute," I say, inhaling the heat that feels like those August days when you can't breathe because the air is nothing but a hot fog, almost like an exhalation. I pour the last of my Tab in the shrubbery and walk inside feeling frumpy in the chinos a girl on my hall insisted I wear instead of my purple fake-leather pants that resembled the pair Peter Frampton wore on one of his album covers.

The air-conditioning is no match for the heat slipping in from outside and the loamy breath of single-minded frat boys, bodies shoulder to shoulder as the night deepens.

I'm not sure why I'm here in this South Carolina college town so small there isn't even a Burger King. It is 1979, and the nearest McDonald's is a half hour away. This is what I think as I take the beer and pop the metal tab, which curls like a sharp tongue. I pull long sips from the can. Cold, yeasty relief: my lover, my cure, my confidence.

The music changes and The O'Kaysions are singing "Girl Watcher," and everybody rushes to the wood floor to shag, a dance I'd never seen in Georgia but is the official state dance of South Carolina, learned mostly in a town called Ocean Drive, near Myrtle Beach. I don't know how to shag and am not keen on learning. It looks stupid, like Izods and Docksides.

I want to go home. I would rather be at the YMCA, in the gym standing against the wall while a rock band plays "China Grove," and people dance any old way they want, throwing their bodies around or barely moving at all.

This shag thing seems to have a formula: upper body relaxed, one hand holding the partner's, and each person shuffling from foot to foot as if their shoes—always flats—are magnets and the floor is made of metal.

The man leads. It's almost like a slow jitterbug, and it seems corny to me and I'd rather hear Boston or Journey than these bands from the 60s. I'm not in my element. I drain the can of beer and accept another. I can feel the alcohol in my blood beginning the seduction of my sanity.

It would be like this for years, but I wouldn't know it. I would crave this booze, this buzz, the way a newborn needs milk to survive.

My first shag lesson would come tonight, along with other lessons, ugly ones that haunt me to this day, staining my good name: first this man who is holding his hand out to me, asking me to shag, later by others offering their beers and empty promises.

"Ready for another brewsky?" my date shouts from the din of music and laughter.

Yes, yes I was. Two beers down and I am ready for more of anything to transport me from this house, this college, this town. I take it, hold it up as the foam runs down my forearm, as this man grabs my hand with his own, which is too soft to have ever known a day's work. He tries to teach me to shag and I laugh and stumble and somehow get a few steps right. I am feeling better, too good now, as the music ends and everybody claps. I never understood why people clap after dancing. What is the point? Who are they clapping for? Themselves? The stereo?

My date returns to the bar and I go back to the porch where a girl from my dorm is smoking and gossiping with three other girls. This is better, I think, and am relaxing and taking drags off a girl named Claire's Virginia Slims Menthol Lights, the nicotine mixing with alcohol so that I feel beyond tipsy, almost drunk.

My date sashays outside. He is trying to be Mr. Hot Stuff in front of the ladies. "Hiding from me again," he says, smooth as glass, winking at Claire. "Come on back. I don't want my brothers to think you're free. You're mine tonight, sweetheart."

"Sixty Minute Man" pulses almost sexually from the speakers and the floor becomes a sea of pink, green, Izod and madras shirts, Docksides and Topsiders squeaking on the sticky floor.

"In a minute," I say, gulping the beer, feeling a comforting burn in my cheeks and better by the minute. It was the same feeling I had the fall I turned 16 and decided I was no longer willing to be a high school Goody Two Shoes. All my friends drank. They split six-packs with boys or each other and drove around until the cans and bottles were drained and the hormones had peaked. They parked cars by the big lake in La-Grange and let the boys feel them up, sometimes even allowing them to slip a hand beneath their waistbands.

I never did. Mama scared us. She said our reputation was all we had, and to lose that meant losing everything. "Your name is important. Once it's cheapened and lost, you'll never get it back."

* * *

My friend Gena had a purple Vega and we'd drive to Poor
Boy's Two, the name of a shady little convenience store known
to sell six-packs to minors. We'd ease up to the drive-thru window, our hearts pounding. The owner didn't want us coming
in. He'd brown-bag it, double charge us, and tell us to hurry it
up before the cops came sniffing around.

All I could think about during the summer before entering my
freshman year in college was the refrigerator, the tiny brown
box all newcomers receive with a $50 deposit. My own cube of
cold space to stock with anything I wanted.

That was a no-brainer. A given.

I imagined going to Kroger, the brand-new checkbook in
my purse, bank filled with the money I'd earned that summer
waiting tables, lifeguarding and teaching swimming lessons.
I'd walk down the coldest aisle filled with nothing but beer and
wine. Mama and Daddy would never know.

I'd select pony Millers, Schlitz and wine coolers, the official
beverages of my teen-aged years with dear friends Jill and
Margaret, and consumed while riding in Jill's brown Pinto. We
were cheerleaders for the Grangers, a team that was always
winning and going to the state play-offs. We dated some of the
players, but mostly I liked that scrawny twin who sang in a
band called Snatch and played lead guitar.

I envisioned him as lead singer David Pack from the group
Ambrosia. They had the same sweet voice. I'd go to his gigs
and drink fairly responsibly with the other band member's
girlfriends. We all had 70s Farrah hair, and I often wore my
purple fake-leather pants and heels. We'd sit up front, where
people would make no mistake: We were with the band. We
were the girls they'd go home with. Not those in the center of
the hotel lounge, but us. The girls with long, thin legs, frosted
pink lipstick, our hair with wings sprayed stiff as pine needles.

I was careful about my drinking then. Mama would sniff me
like an old dog does its bed before lying in it. She knew, be-

cause she wasn't a virgin to alcohol, that it loosened inhibitions and might make her daughters realize they had urges between their legs. God forbid they drink enough to let a boy have his way with her.

So she twitched her long nose and smelled us, me in particular because I was 16 and out of braces and entering a stage where parents had begun saying, "We'd never have believed it, but Susan Gambrell is turning out to be quite a looker."

I was unfazed by my long legs and little ass, attributes I'd kill for now. I paid them no mind when I saw them tanned and lithe in the mirror. All I could see were the flaws: the big ears, the flat chest, my mother's nose, arms way too long for my body, olive skin fanned with pimples in the oily zones.

I was awkward in my body. I didn't feel pretty, not unless four pony Millers, condensation running off the 8-ounce bottles, found their golden way down my needy throat. I knew that once the four beers were in I was beautiful and the curtains of insecurity would part like those on a stage. My skin would tingle and the beer lit my cheeks like pink roses. The feeling was magical, giddy, and I could be anything or anyone as long as the beer didn't run out.

There wasn't enough time to drink all I craved during the high school years. Mom and Dad never went to bed until I came home, the loud, often mufflerless Vegas and Firebirds pulling up our steep drive and some guy with a thick neck and questionable blood alcohol level would try to walk me to the door, sticking his tongue in my mouth along with the Wintergreen Certs.

Mama would be in her thin gown and pillow-pressed face. I would see her breasts beneath the fabric, knowing she was tired but too curious about her daughter's condition to go back to bed.

"How was it?" she'd ask, walking toward me, her feet silent as they sank in the green carpet. I'd hear the hum of the refrigerator and my father's barn-animal snores.

"It was pretty fun," I'd say, trying not to exhale and hoping the mints covered my tracks. "I'm tired. Good night, Mom. I love you." I'd hold my breath and kiss her soft cheek.

She wouldn't let me pass without a hug. I'd grind my teeth into the mint, hoping to squeeze out more wintergreen and mask the traces of my indiscretions. Most of the time, it worked. Or at least I thought it did.

Maybe she knew but realized I was sober enough to get home in one piece, clothes on and walk like a debutant to bed.

No more pretending now that I'm free. No more holding back. I am on my fourth beer and shagging like I've been doing it for years. A disco ball glitters above the floor, and I never noticed it earlier. I tilt my head and stare until I'm dizzy and all the colors of the sunset mix with the untamable hues of the ball. A hand, my date's, passes me another beer, and I think nothing as I crack it open, drinking and dancing way into the night.

The last thing I remember is falling onto a sofa pushed back against the wall to make room for the party crowd. I feel sick and heavy, as if I can't take another step. The room sways and my stomach recoils. A girl from the dorm, older and wiser, takes a wet paper towel and presses it across my forehead.

"Are you going to throw up?" she asks.

I try to answer but can't talk.

"It's OK, Susan. I'll take you to the bathroom. Happens to all of us until we get the hang of it."

I remember nothing else. Just the cold paper towel, the kindness of this upperclassman handing me a Coke, the bodies blurring as they continued dancing, and the struggle to keep from vomiting or falling asleep.

After that, the world goes blank. Black. A deep, dark hole of nothingness. Maybe the party kept going. Maybe not. Probably so.

When the early sun of a Sunday morning finds its way into the creases of my closed eyes, I awaken in a panic. My head throbs each time my heart beats. What time is it? Where am I?

Something isn't right. Something horrible has happened. What? What did I do? Why do I hurt down there?

I am in a bed, oh, dear God, and not on the sofa where that

nice girl from the dorm put me with the Coke and a couple of wet Bounty paper towels. The 22-year-old man who'd plied me with beer and beach music lies next to me sleeping on his side, breathing so quietly one might think him dead. I feel his calf and peek under the covers and see that he is naked. Acid rises in my throat as I quickly move my leg. *How did I end up here? Oh, God, oh, no, oh, please, God, don't let this be real.*

I feel a rush of cold air between my legs and realize my underwear and chinos are gone. My bottom hurts. I feel sticky and sore. This can't be happening. I don't remember even kissing this man, much less getting into bed with him.

Please, God, don't let him wake up. Please. Tears fall down my shamed face and I want to run home to LaGrange where the boys I knew didn't do this to girls. I want to climb in Mama's lap and nestle against her sheer nylon nightgown with my head on her breast and listen as her heart thumps the slow tune of love and reassurance.

I tiptoe around the room, pale pink blood running down my leg from my most private, aching parts, and find my pants but not my underwear. I wonder later if it wasn't part of the fraternity ritual after raping girls. Keep their panties. Hang them somewhere like a trophy.

Only I don't realize I've been raped. In 1979 if a girl drank too much and woke up without her panties and in bed with a man, then she was a slut and a whore and her name was forever tarnished.

I run as fast as I can back to my dorm, slip in the side door, climb into bed and cry until sleep relieves me of the guilt. But only until I open my eyes three hours later.

I cannot go into the cafeteria for lunch. Even if they did vote me second-prettiest freshman just a couple of days before.

What in God's name would they vote me now?

Twenty years later they would have a name for this. Rape. Maybe statutory or date rape. And the man-boy who'd entered and destroyed my innocence would have a name, too. Date rapist. He'd go to court, his lawyers trying to prove consensual sex and airing everything they could find about the woman pressing charges.

He may get a fine and community service. He may get nothing.

But the victim would get everything. A reputation she could never shake. Decades of guilt that would be hard if not impossible to overcome.

When the Bough Breaks

Why aren't I dead? Why am I at the Comfort Inn & Suites at 11 AM trying to get a room, smelling of last night's wine, bleeding and bruised and with a six-pack of Miller in my hand and a duffel bag in the other?

"You're Susan Reinhardt, aren't you?" the young clerk trying to check me in early asks. "I love your column. You are so funny. Mom and I read you every morning and nearly pee in our pants laughing."

I smile because it's expected. Inside, I'm rotting. My arms are swelling: biceps and forearms raw as uncooked meat from the beating with the back of a hairbrush. My eyes are bloodshot and my hair is covered in spilled Yellow Tail Shiraz and what appears to be dried vomit.

"Thanks," I say to the pretty girl trying to find a clean room hours before the normal 3 PM check-in time. She would type in her computer, then glance at me, sizing up the pathetic condition in which I'd arrived at her hotel.

"I think I have some sort of flu." I am lying. "I just need to get some sleep." This part is true.

"Let me see what I can do," she says, and I tell her I'll be out by the pool if it's okay, and she says, "Sure. Whatever we can do to help, Mrs. Reinhardt."

"Susan. Just call me Susan."

Always smiling. Always onstage. Always trying to put on

the outside face my insides don't want to wear: roses and Gerbera daisies, when beneath the skin and Estée Lauder foundation, the 36-D bra, lay snakes waiting to release venom, fighting with a soul that searches for gratitude and God.

I find a chair, the kind with plastic strips horizontal across the white framing. The kind that if you're fat or if the chair is flawed, your ass slips through. I have a thin hotel towel that the blonde who likes my column gave me. I spread it out and set the six-pack by my side.

My head is like its own heart outside my body, beating in the heat of a midmorning promising a July day like the kind we had in Georgia, the days when no one could catch her breath it was so hot.

Already, it must have been close to 90 degrees. I twist off the lid of a bottle of Miller and drink half of the pale, gold liquid in one gulp. Almost immediately it mixes with last night's near "accidental" suicide and gives me the illusion that everything is all right. Everything, I tell myself, will be fine. Sleep. That's it. A couple nights of rest and good as new.

It's not quite noon and my kids are safe with their father who is a good man when it comes to raising children. I didn't want anyone to see me in this condition, especially my two children.

If only I could lie down for two days and not wake up, then my mind would clear and I wouldn't think these crazy things people who have it so good in life have no business thinking. Depression is the dark blanket no one wants to cover up in.

Ego, my daddy calls it. Dwelling on oneself is nothing but ego. Humility—he likes to say often that the only way to live right is through humility. "Remove self from your life and you'll fulfill God's plan. Self destroys."

Yes, Dad, it does. It tries, anyway.

I have the Millers to stave off the black blanket of depression and the memories of last night's insanity. There are four beers left, and maybe it will be enough. Probably not. The sun burns through my skin like a torch moving in closer. I am drifting in a sea of last night's leftovers and the cold, cheap beer of my teens. Miller High Life. Brown Pintos, Gremlins, a purple Vega . . . good times. Boys who grinned with the shyness of youth and who wouldn't look at women as things to hunt and capture for years.

I close my eyes and see red and orange swirls because the sun is bright and I have no glasses. Time is something I don't care about. Who knows how much is passing. I drink all the beer and jump into the pool, sinking to the bottom, wondering how long I can stay there, once again realizing no matter how bad the inner pain, the will to live is much stronger than the desire to die.

I know a great man whose entire family committed suicide over a span of twenty years. First his mother, then his twin brothers, followed by his sister and finally his dad. He tried it twice, but is happy now and wrote his memoir. He is known as the Sole Survivor. I did a piece on him for the *Washington Post* and dozens of other papers, and for a while he was on all the talk shows.

He isn't going to follow his family's tradition, he promises, and I believe him because he is strong and got therapy and found meaning in life. He knows he was spared for a purpose he intends to discover and fulfill.

Wasn't I? Shouldn't I be dead? Not that I wanted to die, because, really I didn't.

Already, the sun has dried me from the pool water. The sweet girl comes out and says she's managed to get a room clean and ready. "You can sleep all you want," she says, and I smile at her as if the night before was just as wonderful as she must imagine my "charmed life" to be. How could a woman be funny if her life wasn't one big run of happy-go-lucky days and hijinks and capers?

I'm on the radio a lot of mornings, cracking jokes, saying wild and supposedly hilarious things, or so they tell me. The hosts keep inviting me back. I deliver speeches all over the country that are more like stand-up comedy routines. People must think I have no problems, that life for me is one big sitcom of joy and joking and Lucille Ball–type activity.

They know nothing of the darkness and periods of self-hatred and shame, the guilt—a gift that keeps on giving—that has followed me since junior high.

I rise from my chair, the backs of my thighs stuck to the plastic strips and wet with heat and sweat. I find a pair of shorts and wonder how in the world I had the foresight to pack anything during last night's dash for death. Or was it just a sprint for attention? *Notice me. Save me. Please. Help. Please, someone, can't you see? Can't you fix this?*

I stagger down a hill to Eckerd Drug where there is a beer cooler with six-packs of Budweiser Select. I'm messed up as hell and yet sane enough to consider the carbs in my choice of beer. Why? People think the weirdest things at the most inappropriate moments.

I stumble back up the grassy hill to the hotel and decide it's too hot and I'll drink in the room. The clerk is so kind. She must know I'm drunk, but says, "It must be hard, your job. Everyone needs a rest. You just let me know if you need a thing."

I think I hug her. That's how I am. A hugger. It's not fake, but real. I like to hug and be hugged back. The governor didn't want me to hug him and neither did David Sedaris, but I understand some people just aren't raised that way and have their own aversions and peculiarities. It's all right. Everything will be all right. Yes . . . in a day or two.

I turn on the air-conditioning and breathe in that distinctive smell that all hotels with decent ratings have. I adjust the fan so the white noise is comforting and drowns out the sound of cars and people walking on floors above mine.

Sleep. That's the cure. Sleep. I take out a beer, maybe it's my second of the new six-pack, but I don't finish it. An hour passes, or maybe two, and a loud knock that's more like pounding awakens me from the fog of drunkenness and last night's excesses.

"Susan!" I hear a familiar voice shout. "SUSAN!!!!"

Oh, please, God, no. It's my mother. Then I hear a deeper voice, and panic. My father is with her.

"Let us in. We need to help you, honey, please."

I stumble out of bed and hide the beer, what's left of it, and unlock the door, run and jump back in, pulling up the sheets to cover my arms, which are turning a purplish blue. My wrists seep blood from the Band-Aids that lost their stickiness at the pool.

I hide them under the cool floral comforter.

"Come in," I say weakly.

They do, staring with frowns of concern on their faces, almost blank in spots, as if waiting on me to fill in the canvas of their unasked questions.

"You need help," one of them says, as they sit in the two chairs at the small round table near the window. "Stuart called us. He didn't know where you were last night. He said you've been drinking again and are out of control. We thought all this was behind you, Susan." Their voices are calm and kind.

I try to control my mouth and facial muscles so I don't slur. "He's wrong. I'm just tired. I can't sleep and needed one or two nights just to get my bearings and wits about me. That's all."

They could smell the beer, the fear and the pummeled flesh hidden under the sheets, oozing out like secrets that can't be kept.

"Where is it?" Daddy asked.

"What?"

"The alcohol."

Mom stares like she did when I was in high school and she wondered what I'd been up to. "I don't think she's drunk, Sam. Look at her eyes. She's on something. Pills. What have you taken, Susan?"

Dad moves toward the bed. "You're eyes are miles away. You need to tell us what you're on, Sugar, 'cause you look stoned out of your mind. We've got to get you some help."

"I just need sleep."

Mama's face reddens and the anger rises and can be seen in her chin and its jutting position. "You wanna be like my daddy? Fine. You can lay up here like some drunk and let the courts take your kids or you can tell us where to take you."

"Home."

"You can't go home," Daddy says. "Your children can't see you like this. Tell us what you want."

"Sleep."

My poor mama couldn't let her anger go. She was reliving a nightmare, had seen her own daddy drunk and passed out and unable to do more than lie on the couch and sleep off bad hangovers. My own father had seen it, too. His daddy was a weekend drunk. I got the gene, the curse, the weakness, whatever anyone wants to call it, but its roots, I know, are planted in dark soil of depression and fertilized with insecurity and self-doubt.

Neither wanted to see their daughter—their humorous, seemingly successful, award-winning, published-author daughter—like this. What had happened? She'd been sober for so long. Wasn't that part over? Hadn't she gone to AA and straightened out her life years ago?

"Oh, let her go home, Sam," Mama says, chin still jutting with fury and disappointment. "Let her just ruin her life if this is what she wants to do."

I knew, even in the haze of my fried brain, she didn't mean it. I knew she was simply rewinding her own past, seeing the ugly parts of her childhood.

"I'll go," I say, voice cracking. "You can take me to Brookstone. It's where I went last time."

They remembered. It is the psych unit at a local hospital, and if I'd been in my right mind, I'd have told them to take me somewhere for substance abuse and alcoholism. But I knew my insurance wouldn't pay but for a few days in Brookstone, so I said I'd go. I sure didn't want the traditional twenty-eight days in a real treatment center where they make you look way too deep within your soiled soul and scrub toilets and everyone yells at each other like in the Sandra Bullock movie *28 Days*.

I wanted a few days of insurance-paid R&R. I knew after that, my wonderful HMO would boot me out, and that was fine. Just fine with me.

I pull off the cover and try to walk but am too drugged and drunk. I manage to slip something over my shorts and top and allow my parents to dump the leftover pills from my purse and empty the bottles of Bud Select from beneath a wad of towels I'd hid them under in the bathroom.

Off we went, out the door and into a blinding white sun I wanted to yank from the sky and bury. I don't remember seeing the clerk or telling her good-bye. I wanted to because she'd been so kind, but when I ask my parents' permission they hold tighter and steer me toward their car.

We must have sneaked out the side door, them not wanting the town to see their daughter as their own parents had been. A drunk. A mother of two with a decent job and good life . . . drunk. And on pills. Drunk and drugged out. In their minds, you couldn't get much worse than that.

We drive in silence to the hospital unless Dad asks for directions, and I try to hold myself up and tell them to follow the signs with the big H on them. I needed to sleep, but they kept waking me up as if it was some sort of punishment.

Finally, we arrive in the emergency room where we stay for hours, answering questions and taking vital signs, and hearing how after swallowing so many different pills, I had no business being alive and it was a damned miracle. But I knew hospital staff always told survivors they were miracles, so I didn't put a lot of stock in what they were saying.

After about 7 o'clock I beg my parents to go home because I don't want them driving in the dark down the mountain to Spartanburg, South Carolina, an hour or so away.

"I'm fine. See? I'm checked in." I show them the bracelet with my name typed in pale purple letters, hug their necks and say my good-byes and I love yous. "Thank you for everything." I smile, as if part of my job as a dutiful and obeying daughter trying to please, always trying to please and make everyone happy. It's what I was raised and paid to do. Smile. Laugh. Be pleasant. Always. No matter what.

At the time this was happening, I hated my husband. He had called them when he must have known that all I needed—

or thought I needed—was two nights of rest in a fairly nice hotel. I'd tried the night before to treat my fatigue and depression with red wine. The TV and news reports all said how good it was for you. If one glass is good, more is better in my twisted mind, and a couple bottles later I was insanely drunk and depressed and decided to destroy myself, but not enough to die.

I just wanted to clear away the thunderclouds within, bleed out the bad.

I remember waiting until the kids were asleep and then the world swaying like a hammock and blurring. It went like this:

Two bottles of pills are in one hand. A dull razor blade and pair of scissors in another. I swallow the pills and hack at my wrists, but even through the distortion and anesthesia of alcohol, Ativan, Benadryl and whatever else was in my junk drawer, the pain of the cutting is too much to bear.

I want to live. I want to die. I want attention. I want to be left alone. I want the darkness to end. I want the light to enter. I want my parents and husband to see my unhappiness, but I don't want the kids to see anything but a mom who takes them snow tubing and roller-coaster riding, one who body surfs in the ocean without fear and with a face wide with laughter, eyes crinkled in mirth.

I have every right to be grateful. God is good. My kids are beautiful, as is my home. I have a job many would love and great friends. Only a few people hate me, and if others do, they don't say anything, which is nice.

And yet I'm trapped in a cycle of hell fueled by depression and an off-and-on battle with alcohol. Am I an alcoholic? Maybe, whatever the hell that is I certainly qualify on most occasions, this being one of them.

The pills begin to melt reality and the blood leaks from my wrists, though I'm cutting wrong and superficially, which I know because, really, I don't want to die. I want someone to listen. I want my parents to realize I'm unhappy, that I've chosen a life I can no longer live, at least part of it. The husband part. I am sure at this point in my marriage that I want out, but know I'm trapped by fear of their disapproval and of hurting my children and the rest of the family.

"He is a good man and father," they have said, and I know they are right. He's good to our kids. Still, in my messed up, mind he is the cause. I'm too confused to see my own part in the destruction of the union, and he won't recognize his part either. We are on that hamster wheel that repeats the same arguments for years and years, nothing ever being resolved. The tapes play, a needle stuck in the groove of a single tune.

Maybe this is distorted. Everyone has gifts and weaknesses. We are all a mix of good and bad, positives and negatives. He was forced to live with me: an imperfect, on-and-off-again alcoholic who at times was unmanageable. I had to live with his anger, the tiptoeing on pins and needles and hot coals, afraid if I said or did something wrong he would explode verbally.

His fault? Maybe. My fault? Maybe.

The blood is pooling and I ask him to take me to the hospital but he doesn't, thinking I'm crying wolf again, so I get in my car, screwed up as hell, and drive to a friend's house. Maybe he'll take me. He's my best friend, a great guy, but when he sees me he is afraid. He gently puts me to bed and then takes the futon for himself. I may be dying, but he doesn't see it and neither did my husband. Maybe they just didn't want to see it.

Five hours later I awaken. I am not dead. Good. This is good. I didn't want to die. Really. I only wanted someone, anyone on this planet, to realize that I was alive and hurting and wanting out of my marriage or out of my head or out of something that didn't feel right and hasn't for many years.

My sister got a divorce and it nearly killed my parents. They broke like speared bulls and fell to the ground in prayer and heartache. They turned to God and church and found their peace, but not without a price. Mama's blood pressure rose and Daddy's nerves went to hell.

My sister turned to a Christian singles online dating site and found her a second husband, a fine man who didn't treat her like shit or yell and curse and make her work out to the point she had nearly zero body fat. The first husband had wanted her blonde, rail-thin and stripperlike, and for years she conformed.

She finally had had enough and now is blissfully happy with her tall and adoring new husband, and her children are not in boot camps and prisons like I'd been taught to believe of the "victims" of torn, one-parent families.

I am not happy but not strong enough to leave. What is wrong? Why can't I stop feeling sorry for myself and realize life is good despite a husband I'm certain belongs with someone else, someone not like me?

I adopt a child in a Third World country and help the poor and give to various charities and do all the things those into themselves are supposed to do to get out of the Me and seek humility to feel better.

Love others. Help them. Forget self. Kill ego.

It wasn't working, nor was the Lexapro, the Effexor, or any of the medicines the doctors prescribed to straighten out my hormones and serotonin levels and prove to my brain that yes, life is good and I'm one of the more blessed in this crazy world.

Only my brain wouldn't listen. It wanted wine. Beer. Pills. Escape.

I wanted out of my marriage. I loved him, but couldn't stand the arguing and feelings of inadequacy. I didn't want my children to suffer, as my parents had promised would be the case, should I divorce.

"They'll be into drugs and drop out of school," one said.

"Statistically, they'll be in jails and juvenile detention centers," the other assured. It went on from there.

"The Bible says no to divorce."

"Children need a two-parent home."

I need a sharper razor blade and strong pills and someone to take me to the hospital and call my parents and tell them I cannot live this way a moment longer.

The kids are safe and soundly sleeping, and my husband is downstairs watching television.

I cut at my arms with scissors and Bic disposable blades and then decide the pain isn't worth it, because, really, like I said a million times, I did not want to die. On the counter is a hairbrush, heavy and black, next to the sink. I take it in my hands and beat my arms as hard as I can. I feel no pain, only pressure, so I keep striking over and over and over until my hands ache from the constant hitting. Release, I'm thinking, trying to beat out the demons within.

I pack a duffel bag with things I'll need in the hospital. They will pump my stomach and call my parents and then everyone will know why I have to leave my house. It will all work out. I get in the car, turn the key and back out of my driveway and so-called charmed life.

No one follows me.

Seventeen hours later I'm in Brookstone telling my parents good-bye.

"It's gonna be all right," I say and deep down believe it, know it to be true.

The Cradle Will Fall

Brookstone is the last stop before state-run institutions, death, disability or a lifetime of electric shock treatments and medicines that may make some well but are intolerable for others. I could envision myself as a dry-mouthed, twitching woman with mumbled thoughts and paranoia if I didn't hurry up and get out of here.

Sure, the staff may be nice and eager to help, but I didn't want this kind of help. I wasn't hearing voices or running for the Senate in some state of mania. I was simply a depressed and exhausted substance abuser who needed R&R and maybe someone to force me to stop drinking red wine the color of day-old blood.

I curl fetally onto the vinyl gurney, rustling the scratchy white paper, and wait for a room to open up. A man comes in. He is splotching and smiling and turning several shades of red. A book by Augusten Burroughs called *Dry: A Memoir* is in his hands and he is saying he enjoys my column and figured I'd like the book, and by the way he's also a real estate agent if I'm ever in the market for a new home and is also gay so don't worry "I'm not hitting on you."

Not that I thought anyone would be hitting on me in a mental ward with my wild, dark-circled eyes, hacked wrists and arms that look as if they've been hammered by an angry roofer.

"Anytime you want a new start," he says with a wink. So cute. All the gay ones are so damn cute and understanding and easy to talk to. "New homes are sometimes the cure."

New home? I'm in the market for a new life, a way out of this pitch-black tunnel, but I take the book and thank him and promise to read it and will. At some point.

Maybe I will buy a small house or condo, start over and see if that helps. I could paint the walls that new trendy color of coffee shops: low-key orange and butternut-squash, and sponge and texture them like they do on the home improvement shows. No one would scream if I nailed holes in the walls or bought things at yard sales and thrift shops and painted them all different colors with swirls and stencils, maybe flowers and abstracts.

I close my eyes but sleep won't come; it rarely does unless I pour wine and pills into my body. By now the beer and drugs are wearing off and I've been in the emergency room's holding cell for nearly ten hours, waiting on a bed to open in Brookstone, waiting for someone saner than me to move through the gates of newfound wellness and check out. Those who leave the South Tower, reserved for the truly screwed up, are medicated and pharmaceutically lobotomized to the point that they graduate to North Tower where they give you plastic forks instead of just spoons to eat your meals.

But they want me in South, at least for a while, to make sure I don't find a way to hang myself or kill off another patient, not that I would.

Around 1 or 2 AM I'm wheeled upstairs to the sixth floor where everything is triple locked and coded, with warning signs posted everywhere about NO ACCESS and how the police will restrain any intruder without permission to enter. I am helped into a stiff bed and notice first thing there are no shades, no curtains, no blinds. A half moon shines directly into my eyes and I feel doomed that day or night, sleep—what I need most—won't come easy.

There is no darkness except in my heart and mind. I stand and try to put a blanket over the window to block the moon and the promise of morning sun, which is destroying me and sizzling my brain along with the Shiraz and depression.

I hear my mother's voice calling up the mountain. *Just pray, Susan. Pray. God is good, God is good, He is here; He is always listening. Ask, Seek, Find, Heal.* I am on my knees in prayer. Please, please. Please. Help.

I feel nothing and can only sweat the poisons from my pores and listen as one therapist and doctor after another quizzes me as to why I tried to kill myself and why my wrists and arms were sliced and pounded.

"To let in the light," I tell them, staring off through the bare, moon-drenched window. "I wanted someone to see how much I hurt inside and how tired I am. Nobody would. No one believed anything I said about what it was like to be trapped in this freaking hell."

They wrote frantically in their charts and one even took a Polaroid and I'm sure I showed teeth because that's what I'm supposed to do—be happy, be funny. Even while in a mental ward and wearing a tired face with no makeup other than lipstick that I put on every hour or less because I have a lipstick disorder. No matter if I'm dying or going insane and curling like a *C* in a bed with no blinds and no cords or devices with which to kill myself, by God, I'm going to have my lipstick on.

I answer a battery of questions, wondering why they can't wait and do this in the morning, but by the end of the session, they determine that after breakfast, if I've not tried anything stupid, they will move me to the North Tower. A promotion. Yeah! I'm being promoted from Super-Crazy to Semi-Crazy.

That night I don't sleep but roll around in the bed covered in plastic so no one can pee or vomit and ruin the mattress, and sweat like I did on that pool chair at the Comfort Inn. I squeeze my eyes closed and taste the bitter aftereffects of Miller High Life. Maybe I fall asleep, but it's hard to tell because every fifteen minutes a nurse's assistant shines a flashlight at my chest to make sure I'm still alive.

By morning, just four hours after I get in this damn bed, they hand me a little paper container shaped in ruffled ridges like a teensy chef's hat and containing at least six pills, and they watch like hawks as I swallow. They ask to see inside my mouth and beneath my tongue.

They try to weigh me but I refuse, and they say too bad and put me on the scales anyway. After that, they do the vital signs and exclaim a fast and irregular heartbeat and I tell them it will all pass with enough rest. Really.

"Is there any way you could maybe not come in and shine that giant flashlight in my eyes every fifteen minutes?" I ask and try to smile, be polite and onstage as always.

"It's to make sure you're not dead," the humorless nurse's aide said. Standard regulations, I'm told. On the North Tower, they shine the light only every half hour. Whew, what a vacation North is going to be.

I try to return to my room and begin a wobbling walk (from the pills) until a gentle-faced male nurse leads me to the breakfast area where the others are gathered. They are like me only worse, or so I tell myself, and yet they're kind enough that I feel a liking for all except one who keeps saying we're cousins over and over and that she swears she can see wings sprouting from my shoulder blades.

"I know you're the Black Angel," she says. "I know about you. I see your wings. We all do and have been awaiting your arrival."

I can't wait to get to North, hoping nobody sees wings on my shoulders or says things about Black Angels. I stare at the food and try to cry but the drugs have numbed me to the point where it's as if I'm starring in a modern version of *One Flew Over the Cuckoo's Nest* and Nurse Ratched will appear at any minute.

I feel very little, like a brain-dead little zombie unless I look at my arms, but I don't. I cover them up in black long-sleeved shirts even though it's 1,000 degrees outside.

Breakfast is bizarre and the other incarcerated nutcases like me either poke at their food or try to eat everyone else's. I am famished, and the parched skeletal woman of an undetermined age next to me gives me all her sausage and waffles and blueberry muffins. She just wants to get out and go smoke and retreat to her singlewide where she can cook up what she truly craves at mealtimes: crystal meth.

"I ain't hurting nobody but myself," she says and many of her teeth are gone or in stages of packing up and leaving her gums for good. "This place is a shit pit. My babies need me back at home."

I can't take much more of this: I'm furious with my husband for sticking me here and for calling my poor mother and daddy who've already lived childhoods from hell with alcoholic parents. I am reminded of the phone call that came in the dead of night when I was ten years old.

Early the next morning Daddy sat us down and told us what had happened. His eyes were red and swollen from crying and his hands shook. He faced us bravely, though trembling, and said his father had died, that Pa-Pa had been shot and so he needed to drive the four hours to Granny's house to help her and my aunt and uncle deal with everything.

I learned later that week what had really happened. Pa-Pa was in the war and had a bad leg that gave him fits, as did the memories of the living nightmares young men in combat must see and endure long after the gunpowder and bomb smoke clear. Pa-Pa drank every night and cleaned his gun and ate my granny's fried chicken, and every morning got up with his hangover and heartbreak and went to the textile mill to do his blue-collar job until one day it became too much.

He was hurting on his final night, his leg so painful he could barely stand it. The doctor had told him it might have to come off. He poured one whiskey after the other while Granny cooked and read her Bible and figured it was a night like most others when Pa-Pa fell into this kind of mood.

Aunt June was there and nothing unusual was happening until they heard a loud boom, the unmistakable explosion of a gunshot blast from my Uncle Steve's room. Granny screamed for June, the registered nurse and strong one in the family. She rushed in, fell to her knees upon finding Pa-Pa lying in a puddle of blood on the hardwood floors part of his head missing and brains everywhere. She called my daddy and before Granny could see her husband like this, scooped up skull bits and brains and crammed them down the bathroom drains.

He had a pulse, but by the time the ambulance arrived, Pa-Pa was gone.

Was it suicide? I think so. Others say no, that he was just drunk and cleaning his guns. Amazing what denial will lead a person to believe. Denial? Is that why I'm here? Pretending to be tired when maybe, just maybe, they are right and I'm super-sick and need to pack all my things and move into a place like this forever? Could this possibly be correct?

The family history is mostly what I told them when they questioned me for two hours in South Tower the night I finally got a bed. "Does suicide run in your family?"

"Yes."

"Who?"

"My grandfather."

"Anyone else?"

I was afraid to answer. "Not exactly."

"What do you mean, 'Not exactly'?"

I no longer smiled or pretended to care what anyone knew or thought about the girl in the newspaper who made people laugh. Here I was the girl who was very sick and who would break if not fixed.

"Tell us, Susan. What do you mean 'not exactly'?"

I tried to sit up but the room was like a Tilt-A-Whirl. "My dad. He sort of messed around with it a little."

The doctors looked puzzled. "Messed around with what?"

"He took some pills. Lots of them and parked the car in a ditch and chased them down with a bottle of liquor." It was in uttering these words I realized I'd done the same thing. "He's a Christian now. Not the same man at all as he was back then. He woke up five hours later and couldn't believe he was alive."

Our stories were eerily similar. He drove to my Mama Callie's, his grandmother who was very tough and strong, and told her what happened. She put him to bed for four days. I really think people just get tired. I'm fairly certain half the people up here in these towers are simply exhausted, overworked and overwhelmed.

"If someone had just put me to bed for a few days none of this would be happening." Or maybe I'm in denial.

More writing in the charts. "I don't know," a dour-faced doctor said. "I believe, from all the questions we've asked and you've answered, you are suffering from Bipolar Disorder."

I wanted to die right then. I knew bipolar people, and while creative and interesting, some led tormented lives of hell and tampered with or refused to take their meds and would end up right back where they started. I knew they ran for governor when manic and bought yachts, and then when depressed, they wanted to die and couldn't get out of bed for days. They went on spending sprees and flew to Vegas. They were out of control with the highs and immobilized and suicidal with the lows. I never spent more than half a day or so in bed or over $200 at a time on some good deals on eBay or the department stores.

I was not that. I was a lot of things. But not that. Not bipolar.

No point in arguing. The meds in the baby chef's hat erased any combative energy a fighter could possess. "Whatever you say. You're the professionals. Bipolar it is." The doc in charge took a deep and satisfying breath, after having been designated by a loony as correct in his diagnosis.

"It's more common than you think, and lots of very intelligent people have it, this Bipolar Disorder, that is. It's hereditary at times, and not your fault, and the good news is we have so many new and wonderful medicines to treat it."

I thought about my bipolar friends, wonderful people, but who had fits with some of their meds.

"That's great," I said, hoping to get to North Tower soon so I could call my mother and tell her and daddy not to worry— that I was bipolar and had six pills a day that would cure me and all would be back to normal.

"There are many degrees of bipolar and we'll go over them later. We're moving you to North and you'll be assigned a

caseworker and she'll get you started on a new way of living."
The doctor smiled but it was fake. I know fake from real. I
smiled back. Mine was real.

I made it to North by lunchtime where all the tamer victims of mental illness and excess glared and wondered what we
all want to know: "What's she in for? What has she done?"

My wrists were bandaged, obviously cut, and my arms covered
in the sleeves. I wore my long dark hair piled without thought
or combing in a big brown clip and sprigs sprouted everywhere.
My face was bare with the exception of lipstick and eyeglasses.
Beauty Tip Number One for those who've wrecked their lives
with too much booze and not enough sleep: Wear eyeglasses.
They hide almost everything.

Everyone's food once again looked exceptional and I'd
never been so hungry. Most of the patients, just like in South,
didn't want to eat. Those like me who did, ate everyone else's
meals. It all boiled down to which pills were in the miniature
chef's hat.

A man with a semibald head and a ponytail with what was
left, eyed me from across the table. He had scabs all over his
face and a nasty sunburn. I was certain he was gay and in for
the depression associated with either HIV or full-blown AIDS.
Wasn't that how those sores crop up? Those scabby things
from the final stages of AIDS?

He wouldn't stop looking at me and so I gave him a smirky,
"look-at-us-fools-in-here" kind of smile and went about eating
everyone's food, including his. I put up my tray and tried to be
funny, though not 24 hours had passed since my admission.

"Anyone with any CONDOM . . . ENTS, hand them over."

The others laughed at my reference to condoms. They offered up little tubs of butter and pots of cream and packets of
sugar. A sweet woman named Phyllis who heard voices saying
they would kill her helped me put away all the condiments. We
liked cleaning the long table, and I would catch the man with
AIDS watching with a certain amusement.

After that first lunch, I tried to go to my room and lie down because this section of the ward had blinds. Maybe I dosed, maybe not. A ball-busting and intelligent woman bounded in and announced she'd be my caseworker and had an armload of material on my new disorder—BiPolar II—which, she said, was more manageable and less serious than the classic BiPolar I, formerly known as manic-depressive illness.

"I have it, too," she said and I wanted to hug her because she was so honest. "If you take your meds, you'll lead a normal life. If you don't, you'll end up here . . . or much worse."

I nodded and reached for the papers.

"Read the material and I'll come back. By the way, I love your column."

Damn. Why couldn't I get away from this? I pictured word getting out to my editors that I was a bona fide nut job in a mental institution and then receiving my pink slip, only it would be a thick folder of legal papers so I couldn't sue them for ditching a crazy woman. No way in hell they'd keep a depressed, bipolar on staff. Would they? Or would it be a sign of catering to those who are different: the underdogs, the minorities, women, Asians, Hispanics, African, Native or just plain old insane Americans? After all, Corporate America DOES have its perks, supporting diversity being one of them.

This was a small town and word would get out, so instead of lying and pretending I wasn't Susan the columnist but looked an awful lot like her, which I'd done a few times before, I admitted it all.

I asked the caseworker a trick question. "Can you drink with all these medicines?"

She thought for a moment. "An occasional glass of wine would be fine."

This was music to my ears, the sweet melody for an alcohol, wine-craving soul. Whatever she said I had, I'd agree. Bipolar? Why not, if I could drink and no one was even considering what I thought was my real diagnosis: Alcoholism brought on by depression.

Manic? I get happy sometimes and hyper but a true manic

person goes and does completely irrational things, or so I thought, and I'd kept the same job for twenty years and the same husband for eighteen, so something had to be working. Right?

Maybe not. Variances, she said, are common and there are many degrees of Bipolar Disorder. Some were on broil and others, Bake at 350. Maybe mine was a slow-cooking form of brain sickness that would take over like Georgia kudzu if I didn't down these six pills that made me feel like shit and eat like a sumo wrestler.

She asked me to sign a copy of my newly released book, which I thought was nice and rather odd, but later that day, word got around that I'd written a collection of funny stories, and by nightfall, lots of people had copies and I had one of my most successful book signings ever—in the rec room of the Mental Ward.

Life is strange that way. You just can't predict things.

The day was surreal, for lack of a better word, and I felt as if I was watching some movie set in a modern-day institution. I was Angelina Jolie in *Girl, Interrupted.* Only not as thin or beautiful. That afternoon we had group therapy and were taught things like coping skills other than drinking, cutting or, in one man's case, walking out in front of traffic and hoping to become roadkill.

We learned to diagram our lives as we would a sentence and get to the root of things without toppling the trees. We could deal with life's stresses if we took our meds and deep breaths and kept all doctor appointments, or so they said.

"The med sled comes three times a day," said the man with the AIDS-looking sores. I immediately liked him, mainly because he had a calm sense of humor and a balance that threw me off guard. Why in the world was someone like him here?

I learned later he was an attorney and not gay and didn't have HIV sores. His wife of more than twenty years had bolted, and when he returned from a trip to help the poor Hispanics in Central America, scuffing his face while building Habitat Homes, she had packed up and moved in with another man. As a result he decided to walk out in front of an 18-wheeler until a friend heard the news and dragged him to Brookstone.

We took our meds and sat in a room where a social worker with a sweet voice one would use for kindergartners handed out wooden objects, plastic wind catchers and beads to carve, paint and string. This was art therapy. Later, we wrote out lists of affirmations and shared them with the group.

I am good. I am worthy of life. I am loveable. I am kind. I am generous.

I kept making wooden boxes and earrings for family members, as if they would love having reminders and mementos of my time in the Hopper.

In the mornings, a frightening woman would arrive with misery etched on her face and ask us to gather in the rec room where she turned off the TV and put on a CD from the *Big Chill* and started a slow-motion series of geriatric exercises to "I Heard It Through the Grapevine."

The man without AIDS and who was not gay began to clog when she wasn't looking and I couldn't stop laughing and had to leave the room. I'm certain they wrote in the chart that I had a manic episode because that afternoon, my chef's hat had seven pills in it instead of six and the caseworker was far more inquisitive as to my moods.

Can I help it that I laugh? Can I help it that humor heals? Or that the man clogging while the nurse was trying to dance cracked me up?

I stayed nine days and gained 12 pounds. I fell in love with the staff and most of the patients and even getting to know their families. Many of us still keep in touch, sharing the ups and downs of depression and mental illness and the often difficult effects of the medications we took to make us whole again.

Nothing is perfect, but I'm learning to find joy and meaning in life and to slow down.

It's not hard to believe that if I don't pour wine down my throat, I won't slice and pound my arms again. It's even possible to believe there are chances to heal, to fold the dark wool blankets and tuck them into the attic.

I may be Bipolar or it could be classic depression, doctors aren't in agreement. Whatever it is, I learned many lessons in Brookstone. One, that people care and are here to help if one is brave enough or has family courageous enough to intervene.

And two, you don't have to die, and life can and will get better if one seeks help. It may take a while, but somewhere around another corner, maybe a mile, or even ten down the road, a breathtaking moment or realization will make pain's price worth it.

Living is the choice I'm making. Laughing. Smiling. Being funny. Wearing my lipstick outside the lines. I'm also trying to be real, showing people the other side of the girl who is paid to bring on laughter.

Going into a psychiatric unit was a time in my life I pray doesn't need repeating.

Yet I know for sure, it always bears remembering.

A Symphony of Seasons

Summer

If I could freeze-frame a slice of time, it would have to be the days of blue-skied grace wedged between the moments before a season takes a final bow.

Perfection often appears in the pauses, the lulls prior to change when the world shifts gears, abandoning the stage for a costume change.

It seems to happen each year around September, when the weather turns perfect, and office workers slip away from their desks to catch a glimpse of summer's final curtain call.

I play hooky for the show, often taking my lunch by a lake where everything beautiful captures itself in the mirrored surface of the water.

Ladies in business suits and sneakers walk the dirt path strewn with the first casualties of summer, dried leaves falling at random.

I sit under a tree whose canopy reminds me of hair in early middle age, losing hue at the crown and edges, showing signs of letting go while I'm trying to hang on to summer.

It seems the world is made up of people who claim favorite seasons the way some take over certain pews in church. Maybe there are summer people, fall people, winter and spring people. If so, I'm a summer, and seeing tarps covering sparkling swimming pools, watching the sun clock out earlier each evening and hearing the diminishing melody of the insect's nightly choir rehearsals drape my mood in melancholy.

I watch from the bank of the lake as a man in a white T-shirt and shorts aims his kayak and joy toward the water's edge. I see mothers strolling happy babies and couples clasping hands as they walk along the perimeter framed in cotton clouds.

I lean back on a park bench, thinking of a man who once told me you could slow time if you sat on a bench, so I sit and stare at the endless stretch of sky so blue it appears to have been washed and waxed. The wind, instead of blowing a hot yawn, offers a cool whisper of what's to come.

Days don't get any better than this, even when one sees the signs of change: the confetti of fallen leaves whirling in the air, the grass turning hard and brown, the flowers along window boxes struggling to stay alert, offering their last encore of pink and red smiles.

A lawnmower sounds in the distance, muffled by urgent calls from birds making plans to fly south.

A few days earlier, I was at a middle-school football game, the sun so hot many carried umbrellas. It won't be long before those umbrellas are replaced with wool blankets and mugs of hot chocolate and coffee.

It won't be long before I see the explosion of color: the quilt of red, gold and sienna hugging our world before the blasts of cold and winter's bitter beauty. In a short time, smells of wood smoke will trail wind, signs of autumn and those anxious for it to begin anew.

I try to feel the excitement, a bit of fondness for fall.

On the lake, the water ripples, invigorated by a sudden, hic-coughed breeze. I wrap up my leftovers and head back to the office, the sun still holding summer in its hands.

In a few days, according to the calendar, it'll be fall, the season I used to loathe, feeling that with each bleeding leaf a part of me died along with it.

Autumn reminds me of saying good-bye too soon. But the truth is, it's not unusual for people like us to turn our heads and look back one last time as we do when autumn nudges summer to the back of the line.

Not long ago I got a phone call from a man named Charlie, the man with theories about benches and slowing time. He lives in a nearby town and wanted me to write about the bench he's planning to order and cement to his lawn, wanting to extend his life by sitting and doing nothing but enjoying the days.

Charlie and I had one of those wonderful conversations in which a person realizes she's listening to wisdom. He said he's getting up in years and has invented a way to tie the hands of a clock so they don't run up and down its face as if it was a race.

He told me about the bench he bought, similar to those at bus stops.

"Only be sure to put it in a place where a bus never comes," he said. "That's the key. Otherwise, you're once again in motion. Motion is the enemy of extension." He promised that as soon as his bench comes in he's going to call and we'll sit a spell. His reasoning is that as he sits, doing nothing but watching life all around him, the world will halt on its axis or stall long enough to grow sluggish.

Charlie will breathe in the smell of summer and lengthen his enjoyment of all the things in life one wishes to freeze before it ages, changes or gradually disappears. I didn't know then that Charlie was dying. He kept that part to himself, and I never heard from him again.

I'd forgotten about his bench theory until we moved into a new house that summer. Shortly after our move, I walked to the end of the cul-de-sac and there it was. A bench. A curved cement seat planted directly beneath a Norway spruce. It was the kind of bench Charlie would have wanted.

Fall

Last Sunday evening I glanced around at the beauty of the dimming day and took a seat on that bench surrounded by smells of fresh mulch and evergreens. I drank in the youth and innocence of my children's faces, the pure joy of living and not having known enough disappointments to rust the heart.

So this must be why Charlie wanted a bench in the middle of nowhere in particular. He didn't want everything to end too soon. Like summer has. Maybe he, too, grew sad when a season wore itself thin.

Children are already in school, even when the air is too thick to breathe and the Saturday and Sunday sun lingers all week in the heat of their cheeks, along with the smell of swimming pool in their hair.

The scrapes and scratches of summer remain written on their skin.

I stared from my perch, waiting to see if a flower stood alert or if its petals would fall. I heard children riding bikes down the road, taking one last loop around the neighborhood streets until the day was lost to baths and homework, schedules riding piggyback with freedom's last gasp.

Even sitting on this slab of cement, I could see a season slipping, giving pieces of itself to the yellow squash in a neighbor's garden. Or weaving with last bits of steam through the faint cicada songs and trailing a finger of cool air, tickling its way through an August night.

Fall was on its way. For the autumn people, summer is the misery before glory, the spell of endurance before they enjoy what they live for: lighting a fire in the fireplace. Pulling out wool sweaters and blankets. Sitting in a football stadium and drinking hot chocolate or coffee to stay warm.

They like the days when the air feels laundered, the sky a blazing blue that only fall displays, as polished as the jeweler's stones.

This is a season I used to dread but am learning to appreciate, especially after weekends when the edges of summer waltz with fall, one giving warmth, the other luscious color.

Fall used to remind me of death, nature's corpses in the form of lost leaves and withered vines signaling the end of daffodils and impatiens planted with eagerness after last frost. I'd watch the one-shot flowers collapse, the bees flying zigzagged in a final spree.

Fall may spread a patchwork of color across the mountainside, but the beauty of each topaz leaf and ruby-red bush seemed as cruel as the glittering ball gowns on Cinderella's stepsisters.

I'm a Summer person, a Georgia girl who relishes May through August and the shucking of shoes, the first blinks of lightning bugs, the chorus of eager insects trying to live and love and do it all as if the next day was their last.

The sauna breath of an afternoon is for me as comforting as a heating pad on sore muscles. The flowers and emerald leaves, tomatoes going from green to red, tulips and wildflowers offering snapshots of God within every bloom. Children in swimsuits and sunburn, roaming the streets until after 9 PM.

Summer was a season of more; fall, a season of less; winter, a time of death; spring, the months of renewal. That's how I'd always thought of this, though the older I get, the more I have come to appreciate autumn. No longer is it the months of taking, but I can see it as a period of giving.

Certainly life leaks out of things, but in that slow evaporation the full-color veil lifts itself from death as a promise. Its beauty doesn't disappear but changes. It's no longer a virgin green leaf or the first pink petals of a dogwood. It's no longer a Bradford pear like a bride in white.

These are the months when people carve pumpkins and drink cider. Spend time with their families and friends, and when life is pulled by forces of temperature and tilt.

It is also the season of state fairs, my favorite autumn pastime, which I enjoy every year at least twice, often more.

This past year we attended the North Carolina Mountain State Fair. It was midweek, around 3:30 PM, and the grounds were nearly deserted—the way old people and mommies like it. The quiet hung over the midway ever so slightly, like something napping after many days of exertion.

Clouds played bumper cars in the sky, hiding the sun and catching heat, letting autumn cut in line.

We stood in the sawdust and earth as the place tried to shake off fatigue from the previous night, everyone involved bone-tired but dedicated, all waking up like a row of toddlers after naptime.

The fair has always reminded me of life boiled down along a single, expansive field. It's a place where the farm and the city hold hands—private-school boys in their Tommy cargos pet the sheep that are fed and raised by the 4-H'ers in their denim overalls.

It's where animals are as much a part of the show as people. Where a woman's quilt and a man's beefsteak tomatoes are all eligible for glory and ribbons.

The fair lives up to its name. Everybody has a shot, a fair chance. Grandma with her killer cornbread and Mary Lynn's new boyfriend who isn't leaving until he wins her a stuffed bear bigger than his car.

Around 4 o'clock the rides and attractions along the midway groaned to life, metal and machinery cracking like the lid on a slow-opening can. Ticket booth tenders raised their little glass windows. Hands clutching money slipping in; hands offering tickets fluttering out.

A Ferris wheel began a slow spin, rising and dipping, its operator sun-baked and dirt-caked and trying to keep the ride moving and people smiling.

Men and women selling chances sipped their drinks and lit their cigarettes, and at some point in between, called to those walking by.

"Winner every time. Pay one price and everyone goes home happy."

Kids threw darts at balloons and five-dollar bills down the drain. They thrilled at the pop of rubber and the sight of a tattooed arm sweeping across the prize board. "Pick a prize. Any prize along this row is all yours."

Grills shot plumes of smoke that smelled of meat and onions; fryers crackled and the music beat louder as the hours matured into a rich darkness scented with all things sweet, fried, battered and dunked.

Throughout the night, as her mood struck, a 40-something

schoolteacher and neighbor of mine returned to the flying machine, paying her tickets and lying on her stomach across the seat. She squeezed her daughter who was next to her and waved to her husband on the ground below.

In the air as the ride lifted her skyward, the woman with graying blonde hair spread her arms as if she were a bird.

"I'm Superwoman!" she cried, voice fading as the ride took her farther away. "Look!" she called the next time she came around. "I'm flying!"

My children and I drank Cokes and found a seat on an empty bench while we watched the lights blinking on and off, the night in slow motion when viewed from the edge of a bench.

Charlie was right. You *can* slow down time if you find the right bench and hang on to the moment the way the flying lady gripped the handles of her ride.

Winter

Winter comes and the melancholy arrives with the shorter days. It's the season of slow, when we think this frozen earth, this feeling of bleak and gray will never end.

Wintertime Sundays always meant one of two things while we were growing up in West Central Georgia. After church, if it was pretty outside, we might jump in the station wagon for a family drive. If the day stuck with a Great Britain–like dreariness, after we ate my mother would scrape the leftover rice and gravy from the plates, wrap the fried chicken or roast beef with the quick tear of Reynolds foil and run a sink of soapy water. Then, around 2 o'clock if the steel sky hadn't given way to a slice of sun, she'd go to her room and ask my sister and me to play quietly upstairs. She'd spend several hours napping away the doldrums of winter.

She wasn't depressed. She wasn't unhappy. She was simply sick of winter.

This was Georgia where summers never seemed to end and clung like a morning moon too stubborn to retreat. Winters, though short-lived, brought little more than unpredictability. We endured weeks of dark clouds and no beauty beyond the music and cadence of cold rain—the way it pattered against windowpanes and tapped on the roof, as close to a lullaby as the sky would offer.

We rarely got snow in our part of Georgia. Every five or so years we might get an inch or two, and watching it fall in huge, wet flakes was as beautiful to those who hardly ever saw it as a stretch of bleached white sand surrounding an impossibly turquoise sea.

When the snow lay against the clay earth, covering the dead grass and decomposed leaves, we'd stare as it piled up and dressed the world in white. It was what made the winters bearable.

I hear people from up North moan and grumble when forecasters predict the storms that snag lives, slow the world and tangle schedules. For many the falling snow is winter's pest, like summer's mosquitoes. For people like me who grew up without it, snow was like confetti and fireworks.

Winter, with its bone-thin trees and snaggle-toothed landscapes, is meant to wear white. Some of us who hate the cold and clouds, the rain that hovers at 34 degrees, can tolerate the season only so long.

By January we are dreaming of the Keys or the Caribbean. By February a lucky few are there.

I often spent the winter days as my mother used to—in bed with a good book, staring at the naked trees and imagining them ruffled in green. I would wait for spring like an eager schoolgirl for the last bell.

Spring

Spring would come before winter ended—another pause before the season changes—a sampling of beauty with 65-degree days in mid-February. A chance for long walks and hikes, hours spent outdoors aching to plant but knowing it was too soon.

I wanted to call Charlie and tell him that winter is the way to slow time. That it works better than a bench.

But when I dialed his number and reached his wife, she said he was gone. He had passed away, but not before he got his bench where he spent many of his last days in the quiet stillness pondering the mysteries of the world and what lay ahead.

He knew that the end of winter, like the end of life, meant spring was coming. He knew of renewal, of chances for rebirth the way new life finds its way into the barest of trees, nudging the branches with polka dots of green, ready to unfold as the days grow warmer.

He realized as he took his last breaths that this wasn't the end, but instead just another season. I believe it was his favorite.

I'll Love You Forever

Written for my wonderful son, Niles, shortly before his baby sister entered the world, and later, as he changed from boy to teen, almost as if overnight.

These are the last few months of just you and me. Of the nights we share after dinner, laughing about nothing and playing Knock-Knock until both of us are hoarse with silliness.

Your baby sister or brother will be here soon, a period of great joy but also of divided time when a mother's attention spreads even thinner and the necessary often replaces the fun and frivolous.

For the next few weeks, I count our every minute as a gift, the uninterrupted attention as something that will never again come so readily, so freely. Many nights, after you've fallen into the dreamy sleep of children, I tiptoe toward your bed and watch your face in the glow of the moon, slipping through cracks in the shade.

Many nights I can't resist and place a hand against the curve of your cool cheek. And like the mother in the book *Love You Forever*, I long to scoop your relaxed little body into my arms and rock you. Just as I did not so long ago.

Has five years really passed so quickly? Could you possibly be old enough to play T-ball? Lying in the outfield as the balls fly and skitter while you roll in the dirt tired and bored, sitting up only to check under the bases for worms and bugs? Could you possibly be old enough already to start kindergarten in the fall?

I make promises in the dark: That I will always tuck you in with books and laughter, no matter the other demands of the day and child to come. That I will always find pieces of time for you, an hour here or there, maybe only thirty minutes, but I'll catch it, trap and treasure it, no matter the crowded slates that leave a parent feeling drained and guilty.

Seeing your peaceful face makes my throat knot with the oncoming tears, your beautiful profile, that of a sleeping child being one of the most serene on earth. It's like watching an angel, something extraordinarily innocent, and all of the day's frustrations sink with the sun and are silenced within the quiet corners of a child's room.

Sometimes, as I'm standing over your bed, I notice your hair slicked back with perspiration, matted from the sweat of a mother's worries and extra blankets.

Sometimes, it's too much for me.

I can't resist and crawl underneath the covers until my body is spooned against yours. I try to match your gentle breathing, and I feel tugged from places deep within my chest, like an anchor slowly dropping, weighting a parent with a love she can never fully explain or begin to understand.

It is a love that gives and takes. And in the hush of nightfall, knocks us cold with fear.

We love and fear, mostly fearing what we love. This is the moment when I'm most vulnerable to the thoughts I easily push back in daylight, when I inch closer to your warmth as a chill surrounds my heart.

This is when all the visions of lurking dangers crowd my mind. When the news on TV about children missing, the suffering and the madness of the world shoots images like a frightening montage of what can happen. We always think, "That's other people. Not us." It's at night when I see your smooth-and-flawless face I begin to worry.

I scoot in tighter and pray for another day, another year,

even going as far on some nights as asking God to grant us both a long, happy life. Selfish, maybe, but necessary for peace of mind.

I hook an arm around your tiny waist and feel your little-boy bones and baby-soft tummy, still round and free of the taut muscles to come later. I bury my face against the back of your hair, smelling the apricot shampoo and leftover sunshine.

Sometimes, I hold your hand and listen as your breathing changes, as your eyelids flutter with dreams known only to little boys. You don't move or stir. This is your gift to me.

Before I know it the years have run as if in a marathon and you are 7, 8, 9, and now a boy entering middle school.

Tomorrow is your first day at this place we used to call junior high school and you can't fall asleep. I enter your room, just like the mother I used to be, the mother in *Love You Forever*. Your legs thrash, twisting the covers, hands flipping and pounding the pillow. You are nervous but won't admit it, only that your tummy hurts. That former child's belly is now hard and flat, the beginnings of adolescence hardening a child physically, and often emotionally.

This is the evening of one of the biggest milestones in a child's life. Middle school. I don't tell you how difficult it was for me, the teasing, the girls who left me out of their inner, popular clique. I tell you about my best friend, Margaret, how if you find one or two really good friends, the rest won't matter.

I still think of Margaret and how our friendship saved me from what could have been three years of angst, of changing into a blue- and white-striped and ultrahideous polyester gym suit while the popular girls laughed because I had no breasts, just an empty training bra.

I realize your worries have swelled with each story a neighborhood kid has told, as if sitting by a campfire and seeing who could outdo the others with gruesome tales of ghosts and monsters. Only, in this case, the monsters were bullies, certain teachers and the cruelties that can befall one at this stage of life.

"Mama," you said, your former apricot shampoo now the more grown-up scent of Pantene, hair slightly damp. I can smell Arrid XX as I try to scoop you near me, and you say, "Mom," in that sing-song, go-away-I'm-fine voice.

Then you throw me the bone I've been longing for.

"Tell me," you say, yawning, the thrashing silenced. "What is middle school really like?"

I thought for a moment, breathing in the night and choosing my words carefully. "It's freedom. It's having choices in the lunchroom instead of mystery meat." I see a smile, though faint, inching across his face. "It's getting to change classes and not being stuck with the same mean old teacher. You'll have to study harder and some of the kids will begin acting out and putting on the peer pressure, but you stay true to who you are and it'll be fine. I promise."

As I said this, I knew in my heart that compared to other kids the change from elementary to middle would be twice as hard for my child. We'd moved from the city to the country and most of his friends were going to the middle school in town. We'd found a house we loved with weeping willows, mountain views and enough cul-de-sacs to ride bikes and skateboards and send the children outdoors roaming like we did as kids in the 60s and 70s.

It felt like the right decision, especially after having been told, as mothers long to hear, of the strength and dedication of the school system in that district. I assured my son he'd have every opportunity he wanted. But these weren't his fears.

His monsters were basic.

"What if I can't get the combination open on my locker?"

"Oh, the teachers will be more than willing to help you," I said, patting his back, which felt like the skin of a tight drum, his shoulder blades protruding with the sharp angles of adolescence.

"What if I can't find my classes?"

"They'll walk you through it all the first day. You know that, honey."

I stayed with him until his breathing slowed and the rhythm

of rest overcame his anxieties. Even at this age, a sleeping child, a preteen, is a sight worthy of tears. I let them fall, lying with him long after he'd finally gone to sleep.

The next morning he rose before the alarm shrilled, dressed in new shoes and ate his Honey Bunches of Oats. He spent a lot of time in the mirror, wetting and rewetting his hair, trying gel, then washing it out, changing shirts several times.

We drove through a tangle of traffic to the doors of this new world. I knew, as I saw him disappear in a sea of back-packs, that when he came home, he'd have dozens of stories to tell, and that he'd say "Middle school is a whole lot more fun than I thought it would be."

At least I hoped that's what he'd say, but the truth was, it was a day as heart-wrenching for me as when I dropped him off on his first day of kindergarten. I spent most of it at work, obsessing and trying not to. I watched the clock. At three, I raced to the school and waited in a long pick-up line, knowing that these very parents, once settled and confident, would send their charges home on buses or would carpool and this snarling jam of cars would thin.

I finally moved closer to the circle where kids waited. There he was, his backpack half his own body weight, a trum-pet case in one hand. As soon as he got in the car, four words summed up his day. "Middle School is awesome!"

Relief washed me like a warm shower. He continued with excitement, "They have pizza and a Coke machine. We get to change classes and it's so much cooler than elementary school."

I thought my worries were over. But they were only shift-ing, changing course as my baby had grown from toddler to boy to teen. New worries would soon come. Peer pressure. Lingo I didn't quite get. Everyone called everyone else "gay," only it didn't mean homosexual like it did when we were young. It meant, dumb, stupid. The kids said it all the time.

"That show is gay. Those pants are so gay. I hated that movie. It was gay. My spaghetti was gay . . ."

Then it was raw. "Man, this is a raw Vince Carter jersey. Those golf clubs are raw. I'm so raw, dude."

Fads and styles changed quicker than the seasons. Dress styles were first to knock me for a loop. I mean, granted my bell bottoms with the studded tic-tac-toe butt were one thing, but the pants these boys were wearing?

Seemed every time I looked at a boy in middle or high school, all I'd see was his crotch down near his knees. Soon, my own son picked up on the fad and I had to endure months of saying, "Wear a belt or else!!!"

The question being, should this be a point worth my motherly battles? Or should I let it go, figuring, "Hey, my kid is an honor student, a musical standout and athlete, and if he wants his boxers to claim space where Levi's pockets should be, who am I to say, 'Forget that, son. It's way too gay and raw'?"

"Pick your battles," my dear friend Nancy said. She's the mother of a preteen, too—a boy who doesn't sag, but most of the other kids do. She's lucky in that he's into golf and the preppy look. She's more than grateful his skateboarding days and accompanying attire are over. "Wait it out," she said. "It'll be something different in a matter of weeks."

I used to complain about girls and their crack addict–like clothes. But now the boys are going gung ho with their sagging fad. It seems that if the pockets of their cargos are around their kneecaps, then all the better.

What are these middle-schoolers thinking? Since I don't smell pot or beer on the kids' breath, shouldn't I just let the chips—or jeans, as it may be—fall where they may?

I try to think about how bad it COULD be. Remember the hussy girls who wore low-riding jeans and let their thongs show?

Maybe I should just let this slide, literally. I mean it's not a tattoo or tongue piercing. It's not lost virginity or STDs or even drugs and alcohol. This is why the other day, upon noticing once again my child's crotch was around his knees and he was doing that funny walk they must do to keep their pants up, sort of a Quasimodo hunch and drag, I did what Mama would do and decided a dose of religion was in order.

"Son," I said. "We're going to church. You might want to stay home if you can't dress any better than that."

His face fell. "Good. I like going to church," he said. "They have great donuts. It's not what you wear, anyway."

How could I argue with that? The boy was WANTING to go to church even if it was because they gave out free food and hot chocolate.

"Could you please wear a belt?"

"Can I get real coffee instead of hot chocolate?"

Everything is an argument with a child this age. Trust me. If it isn't, you either got yourself a miracle or a future serial killer.

"I bought you a belt at Target. Where is it?"

"The dog chewed it in half."

"Couldn't you at least look decent for the Lord?" I asked, sounding like my nagging mother.

He shrugged. "I haven't been suspended once this year and I don't smoke or drink."

"Wow. How old are you? Twelve, thirteen?"

"Middle school, Mom. It isn't easy. Really. Some days are so gay it sucks. I don't mind going to church, though. It's raw, dude."

"Please call me Mama."

He got in the car wearing baggy khakis and a wrinkled *but* collared shirt. The poor child had tried. And as long as I don't see a bare crack, I'm promising to not care less. This too, shall pass.

I'd do my best as a working mother, *spending* more quality time with my child instead of nagging at him all night and day. I cooked up a plan where I'd be the Rawest Mother of the Year. I'd buy us a couple of tickets for a Pro Basketball game to see the Charlotte Bobcats play the Chicago Bulls.

It would be one of those MasterCard TV moments for sure.

Priceless. I would be the cool mom taking her son to a pro game. I scored the tickets, and there we were in the oxygen-depleted upper levels of the Charlotte Coliseum: my boy, wearing his extralarge Bobcats jersey and a size "Hefty Lard Ass" pants that sagged to his knees. It was just he and I, having a grand old time eating $7 hot dogs and drinking $5 Cokes.

The game between the Charlotte Bobcats and Chicago Bulls had gotten under way and I was pretending as if I knew all about sports and Pro Ball. A mom is always trying to impress her adolescent son, an impossible task. I leaned forward in my chair and shouted, "DEFENSE! Block those cocky, mean old Bulls. Come on now, Bobcats, you know you can't give Scottie Pippen the ball. You gotta watch out for Rodman, too. He'll sneak up and slam one in."

My son said nothing but stared at me blankly. The Bulls scored, but the Bobcats ran the ball back down court and sank a 3-pointer. "That's how to show those Bulls," I yelled. "You boys can take on Pippin any day!"

My son gave me a puzzled look and a slight smile. The young man next to me, who had Down Syndrome and a vast knowledge of sports, could contain himself no longer.

He turned to me and poked my arm. "Scottie hasn't played for the Bulls since the early 90s . . . and neither has Rodman." He rattled stats faster than anyone on ESPN could ever begin doing. I was beyond impressed, but couldn't stop laughing at how stupid I'd been about sports. The young man with Down Syndrome then started cheering and so did my child, which is a breakthrough for some of us moms with adolescent boys who seem hard to please at times.

Mothers of this age group often have it tough. Where once our sons would throw their arms around us—even in public—these 'tween years give them the hormones and strong wills to seek out their peers more often than their mommies.

This is how it should be. It's the way of growing up and becoming independent.

I'd been feeling disconnected and wanted to somehow plug back into that direct line of communication with my child. That's why I bought the tickets, and while I'd never been one to watch many sports events, other than tennis or the Olympics, my son had become obsessed with football and basketball. He knew all the names and stats.

He didn't care that the seats were so high that the players appeared like nervous ants in orange. He didn't care that the one taking him to the game was his mom—often a source of irritation and embarrassment. He only cared that he was seeing his first professional basketball game LIVE!

And I only cared that he was happy. He kept grinning throughout the game, cheering and clapping. He even allowed me to take pictures without groaning. Midway through the game, we sneaked into a lower section and found better seats. It was at this point I also began to understand the days of Jordan, Rodman and Pippin were over, just like the days when the Doobie Brothers and Eagles had given way to Usher and The Black Eyed Peas.

I tried to read the names on the backs of the jerseys, but being in my forties with one contact dried up and tossed under my seat, I made a major mistake. The star player for the Bobcats was Emeka Okafor. I heard them calling out his name several times, and thought it would sound smart to cheer for him, since he was actually on the team, unlike Pippin (whom I'd earlier commented on).

"Come on, Okra Crow, you can make it, come on and shoot!" No one said a word. I decided to cheer louder to show my child I wasn't a total fool. "Oh, no. Don't let them take it, Okra Crow. Defense. Give them the big *D*!"

"Who?" my son asked, eyes huge, mouth gaping. "Who are you yelling about?"

"Okra Crow," I said, proud of this knowledge.

"Mom," he said. "Do you mean Okafor? As in Emeka Okafor, the best player on the team?"

"Yes, son. That's what I said. Didn't you hear me? I said 'Okafor.'"

"No you didn't, you said—"

"Hey, I think I see Michael Jordan."

"Yeah. Right. Mom, that's too gay."

I smiled and said, "I have a permission slip you left on my desk about going to sex education classes at the Health Adventure. Maybe you'll really learn what gay means when you attend that."

After the game, we ate a big meal at Jock and Jill's and he actually thanked me for the entire experience. Middle-school boys aren't all the trouble they're cracked up to be. Even when their cracks are showing.

A couple of days later, his first sex education class was coming up and he shoved the forms across the table. "Remember, honey, the human body and its many seemingly strange functions is nothing to laugh about." For nearly two weeks, my son talked about nothing other than his upcoming sex-education class.

"Don't forget to sign the permission slip, Mama. We can't go hear the goods without your signature."

You'd think he was getting permission to go to the beach he was so excited. He thought he was in for a real eye-opener, a revealing unlike anything his parents had tried to discreetly, but accurately, tell him on the subject.

I called Mama to tell her I was afraid he'd start laughing when he heard the word vagina.

"I told him I wasn't going to sign the paper unless he promised not to laugh," I said. "Sex is not a laughing matter." At that point we both cracked up.

"I'll never forget when you were in the fifth grade and I had to sign a similar form," she said.

I tried to remember my own sex ed class, but the only memory flickering through my head was the shocking pamphlet on feminine hygiene and the free Kotex and belt I crammed in my dresser drawer and blushed just thinking about.

"We were all sitting around the dinner table," Mama said, reflecting back more than thirty years. "I wanted to ask you so badly about that class but you weren't saying a word. I kept waiting and waiting. Finally, I just up and asked you how the class went."

I heard Mama drop the phone and collapse onto the coffee table, which is what she does when she needs to laugh real hard and the phone hinders her mirth. After a few minutes of womanly howling, she came back to the phone, trying to collect herself.

"What's so funny?"

"Well, when I asked you what you learned, you just looked at me and Daddy and said, 'All I want to know is how many times do you do it a week?'"

I assured her my son's class was more about voices changing and hairs sprouting in unlikely places; that I was almost certain they weren't going to get into anything too deep.

"I believe some of the boys are starting to stink," I said. "I think they'll just tell them about Arrid Extra Dry." I then remembered my own first experience with deodorant, a jar of something wet and nasty called Tussy, the smell of which makes me want to cry with memories of locker rooms and polyester gym suits. Memories of the developed girls who wore bras and shaved their legs and laughed at those of us who had no secondary sex characteristics to speak of.

Soon after I signed my son's permission slip to go to sex ed, I bumped into my friend Dottie whose boy was in my child's class.

"You're right. That's all they've been talking about," she said of the sex ed sessions—one for the girls and one for the boys. "A group of the boys were telling me they wanted to go into the girls' class and I said, 'Oh, no you don't.'" She and I both fell onto the pavement laughing. "Going there would for sure turn my boy gay hearing all that mess we go through down there, honey."

That night, after my child slipped into an exhausting, sweaty sleep of boys who run hard all day, shower and smell of Pantene and Arrid, I couldn't help it and climbed into bed with him, as if he was once again 5 years old. I was careful, not wanting the springs to squeak and him to wake up and catch me in the act.

He doesn't know this, but I plan to slip beneath his covers, listen to him breathe, watch his eyelids as he dreams until he's long grown. I'll think about the Robert Munsch/Sheila Mc-Graw book *Love You Forever*, and won't be able to stop the words from going through my mind.

Whatever God Sends

Note: I wrote part of this when pregnant and also later, after my diva was first born in 1998.

Here I sit, same seat cushions, same doctors' offices, one year later. I press my back into the wooden chair, heels nervously grinding the carpet and heart racing as if it has jumped the track.

I have been here before, not knowing if I would again face one of the hardest moments of my life. I am wondering, fearing, that I'll hear the same news again.

Today is a cold November afternoon, no sunshine, nothing but bitter breezes that whip and slice through clothing and bone. I am hearing the words of last year repeat themselves in my mind.

"I'm sorry," the doctor had said, patting me. "It just stopped growing. It happens so often. One in five pregnancies, by our best estimates."

I had stared at the black screen of the ultrasound machine, the motionless patterns of what was, what would never be. My baby had died without warning, without the symptoms to gradually prepare a mother for such news.

"It just happens sometimes," the gentle doctor said, and I reached for her neck and hugged her, a near stranger, my mascara bleeding onto her dress.

As I sit here waiting, writing these words on a yellow legal pad as part of the journaling I do while pregnant, my stomach is as queasy as a child's before getting a set of shots. It will be different this time, I tell myself over and over. Last time it was random, right? Nature's way of selecting the fittest, the strongest, the finest. My eggs were old. Now they're even older, but it doesn't matter, there are millions, right? And some still have to be in pretty decent shape.

A door swings open and a nurse appears, chart in hand, and calls my name. I follow her to a corner and step on the scales, something I never do during my regular doctors' visits.

"May I take off my shoes?" I ask, feeling silly but knowing I've gained much more than necessary because I got mad and threw that famous book *What to Expect When You're Expecting* under the bed when I got to the part where it listed what you should and shouldn't eat. The whole book scared the daylights out of me, and though the advice was good and reasonable, my hormones and cravings had other plans.

The doctor gives me a raised eyebrow and a smile, and slides the scales farther and farther right. I exhale every bit of air in my lungs, as if that will help.

Afterward, I move to another row of chairs, another brief wait for the next stage of this visit. A slender woman is seated beside me and we talk, sharing this common condition that bonds all women, women unlikely to connect on any other level. She tells me about her two previous miscarriages; I tell her about the baby I lost last year.

"I wasn't too far along," I say. "Were you?"

"Three months," she says, hand instinctively going to her belly. I feel myself begin to panic, the metal taste rising in my mouth. On this very November day, I am as she was—three months pregnant.

The nurse comes by and I wish the woman next to me good luck, and we wave in that conspiratorial way of expectant mothers. I follow the nurse down the long hallway, staring at the thick soles of her shoes, unable to meet anyone's eyes.

She takes my blood pressure, watches my chest rise and fall

as she counts the respirations. "Slow down, sister," she says. "You're panting as if you've done an hour on the StairMaster. The doctor will be in soon to check the baby's heartbeat. Just relax, hon," She disappears, leaving me alone with my shallow, rapid breathing and damp hands, the thoughts that keep returning to last fall when there was no heartbeat on the ultrasound screen.

"Dear God," I pray silently, "please let it be all right. I won't ask for much else all year. I promise. Well, I promise to try to keep the promise, anyway."

It is quiet other than the distant thumping of footsteps in the hallways, the mumble of voices, doctors talking to nurses, patients laughing, happy with their own news. I stare at the room's four walls. The dispensers of latex gloves. The black cords snaking from machines that tell fates. A box of Kleenex. For tears? For troubling news? For joy?

I focus on the trash can emblazoned with biohazard warnings. The doctor knocks softly, as if not wanting to disturb. She is the same woman I cried on last year. She is kind and comforting, knowledgeable and respected, all things a woman wants in the one caring for her unborn. She is a high-risk specialist, a perinatologist assigned to women with problem pregnancies. My first had tried to come three months early. My second had died. And now was my third time at bat.

She squirts clear jelly across my lower abdomen, then uses a device called a Doppler (not the weather-forecasting kind) to listen for life. I watch her face for clues, but it is relaxed, no frown lines. She moves the Doppler across my tummy, but the only sounds are from my own body, not someone else's. She tries again and again but can't hear a heartbeat. My throat tightens. My head is light. *Not again, please, God. Not again.*

"It may still be too early," she says, as if reading my mind, knowing it has returned to last year, the silent screen, death in the womb. "Let's see if we can get you in for ultrasound."

Moments later I am in another room with the equipment that deals news in glowing black-and-white images. I force my eyes on the screen, a blur of shapes I can't make out. The seconds that pass seem to go on forever until at last I see the unmistakable pulsing of a beating heart, the outline of five tiny fingers and an arm jutting above a head. I see legs kicking and can even count the toes on my baby's feet.

I hug the doctor, this time leaving no trail of tears. I take the printout of black-and-white images, my baby's first portraits, and hold them carefully in my hands as I walk into the biting wind.

It's going to be all right, I tell myself. Thank you, God, I pray, not knowing another challenge was right around the corner.

I am now just over four months pregnant and sitting in the audience at my son's preschool Christmas program. It is December 1997 and tears run down my face as I try to watch and smile, videotape his antlers and Rudolph nose while he mumbles out songs and seems completely uninterested in the entire pageantry of the event.

An hour earlier I was at work, trying to hurry and get out the door when a nurse called my office, but she couldn't reach me so she had a coworker track me down. Urgency edged her voice and she told me to come in as soon as possible.

"But my son is in his Christmas play." I wasn't thinking clearly.

"It's very important."

And then I remembered. Last week, I'd had a panel of genetic testing designed to prescreen for birth defects. I knew then, with a sinking feeling, with breath I couldn't catch, what the call was about. I'd agreed to the maternal serum screening tests that are becoming routine to check for potential birth defects. About 95 percent of the time, the test results are fine. Another 5 percent of women have results that could indicate birth defects such as Down Syndrome, neural tube openings and other conditions, some incompatible with life and characterized by mental retardation and a number of physical abnormalities.

"We have some concerns with your test results," the nurse said. I felt dizzy and sick to my stomach. "We would like for you to come in right away, as soon as possible, and talk to one of our genetics counselors."

I begged her to tell me what was going on. First, she gave the news she considered good. That the levels did not indicate Down Syndrome or a neural tube defect. Then, the bad news. The blood samples did point to trisomy 18. She may as well have been speaking German for all I understood. I did a search in a medical book and froze in horror. The condition was one in which most babies never survive in the womb, and if they do enter the world, they die within days or weeks in most cases.

Within two hours, after my son's Christmas program, attended with tears streaming down my face, my husband and I were sitting in front of the genetics counselor, a woman with enormous compassion.

Trisomy 18, she explained, occurs in extremely rare situations when each cell in the body has three copies—instead of the usual two of the chromosome 18. Most of these babies die shortly after they are born, rarely living past their first birthday.

The tests showed my baby's odds had increased dramatically—from 1 in 8,000 to 1 in 50 or less. It affects baby girls much more often than boys and is characterized by severe physical and mental handicaps.

The doctor suggested amniocentesis, but I didn't want it. The year before, at 35, I'd already lost one baby to miscarriage and, most likely, an age-related chromosome condition. My husband and I agreed against further testing. I'd felt this child move, seen its heartbeat and tiny fingers opening and closing on ultrasound images. If the news was bad, I'd deal with it gradually, believing that by carrying the child, I might possibly reach a peaceful acceptance in time.

"We really should do amnio to rule this out," one doctor said.

"No. I can't. I'm sorry. Are there other options?"

She said there were higher-level ultrasounds that could pick up more on-screen than standard equipment can, but there were no guarantees other than amniocentesis.

"We'll just do the ultrasound," I said, my husband agreeing. A few minutes later a technician wheeled in the machine and once again my belly became wet and cold with gel. The doctor scanned and clicked, freezing images to print out. She nodded and emitted positive sounds.

"Everything really looks fine," she said. "I can't see anything on this ultrasound that would indicate trisomy 18."

They were searching for the usual signs: clenched hands, small heads, severe heart and kidney problems. They had no explanation why the tests were showing something else, something fatal in most cases. Though I'd gone online and read the beautiful stories of children with trisomy 18 who have lived for several years. I was particularly struck by what one parent wrote, daughter in arms:

Sometimes love is for a moment.
Sometimes love is for a lifetime.
Sometimes a moment is a lifetime.

Seeing my daughter on the screen, so active, so vital, gave me hope to continue the pregnancy with joy, with the baby showers and optimism of other expectant mothers. I really didn't think about the possible birth defects or chances for death. I had faith, a mother's intuition, that all would be okay.

On May 11, 1998, my daughter, Lindsey Hope, was born. Healthy. And full of energy. Prayers had been sent. Prayers had been answered. I wept with joy and the appreciation of a mother who knows how fragile new life can really be.

I took my new baby home and within hours another fear set in, a panicky feeling that once again, this time at 36, I had become a new mother. You'd think time and experience would make round two a little easier, but it hasn't. It won't. It won't because I'm a worrying sort of woman who reads too many books about child care and all that can go wrong instead of all that can go right.

As with my first baby, I fall into an exhausted sleep with my face pressed against her crib railings, listening for breathing, watching with worry the staccato rhythm of an infant taking air and wondering if those rolling eyes, those whimpering lips, are all a part of normal newborn behavior.

I still honk at every other car on the road, figuring they are coming too close to the yellow line, too close to my cargo who remains fastened yet fragile, each bump in the road, every pothole, making my heart race and hands reach out to protect.

I still rush my baby girl off to the restroom every time a stranger paws her or coughs within 50 yards, and I scrub her like some crazy woman with a baby wipe or soap or the antiseptic towelettes I collect from multiple trips to the pediatrician's office.

I still fret over everything that either comes to mind or that I bring to mind, all with somewhat conflicting advice and opinions.

Is she sleeping too much? Wetting enough? Is her jaundice getting worse? Is my breast milk thin as water, no more nourishing than Kool-Aid?

Hadn't my own father looked at the spit-up dribbling from my baby's chin and whispered to Mama, "That milk sure looks weak to me." And hadn't one pediatrician weighed her and announced she was losing precious ounces during a time she should be gaining?

How was I to know his scales weren't correctly calibrated? How was I to know that in that office every single scale—a dozen or more—would give a different weight, the main criterion of newborn health and progress in those crucial early weeks.

And why is she so good? Why doesn't she cry more, like my son who suffered from colic and unexplained needs?

You'd think that this time, I'd relax. But I didn't. I don't.

I am, in my husband's words, the "fierce mama lion" who growls and barks orders: "Prop her head." "Make sure to burp her." "Please don't bounce or jiggle or put her in direct sunlight."

As I write this, May is ending, finishing its term with hot

afternoons and not a hint of rain. But I don't notice. The world continues spinning around me, news happening, people triumphing or dying, making headlines, but all I know is that my daughter is two weeks and three days old and this is the world as I see it. The only world I can handle at the moment.

In this short span, it seems as if a lifetime of drama and hilarity has befallen us since her birth at 1:21 PM May 11.

I will never forget the moment in the delivery room, just after an injection of painkillers, when I turned to my husband and promised him a TV upgrade and cable if he'd just consent to naming the child Lindsey.

It was a name that, for me, had deep sentimental meaning. A coworker, H. S. Lindsey, whom I'd worked with for years had died the year before and I wanted to honor his memory, the grace and dignity he brought every day when he walked into the office until he retired at age 70.

Promise cable to a channel-starved man during baseball season and you can pretty much name your child anything you want. Throughout contractions, as I tried to focus by looking at a photo I'd brought of my son and me, a small Rhesus Monkey grinning on my shoulder, I imagined my husband's mind wandering toward TV town at Circuit City.

Panasonic with surround sound? Or the flat-screened version with picture-in-picture?

My thoughts, however, were along these lines: *Should I get an epidural, end this wretched pain? Or should I go for a natural delivery, experiencing everything?* He opted for the Panasonic and I settled on an epidural, and for the next several hours, life was lulled by the sweet harmony of painless anticipation. I didn't worry about trisomy 18. I had a peace that was unexplainable and that she'd be fine.

Then my baby was ready for arrival. I will never forget her quick delivery, the great gushes of amniotic fluid that ended up on the doctor's head and in his ears, despite the protective shield across his face and surrounding his head.

And thus began the roller-coaster ride of renewed motherhood, the hills and free falls and accompanying fears—the thrills and terrors and adventures that tag along when you fall hopelessly in love with a new baby.

The first postpartum adventure hit just minutes after the birth, when my precious daughter wouldn't "latch on" properly, referring to her initial breast-feeding efforts. I had seen all the birth videos, newborns squirming to the breast as instinctively as baby sea turtles scuttle toward the water.

I had envisioned my Earth Mother self, tired and elated from a natural (well, at least my eyes were open) delivery, and my infant looking, finding and attaching herself to me the way warm puppies find their mother's milk.

After hours of attempts, a nurse finally looked at my goods and announced with not a hint of tact: "Well, maybe you'll have to hold them up some. They've probably sagged since your last baby, right?"

Regardless of gravity, my child did finally latch and catch on, which is what she was doing beautifully at four days old, back in the hospital, in the outpatient wing waiting on a heel stick to determine her rising jaundice levels. If it's not one thing, it's another. This time it was jaundice reaching numbers that require intervention instead of just sticking a baby in the sunlight for a few hours.

As Lindsey began her soft, feminine cry, my 5-year-old son gave me a knowing look, far too wise for his years. His eyes grew wide as quarters when I fidgeted and squirmed nervously and finally, discretely, produced nutrition for my daughter's newly perfected latching. Poor baby had just had her little heel stuck with a needle and needed comforting.

"Oh, my gosh!" my son screamed, and the packed crowd in the waiting room turned toward his voice. "Don't anybody look at my mother. She's breast-feeding and her privates are showing!"

Everyone stared and I laughed like the truly insane, the laughter of a woman reeling with hormones.

On day five, my mother appeared at my door, and so did the cable guy. Some nitwit in muddy shoes saying something about wall fishes and hookups, and 700 feet of cable for the price of 250 and instant service with free movie channels. I had a baby to feed, a diaper to change, and stared at him through sleep-starved eyes.

"Run it where you need to," I said.

Two days later another cable guy came over, yanking up what the first had put down, saying my neighbors didn't like exposed wires in their dahlia beds. Well, who could blame them?

"Look," I said. "I'm a new mother. My baby has jaundice. See? Yellow as a yolk. Plus, I have a 5-year-old and a husband, and we need some instant service. I need Nickelodeon!"

Days six and seven of Lindsey's life yielded more chaos, more heel sticks and then home health visits, bilirubin lights and the anxiety that leaves new parents drained and feeling helpless and wondering how in the world a person could survive so much love and its sidekick: worry.

It is the kind of love that some claim as a reason for never having children. They are afraid. Afraid of the intensity of such feelings. Afraid of loving and not measuring up. Of loving and losing. Of just loving.

During those early days, I find myself at my baby girl's bed or with her in my arms, staring at her dark slate eyes, crying because she's beautiful, crying because she's yellow, crying because the hormones need bleeding.

Crying because she's mine.

I give her a full bath for the first time and set out three baby-care books. Why can't I just relax, trust my instincts?

"How," I asked a friend, "do teenagers do it?"

"Ignorance is bliss," she said. "The less you know, the less you worry."

Well, how, I wanted to know, do they figure out all the gadgets, such as the car seat's proper positioning and fastening?

I'll never forget the first time I had my daughter out on the road, looking over and seeing her suspended, almost hanging, from the straps of her Joy Ride. I pulled over and tried to adjust things but only made matters worse. So I did what I figured all mothers do: I drove straight to police headquarters and waited for an officer to appear. I'd done the same thing with my son. It didn't take long.

After a few confusing moments and adjustments, they reworked my Joy Ride and I thanked them and said, "I guess you have parents driving through here all the time with the same problem."

One officer smiled and the tips of his ears grew red. "No, ma'am. You're the only one."

Later that week, I met my biggest foe, known as the Diaper Genie. Four adults couldn't figure out how to work mine, thus I was considering buying an antiquing kit and turning it into a decorative butter churn, until one day I'd had enough and decided the plastic grocery bags at Bi-Lo worked equally as well.

All of these minidisasters, and my baby wasn't even a month old. I was certainly needing a lift the morning I once again found myself at the pediatrician's checking bilirubin levels. I hobbled in red-eyed and the receptionist ushered me into a waiting area and said a few comforting words. She thought I was tearful because I had a yellow baby.

"No," I sniveled. "It's the car seat. The Diaper Genie. The stroller that weighs 200 pounds. The high chair that serves as a swing, a bed and a playpen. These infant must-haves are trying to ruin everything."

She nodded knowingly and as the baby began fussing, I felt at ease offering an aesthetically challenged breast to my newborn, who gratefully accepted. The receptionist paused at the doorway, smiled sweetly and slipped quietly from the room, the way someone will when shocked beyond further conversation.

I'm sure there is now a red sticker on my daughter's chart

that says: "Proceed with caution. Child's mother mentally unstable."

I felt much better when they announced Lindsey's bilirubin levels were down and she could stop the light therapy and our lives would return to normal. Normal, meaning my hovering over the crib and watching her covers rise and fall. Normal, meaning the incessant checking of her blankets and diapers and clothing and reading way into the night on how to care for a newborn when my instincts are begging to be trusted and my eyes pleading for a few hours' sleep.

Lack of sleep is why I washed my face with Palmolive, why I sprayed my son's soiled jeans with GLASS PLUS. Why I brushed my teeth with Myoflex and almost spread Colgate on my daughter's chapped bottom.

Tonight, as I kiss the top of my baby's head, her abundant hair sticking straight up like the down of a baby chick, I feel delirious with the rewards and demands of motherhood and the weariness worn at day's end like a coat of bricks.

Tonight, I will once again take up my post at the crib, face wedged against the railings, heart captured by this tiny child, this gift from God.

It is almost as if my worry, my presence, is protection enough.

Rediscovering My Father's Love

We are in his blue Ford truck, my dad and I, heading north on I-85 toward Atlanta. This is years ago, long before he gave up nightly drinking and became a Baptist preacher, long before he parked the blue Ford beneath a seeping pine and bought a Nissan Murano that looks like something a Jetson would drive.

It's early afternoon and for the first time since 5 AM we are silent as we share the front seat, each aware of the other, stepping carefully around the eggshells that surround our natures. We are both too sensitive, he and I. One wrong word, say, a conversation that heads toward politics, and we are in trouble. He is so far to the right I'm often baffled, and even though I consider myself a moderate Democrat who does on occasion vote for a Republican, I might as well be Gloria Bunker from *All in the Family* in his view of me.

Once, when we were fighting, he called me "Pinky Jane," referring to Jane Fonda whom he loathed during her Vietnam fiasco.

For a while we don't talk. We know better. It's a long trip and there's no point starting out on bad notes. He puts in a bluegrass tape to fill the silence. It is not the kind of music I prefer, though I close my eyes and pretend to enjoy the fiddles and Dobros. Years ago my dad got an eight-track tape player and we listened to the Eagles, Three Dog Night, The Guess Who, and other rock groups from the 70s.

That was his music then. Our music. I can still see the green station wagon with the fake wood along the sides, my sister and I in the backward-facing rear seat singing "Jeremiah Was A Bullfrog" at the top of our adolescent lungs. I can feel the heat from those seats sticking to our thighs as we drive to Panama City Beach, Florida, smell the yeasty scent of beer as Dad cracks one while it's Mama's turn to drive.

I've watched him change with each decade. The rock replaced with country, the silk ties with T-shirts, and the silver Cadillac I called the Pimp Mobile one day became a blue Ford truck. Then came the Murano and a sporty Mazda that sounds like a NASCAR engine warming up.

As I get older, he promises, I will also appreciate the unfiltered and pure meaning of country and bluegrass music, the simpler things in life.

This morning before getting in the truck just after dawn, we drink instant coffee, and later, stop at Hardee's for a biscuit and real coffee. We are en route to Peachtree City, Georgia, from my parent's home in Spartanburg, South Carolina, a 3½-hour trip to see my sister's new baby and fancy 7,000-square-foot house.

We talk and talk, my dad and I, and when we pull into her driveway hours later, it seemed such a fast and easy trip. Both of us let out a deep breath, the exhaust of anxieties that never came to pass, relief that two people who love each other so much might possibly say the wrong thing and ignite or explode—and yet it never happened.

"You and Daddy had a good trip without a single argument," is what he said as we stood at my sister's front door. "Isn't that interesting?" He smiles the way he always does, with only half his face. I love that smile and wouldn't have it any other way.

We hold and fawn over the baby and admire the house and do things one is supposed to do when visiting a new nephew and grandbaby. After a few hours, we head back to Spartanburg, leaving Sandy and her infant and home, and knowing in a few weeks they'd all get the hang of this change in lifestyle, this tilt of the world as they once knew it.

As we drive we laugh about the baby's poor cone head, though in all other physical aspects, he was a perfect and beautiful child. We listen to more music. "Looks like he had it rough coming into this world," Daddy says as I hold near the window's light one of my nephew's photos, the ones hospital photographers take and no mother refuses, no matter how chewed up and spit out her angel looks.

Miles later, during this long drive home, I grow tired and he has decided to cut off the music and talk a while. He rambles on and on about whatever soars into his line of vision.

Planes are taking off and landing at Hartsfield International Airport, and he is saying for the second time that the only airport larger is O'Hare in Chicago. He whistles and I am startled and annoyed. "Here comes one taking off. There goes one landing. The only airport bigger than this is O'Hare," he says again. I tell myself not to lash out.

I remember Mama's words: "Hold your tongue. Keep it hostage and you'll have no regrets later."

When I was little, still in diapers, Daddy would come home from work and lean over my crib, cooing. Mama likes to tell the story of how his elbows jutted out like bird wings if she came around, blocking her from stealing his show.

Later, as I grew old enough to talk and toddle, we'd wait until dark and go out on the carport and I'd sit in his lap, a little girl whose daddy was her hero. I'd study his face and listen as he pointed toward the sky and told me about the stars, the Big and Little Dippers, wanting more than anything to see everything he saw.

When I was in kindergarten, my daddy entered his jazz phase. He had a stack of albums—Peggy Lee, and Herb Alpert & The Tijuana Brass—and I'd hold him around the waist and stand on his shoes as he stepped right, then left, forward and back. Sometimes when I hear one of those songs I can still feel the leather, stiff and warm against the bottoms of my bare feet.

"Now that's a crazy place," he says now, glancing off the interstate toward Grady Memorial Hospital. "Knife fights and gunshot victims all hours of the night. It's a madhouse."

I nod and say, "Ummm." It must be apparent that I'm talked out, but he's alert, drinking a Diet Coke and filling empty space with his musings. He reads the writing from 18-wheelers and billboards.

Years before, during what I refer to as my rebellious period, this would have sent me over the edge. Those were the Lost Years, from age 16 to 25, when I believed I was smarter than him. It was the decade my father lived with a broken heart and dusty dreams, the kind of dreams a father collects in his mind, hoping one day a child might wake up and fulfill.

He must have thought he meant no more to me than a coat-rack, a place to hang my hat when out of money, to drape the heavy wool of failure I so readily cast, and blamed on him.

"Please pay my parking tickets or I won't get my diploma."

"I'm overdrawn at the bank. Can you help me out? I won't ever do it again."

"I had a wreck. I couldn't see in the rearview mirror and hit a fast food sign."

He got me out of all these jams. I expected him to. I never thanked him then. It was his duty, or so I believed at the time. After all, he was a father and isn't this what all fathers were supposed to do?

Now I know better. Back then, I was ignorant of the happiness I stole, unaware of the bits of a man's heart I tucked in my pockets and forgot about, even sat on at times.

Funny I never gave him credit for the good things: the braces on my teeth, the education, the beach trips when he bought us giant seafood platters and virgin Piña Coladas.

"That's how teenagers can be," he told a heavy-eyed coworker one day, a man who feared he'd lost his only daughter. "In the end, if you hang on long enough until she's matured or had kids, she'll come back. Mine did."

When I finally did return, understanding his angle in life only after having given birth to my own child, he received me with arms wide, his eyes bright and forgiving, not questioning, *What had happened to the last decade?*

We are so different, my dad and I, and yet so much alike. I look at his hands as he weaves through thickening traffic. They are wide and the skin is rough and dry. I look down at my own hands and see they are the same.

When he smiles at the two women who drive by, singing and dancing to the music on their radios, I see my mouth is like his, too, sly and tilted to one side.

As a child it's so easy to idolize a father, to place him higher and higher until one day he's out of reach. After reaching my teens and twenties, we allowed our differences to become matches, lighting fires that have never really burned out. That's why we were both apprehensive about this trip, neither of us admitting our fears.

It was on a Tuesday evening when he called my Asheville, North Carolina, home to announce my sister had given birth. I was to drive to Spartanburg the following night so we could travel together to Peachtree City where Mama had been for a week.

This was the first time in ten years I would be alone with my dad, and I felt an enormous wash of anxiety, then guilt for feeling that way about my own father. I packed a travel survival kit: books, magazines, stationery—diversions if the front seat suddenly became too small or the conversation too intense. With us, talk can take strange turns. It may start out pleasant and generic, then, if carried on at length, could cut straight to our differences.

It used to be so easy. We agreed on everything. Whatever he said just had to be right.

As I grew older new ideas surrounded me, ideas that made him reel, made him question his influence. We could no longer discuss things. His heroes were my horrors. My heroes were those he called "liberals," with a tone of disgust.

I allowed our differences to deepen the gully we'd dug, to

rub at us until we were bruised and calloused and sometimes raw in each other's company. I'm not sure how or why it all changed and the differences became unimportant, but I believe it was shortly after my first child was born. Instead of recoiling at the dinner table each time his fork scraped the plate, raking the food in neat little piles, I became thankful he was there.

He had always been there for us. He was the kind of dad men try to be though many never are. He came home at night. He loved our mother. He showed us how to solve math problems, drive a straight shift, play softball and croquet. He sat in the audience at all our dance recitals, the talent shows we entered and didn't win. He stood at the edge of the pool cheering as we swam blue-faced for ribbons and trophies.

He was always with us: In the hospital when we lost our tonsils or wisdom teeth. On the sidewalk of the girls' dorm as he set us free, sleeping that night in a half-empty house, feeling his heart bleed with loss and his eyes wet with tears he'd never show.

We are almost home now and I am ashamed that the prospect of this trip caused me so much unnecessary panic. For now, as he drives and the sound of the wind and engine lull us into a comfortable silence, I think how lucky I am. My dad is alive. I reach over and touch his arm, the hand that looks like mine, and his eyes fill with tears he is strong enough to keep from falling.

Maybe we aren't so different. Maybe he wants me to accept him as much as I want him to accept me. Liberal. Conservative. Baptist. Methodist. What does it really matter if the heart and flesh of two are so connected?

The truth is, no matter how many years go by, I'll always be the little girl in the carport staring into the black sky and hoping I see the same star my daddy sees.

* * *

That day seems like so long ago. My nephew, the one we went to see in Peachtree City, is now 12 and my father is graying and bearded, skin mottled from time and sun, skin cancers burned away at doctors' offices. I wrote a poem for him on Father's Day and he still keeps it, a sign he'd never given up on us.

He is the daddy the child adored. With big innocent eyes, she searched his face for wisdom and security, and finding this, she discovered love as well.

And when he smiled at her, praised the little girl, it was as if a July sun had found her in a dark cold world and wrapped her in warmth.

Later, the girl grew taller, older, and with these physical changes came the storms: the thunder of her anger and the rain of her emotions. The father's forehead furrowed with lines, with confusion and heartbreak. How could this little girl be so unhappy?

He had tried, oh, how he had tried.

Many nights he fell asleep with wet cheeks, the wife next to him offering words of comfort. She'll come around, the mother said. She won't always forget your sacrifices. One day they will all come rushing back, when she has children of her own.

The daughter, though not aware and without malice, continued to rob this life-giver of contentment. She was ignorant of the happiness she stole, the hopes she sank, those pieces of a good man's heart she kept stuffing in her pockets and forgetting.

The man must have thought his little girl was trapped behind the shell of her new selfishness. Hadn't people told him, "It happens. Adolescence. One or two get lucky, but most of us . . . well . . . it happens."

It seemed the child was gone forever, replaced by a stranger the family hardly recognized. Didn't she appreciate the small car he bought? Brand new? Sacrificing his own needs to meet hers? Didn't she care enough to stop coming home after midnight with traces of alcohol on her breath? Or what about the boy with long hair and bad language?

Then one day, and it was years later, he noticed the little girl peeking around the corners, peering from behind adult eyes. Was she back? Dare he dream?

Secretly, the man may have wished his girl to have a child just like herself. A sort of punishment. "See what happens when you give and give and get nothing in return but punches to the heart?"

But she didn't. Her own children were small lights illuminating the pathway back—back to the man who'd given everything and gotten so little.

The admiring girl inside the woman awakened again. She rubbed her eyes and wondered where all the years had gone. And though she longs to take back those years of adolescence and early adulthood—when a daddy turned to father turned to stranger—she cannot.

She can only hope that in all the time remaining, before he is bent and lost with age, she will let this great man know how special he is to her.

How she remembers being the girl counting stars from his lap. How she remembers the love that had always been there, even when she had none to give.

What she would give to be able to lasso the lost years. Instead, she takes the days that are left, and uses each to show him how he still shines in her eyes. And always will.

The years passed way too quickly and suddenly my father was turning 70 a couple of years ago. We decided to surprise him and throw the first birthday party he's had since he was a skinny little boy with big ears and dreams to match.

Back then, he wanted a BB gun and toy soldiers, maybe a new pair of shoes so he didn't have to share with a sibling. When a man turns 70—if he's lucky enough to reach that age and do so in good health—he wants only happiness for his family and maybe another decade of decent living.

The wishes are simple as the desire for the material gives way to things that really matter.

My sister, mother and I decided to surprise him. Around

6 PM, Sandy and I met and prepared his gift. She'd bought a huge basket and we filled it with my father's favorite things: red wine, Bibles and barbecue.

We jumped from a small room and yelled, "Surprise!" and I wouldn't give a million dollars (if I had it) for the smile on Daddy's face. That half-smile, the only one we ever knew or wanted.

He's a man who gives to others and works daily to suppress his own needs, beating back his ego the way a gardener fights weeds. Gone now is the former high-strung man, a corporate engineer with a pressure-cooker job. Gone is the daddy who'd come from work beat and frustrated and pour a double shot of bourbon, sit in his easy chair and listen to jazz or Merle Haggard, depending on his mood, while Mama prepared dinner, the smell of sizzling butter and onions winding through our home.

He was always a decent man, but in the last five years, he's not the same daddy I grew up with. He and Mama had discovered shortly after Dad's retirement a country church in need of a few good men and women. He found a place where he could make a difference, and my parents, along with others from the small congregation, provide a children's ministry that has grown from a few kids to more than sixty.

Most of the children have had tough lives and stay with grandparents. Daddy drives a van and picks them up for church, delivering them early while the members take turns feeding them a hot breakfast of sausage and eggs, bacon, biscuits, grits and juice in the fellowship hall. They've made it their mission to ensure the children are exposed to the important things in life: God, good morals and the occasional outing to an amusement park.

This birthday party for my dad was long overdue. He needed to know how much he was loved and appreciated, and sometimes words aren't enough.

Four bottles of wine, a jug of barbecue sauce, a state-of-the art spatula and a few Bibles later, he was beaming like a boy receiving a new bike. I'm sure he felt special, a feeling every person in this world needs from time to time.

My mother, not to be outdone by the wine and Bible bas-ket, had her own gift. Even though she's a proper teetotaling Baptist, she'd pinned $20 bills all over a thong I'd given her as a joke, as if she was a stripper turning in the night's tips.

"My 70th was the best birthday I can remember," my father said, eyes changing from gray to blue with the dew of emotion.

My only regret was that we hadn't done this sooner, or that I could have found a way, some form of understanding in my youth, to have made life easier on him.

For this is what every good daddy deserves.

Later that evening on the occasion of his 70th, we walk out to the carport and he doesn't show me the stars but wants me to sit with him in his brand-new Murano with the killer stereo system.

"Let's take it for a ride," I say, knowing with full confidence I can—and want—to be alone in a car with my daddy for as long as he keeps driving.

Wings and Ass Bangs

I showed my husband pictures of my high school and college years, thinking he'd enjoy viewing the woman he wed before her cellulite, eye-bags-arm hammocks-burgeoning front ass days.

I recently became the not-so-proud owner of a front fanny, after having made fun in my first book of the white-trash woman who had a giant front region, divided with crack and all—just like a big old butt.

Sure enough, Mama was right. You poke fun at someone's flaws and you'll get the same thing. I got it. A baby front fanny with lots of growth potential. It's depressing, but I cover it up with giant Mee-Maw drawers, the kind I swore I'd never wear.

This age is tough, beauty- and figure-wise. It's along about this time of life a woman of my years begins to unravel, both mentally and physically, and it's not unusual to see one of us breaking out the old albums trying to prove to everyone with a pulse and not on life support her glorious past captured by Kodak. You know what I mean. Nothing like whipping out the scrapbooks with the perky cheerleader pictures and those sorority-girl shots to remind us of the beauty we once had and let the person viewing the books know we had it, too.

I'm not sure why I decided to show the albums to my husband after sixteen years of marriage, but here they were, laid out for his Bausch & Lombed eyes to behold.

It was a time of life—a heyday of sorts—when everything was where it should be, high and firm. Instead of whistling and shaking his head and saying, "Whew, woman, you were a fox," which was the 70s lingo for "hot," Tidy Stu groaned and acted like he was looking at a *Hagasaurus*, as if the very images before him seared his retinas.

I noticed he wasn't staring at my orange bikini and pecan-brown, sun-fried skin. He was focusing on two flaps of hair glued to my skull, a set of wings even Heather Locklear never mastered.

"That's so rednecky and gross," he said, his own head shining from lack of hair. "Nobody had those things where I grew up. What are they? Is it a joke or something? I mean that can't be real."

He was talking about my Farrah hair. All of us hick chicks in Georgia who were trying to copy TV's great beauties had a set of gigantic wings, compliments of Clairol hot rollers and Final Net, and lacquered so that no wind could put asunder.

"They are called wings, hon, and I don't mean to brag but I sported the finest pair in LaGrange, Georgia. You're always puzzled how a goon like me was named Homecoming Queen, well, the wings did it for sure. That and the fact my boyfriend was in a rock band and I carried the black vote on account of Sharlette Willis being my second-best friend."

Tidy Stu is the only man I've ever dated who paid extraordinary attention to my hair. Most men wouldn't notice if you dyed your hair blue, not unless it was your puss fur.

The very first date I had with Tidy, he ran his fingers through my bleach-fried perm and commented the texture was similar to dried-up hay. I kissed him anyway, like a fool, and a year later I married him.

And here he was making fun of my only years of wrinkle-free firmness.

"That's the ugliest pile of shit I've ever seen attached to a skull," he said, and I closed the scrapbook and left the room. His obsession with hair only increased as the years went by and we accumulated dogs, children and more dogs, fueling his latest body-hair quirks. He spent virtually all of his spare time snipping, shaving, trimming, clipping, and either styling or eliminating every hair he saw.

It's almost ended our marriage, along with other things he does. Like shaving with that Norelco Spectra 8831XL that cost more than my engagement ring. He keeps it in the kitchen by the refrigerator and my Mikasa dinnerware, where's he's set up a toiletry shop—no matter that we have a large half bath two feet away and three full-size bathrooms scattered about the house.

I am furious that he's got his grooming station right next to my fine china. The poor man is suffering from Hairanoia and shaves his face six times a day. Just mosies over to the china cabinet and clips his nails, Norelcos his chafed skin and Lubriderms his dry spots. Whenever somebody walks by, his eyes glow a neon greenish hue and he begins a near quiver, reaching for his scissors, plugging in his Spectra 8831XL and growing red about the face.

"Come here," he'll order anyone within earshot. "Get over here now!"

At first we would play along with his hobby, but the more times we walked off with bald patches and hideous hairdos, the more we avoided his Little Shop of Horrors.

It started innocently enough, before I gave birth to children who had hair he could botch and before we bought the Pomeranian with enough hair to keep Tidy happy for a lifetime.

Knowing my mother was a beautician and used me as her dummy, he decided he would follow suit. Every time I saw his hands when they weren't wrapped around his saxophone or penis, they were clutching a grooming tool.

I made the tragic mistake at age 28 of caving in and permitting this budding hairdresser to give me a little trim. "Just a tiny snip in the back," I said. "Just the back, you hear me?"

"Just in the back," he said, growing euphoric. "I'll just cut off all this dried hay you call hair."

"Well, I wouldn't go so far as to call it—"

"I know what I'm doing," he said with the confidence of a man in denial. "It will look a lot better than those $70 haircuts you come home with every other month."

After two weeks of hearing this, I gave up and told this budding Vidal Sassoon to sharpen his scissors and have at it, at which point Mr. No License asked me to take a seat in a kitchen chair while he whisked a towel around my neck with the flourish of a true pro.

I knew this was a mistake and tried to focus on something positive, like what he had done with our pitiful yard, the success of his landscaping and turning a bare mud bank into a green paradise lush with dogwoods and rhododendron, periwinkle and Japanese Maples. I figure he thought he could just up and transfer those lawn-and-gardening skills directly toward a skull. Hair. Fescue. Ground cover's ground cover, right?

The scissors we owned back then were not meant for hair. They'd been used to poke holes in tin cans and leather belts, and to cut plastic, metal and other materials that won't yield. As my husband wielded the dulled and damaged blades, I realized I was doomed. But sometimes a wife is just tired of arguing and gives in for the sake of keeping the peace, and such was my dumb mistake.

The first sounds weren't pretty: a whack followed by a yank of wet hair followed by nervous coughing on his part.

"Only an inch," I said.

Whack. Tug. Chop. Snip. Cough.

I reached back and felt a bare neck.

"My hair! What have you done—"

"I'm not finished," this José Eber wannabe squawked. "Hush or I won't be able to get it even." He cut hair the way men mow lawns, each time around the head, the hairs getting shorter and shorter.

Now for some women short hair is lovely, accentuating finely crafted features. But not for me. I could already feel its ghastly effects: my nose growing another half inch, a second chin rolling out of left field, teeth flaring like a mule's. My heart did that irregular beat thing so I did the gorilla pounding against my chest, then tried to bolt.

"Wait a minute," he said, pressing me back down. "It won't look right unless you let me trim up the sides to match."

I breathed deeply, inhaling the humid smell of hot water boiling on the stove for his mango tea. Meditate if you can't medicate, I said over and over, my personal mantra for those times when I'm out of tranquilizers, and Vicodin and booze aren't options.

I felt a huge tug followed by a hacking of hair, as if he had a sling blade.

"Careful. You have to taper that section. I don't want the sides to look like that *Mary Hartman, Mary Hartman* woman."

Whack. Tug. Chop. Snip. Cough.

"Who's Mary Hartman?" he asked, followed by a hacksaw movement with his scissors, as if cutting down tree limbs.

I reached up and felt two flaps of sideburns, big old nasty Mary Hartman sideburns, then I jumped out of the chair, gasped with disgust as I viewed them in the bathroom mirror, ran upstairs, locked the door and cried for two hours.

Next I plotted sweet revenge. I'd hire a yardman to come in and uproot all his precious rhododendron, deleaf his maples and prune his azaleas to nubbins. Should he press charges, I'm confident a jury of nine women and three sensitive and estrogen-enriched men would acquit, and appearances on *Jenny Jones* and *Jerry Springer* would follow, all the rednecks in the viewing audience cheering at their screens, "You go, girl. He deserved it, giving you those ugly old Mary Hartman bangs!"

In the end, I settled for a trip to Wal-Mart, bought a jug of gel, a can of mousse and some giant hair clips, but it didn't fully work to brighten my mood, especially after two women pointed and snickered at me on the Health and Beauty aisle, and I heard one say, "I thought Elvis died in '76."

This is when I hit the mall and purchased an adorable pair of suede boots, figuring, hey, if your hair looks like a rat's Happy Meal, you might as well direct the eye elsewhere.

And because I threatened to cut off sex for six months for

his ruination of my locks, he stopped chasing me with dull scissors for a few years. It didn't start up again until our children were born, one bald as a Chinese Crested and the other with jet-black tufts of downy hair that had his hands itching to sharpen his blades. I knew what he was thinking. It would only be a matter of time.

Surely I could handle him and ward it off, since my very own mama used me as her guinea pig for ten years, beginning when I was four and she arched and waxed my eyebrows. I was so upset I climbed up on the sink and shaved them both off.

That was just the beginning of bad hairdos throughout my life. As a result, I was semiprepared for my husband's unlicensed and barbaric barbering.

By first grade, I'd had half a dozen hairdos, one of which included a sky-high beehive during my first ballet recital. All the other little girls wore pigtails and braids, ponytails with large satin bows, and here I was with an updo like the singers in the B-52's. Now, I know why the audience was laughing and flashbulbs popped in my direction. I understand who people were talking about when they said, "Poor, hideous thing. What a shame."

Mama explained she did the beehive so she'd recognize me from her seat in the nosebleed section, as we all wore the same pink leotard and tights.

The worst, though, was the day Mama said she was about to make me the cutest little girl alive and took her shears to my scrawny skull and cut and snipped until there was barely a hair left on my head. I screamed and cried and pitched a tantrum that nearly blew an artery.

"It's a pixie, Susan. It's the latest look and you'll be the first to have it."

All I wanted was a giant wool cap and a box of Oreos. Even at 6, I knew the power of comfort food. I cried for hours, my face against the pillows of the guest room double bed draped in my great-grandmother's quilt. Mama grew quite upset and concerned, thinking she'd perhaps given birth to a part-devil child, so she jumped in her aqua Plymouth, lit a Kent, and drove to the drugstore, returning with a bag and a big smile.

"Wait until you see this," she said, applying antibacterial ointment to the cuts on my head where her scissors had nicked my temple and forehead. "You know your mama loves you and has always promised if I messed up I'd fix you right back. Just like when you shaved off your eyebrows and I bought a black pencil and drew you in some brand-new ones."

"All the kids at school laughed at me and you know it," I said. "During recess it ran down my face and Carol Ann uninvited me to her birthday party and called me monster face."

"Well, sugar, don't you worry. Look here. Open this bag."

Inside was what first appeared to be roadkill. I carefully picked up a piece of squirrel-brown hair and pulled it from the bag.

"They're pigtails," Mama rejoiced, clapping her long and lotioned hands. "Aren't they precious? You just wait. Everyone will want them after you wear them to school."

I stared in horror at the two curly sections of hair that came with their own attachable parts. I felt the plastic hooks, wondering where on my quarter-inch hairs these things would clip. Mama rushed over and somehow managed to scrounge up enough hair to get them on, just above my ears, which, by the way, stick out like Ross Perot's.

I stared in the mirror, tears rolling down my puffy face. Mama hugged me, made a big pot of spaghetti and promised no more pixies. The next day I wore the pigtails to school and Mrs. Smith, my first-grade teacher, paraded me around to all the classrooms, showing her other teacher friends. I could hear the phoniness in their voices. "Aren't those adorable?" and then the snickering, and when the doors to their rooms closed, the flat-out howling. My cheeks burned as if I had the flu. I thought any minute I'd vomit. The tile floors swayed and spun and, finally, I dramatically collapsed onto the big square tiles.

It must have been the combination of mortification and the sickening smells of that old school in Thomson, Georgia. My nose filled with odors of old bologna and floor chemicals.

"Are you all right, Susan?" Mrs. Smith asked, bending down where I was splayed like the dead. "Get up. We can't have you scaring all the other children in this school, now just how selfish would that be?"

As soon as she said the words, I threw up. I still thank God for that, because she took me to the office infirmary where nurses gave me ice chips and cold washcloths for my head. They removed my pigtails as carefully as one would a body part and didn't laugh when they put them in a paper sack with my soiled dress.

I got to wear clothes brought by volunteers specifically for children who've had bodily function mishaps and vomiting certainly counted and was less offensive than diarrhea pants. No way could I go back to my classroom where the likes of Cy Gasses, my true love and boyfriend, would see my hair and smell my sour breath.

I guess all this prepped me for this latest phase of my husband's barbering disorder, rearing its ugly head last year when our son turned twelve, our daughter seven and the Pomeranian four, and with more fur than ever.

I like to call this his Barbaric Bangs Period.

It was his mission to give everyone in the family a set of bangs that look just like Herman Munster's, the kind of bangs well-meaning mothers used to pay barbers to cut for their poor sons and daughters, usually the ones in the special ed classes, bless their hearts.

I never understood why if someone's brain wasn't working 100 percent, the parents felt it their duty to snip their precious and challenged child's hair in a straight and geeky line four inches above their eyebrows—a sheet of half-inch-long fringe that did nothing for the girls and boys forced to endure what the mean kids called "'Tard bangs." It was sad that the kids in special education had this hairstyle, and I wanted to make a law against cutting a wonderful child's hair in this manner.

Then, one dreadful night, Tidy Stu up and cuts our son's

hair, giving him a set of 'Tard bangs to rival all others. I almost cried when I saw my boy until I gazed at my husband and saw that he, too, had a row of Munster fringe. You should have seen them. Stu Munster and Son Munster Jr., the 'Tard bangs doing nothing to enhance their features.

That very night, still trembling with the desire to snip, chop, whack and tug, he up and shampooed, cut, shaved and styled our dog's fur, focusing on his hairy buttocks region in particular.

And to do so on the Sabbath! That evening my dog pranced by and I lost my breath. His fanny was shaved like a chimp's hiney and he, too, sported a thick-and-short set of bangs, only on the dog they were ASS BANGS!

Our Pom once had more hair than stocks a wig shop, and to see this newly mowed ass with Three Stooges bangs came as a shock. I should have NEVER bought Stu the Norelco Spectra. Since receiving this gift, he's shaved everything in our home. Children, himself, the carpet, clothing . . . and now the dog.

"I'm calling the Doggy Social Services. Zipper looks awful. Look, he is under the sofa and won't come out."

"He's styling, aren't you, Zip?" Stuart asked.

"He's going to need therapy. And a pair of underwear for sure. He's the only dog in the neighborhood with ass bangs. It's really embarrassing."

Our neighbors, who typically never walked on our little cul-de-sac, all decided to make Hunter's Ridge a destination so they could see the dog with a thick sheaf of bangs just above his little black anus.

They'd stare and then start laughing. I heard one even praying. "Sweet Jesus, whatever's going on in this house, please intervene."

Amen to that, brother.

Would You Like a Waffle with Those Shoes, Ma'am?

The man jumped out of nowhere, scaring me half to death as he wielded his metal weapon of choice: a foot-measuring device.

I was in a department store, obviously broke, as I checked out the 75 percent off shoes in the children's section. My daughter saw the sales sign and sniffed up her nose, immediately running over to the shoe pyramid with no discounts—not even 10 percent—and falling in love with all the $100 hookers-in-waiting shoes.

School was starting soon and all mothers who want to come across as decent and proper usually fork out money for new shoes. It keeps the Child Protective Services workers at bay. My wonderful parents and others at their church collect money to buy the needy kids attending their church new shoes for school. It's just one of those things. New school year. New sneakers or, in my diva daughter's case, clunky skank foot fare.

I wouldn't mind investing money in her feet if she'd wear the selections I buy. But her feet are growing faster than my waistline is and she is only interested in the hussy lineups with high heels and fur.

We were eyeing different things, me choosing sweet sandals and sneakers and she blurting, "I hate those. I hate those, too," when out of nowhere, the shoe man sprung on us like an unseen hornet.

"Please take a seat," this butler-toned fright of a man ordered my child, "and I'll give you a thorough and professional measuring." He took a look at her baby-blue Converse high-tops with the frayed shoelaces and then at my footwear, and his nose twitched as if zapped with an electrical device. Unfortunately, I'd chosen to wear a pair of cowboy boots bought twenty-five years ago when I was a sophomore in college.

"My, she has thin feet," he said, and at that point I realized he wasn't right—a bit "tetched in the haid," as we say down South. His facial features didn't fit his bone structure and seemed disproportionately large on such a small canvas of skin.

His eyes were huge and amphibious, bulging as he instructed Lindsey to stand straight and tall while he did his obsessive-compulsive thing for about ten minutes, proclaiming her arches weak, her feet long and narrow and a size 2.

"What size are those . . . those . . . sneakers?" he asked.

I felt like some sort of neglectful mother. Her Chuck Taylor All Star sneakers were a 13. "Her foot grew overnight," I said. "Seriously, two days ago it was a 13 and she was crying last night saying how bad they hurt, and so I held her delicate feet in my hands and actually saw growth. Really. I saw her toes elongating right before my eyes."

He poked and prodded, taking this shoe job as seriously as if he was at a doctor's office doing blood work for a matching organ transplant.

"You are good at your job," I said, wanting to hurry his odd ass up. "Almost like a shoe scientist." His features enlarged further, to the point that they all but popped right off his head. He stood and went to the back room, that mystery place where shoe salesmen go to find sizes they never have in the style your kid must have or collapsing in the floor will ensue.

He returned with every size I could have imagined: a 13, a 1½, a 2 and even a 3. I wondered why he even bothered to measure if he was fluctuating so much with the sizes.

"Every shoe brand is different," he said. "Skechers run small. Nikes run larger. The human foot is a complex organ with so many bones and opportunities for complete ruination. One can't just run off to some cheap store, grab a pair and hope their feet will last as long as their hearts. No, sir. You see folks in wheelchairs? Many got that way from foot neglect, and the proper shoe and fit is as important—"

"Ohhhh," I yelled, exhausted and in need of a Goody's Powder. I grabbed my stomach, a trick I do on rare occasions such as this one. It works perfectly in getting people on tangents to stop the blabbing. I learned this from Fred on *Sanford & Son*.

Just the week before, I'd spent three hours in a mall shoe shopping with my son, who came away with nothing but complaints. Hey, but no one measured his feet either. When I was growing up, measuring was a must, and it all began with that metal thing and a shoehorn and lots of fanfare and footwear. None of this do-it-yourself stuff that I had grown to love about discount places such as Pic 'n Pay, Payless Shoes and all the outlets where salesclerks don't even come out from behind the register unless for a smoke break.

This man tending my child rattled on for an entire hour, lacing and relacing, explaining everything about feet and shoes I NEVER wanted to know. It didn't help we were the only people in the department and had his full attention. I am certain he had Obsessive-Compulsive Disorder and was not a foot fetish freak. Instead, he examined every centimeter of skin and bone on my child and chattered incessantly about sizing and lacing techniques and the proper fit. She didn't seem to mind this attention to her tootsies, as if she was Cinderella and the Freaky Prince of Feet was about to shower her in shoes.

When I finally got my diva to settle on a pair, I followed this man's tall self to the cash register and proceeded to hunt down my debit card, lost in the bowels of my garbage dump of a purse. I needed to get the heck out of this place before I had a full-blown hissy fit. I realized I was moments from falling to the ground belly-up and feet swirling, upside down bug-style in my ugly-ass cowboy boots.

I swooshed my Visa debit card as quickly as humanly possible.

"GOOD SWIPE!" he shouted out with glee when my card didn't screw up his machine. He moved to the left and placed his knobby skeletal hands on a large box and his entire face lit up, once again overextending his features.

"Would you like a waffle iron to go with the shoes?" he asked, tapping his foot-loving fingers across the top of a cooking appliance that had no business being in the girls' shoe department.

"Do what? Did you say WAFFLE IRON? As in what one would cook waffles in? As in a waffle iron in the shoe department?"

His smile exploded, a real shocker, revealing teeth that seemed a full two inches long. I am quite certain he got the appliance for Christmas and set it on the counter to make a profit, poor underpaid shoe scientist that he was.

"Does it make shoe-shaped waffles or something?"

He ignored me. "It's regularly $99.99 and on sale for $39.99 with an extra 30 percent off."

"I really don't do much cooking," I said, in total shock at the scene unfolding. "Especially waffles. The Surgeon General recently warned—"

"Oh, you don't have to be a cook to do this," he said. "They sell the mixes at the grocery store and you just add an egg and some—"

"Kellogg's frozen waffles are fine by me," I said as kindly as possible, trying my best to leave the store. My gosh, they'd already had last call for shoppers and were beginning to cut off the lights.

"You sure you don't want to get the matching Nike socks or sign up today for one of our cards and get 10 percent off your order, or perhaps you'd reconsider the waffle iron since it's such a good deal and everyone loves a good waffle? It's a great way to start them off in the mornings before school, which as you know rings the opening-day bells in a matter of days."

I knew at that point how to get rid of him. Same way you do a pesky boyfriend.

"You are wonderful. I'll bet you could have any woman you

wanted, you hot little thing. Could I just have a comment card so I can send positive feedback to your manager? Even though you are a true Sex God with all your shoe knowledge and waffle skills, I just want to be friends, you know. It's not that I don't like you, it's really a matter of—"

He did a jerky movement as if pre-seizing and his expanding facial features began to quiver out of control. He dropped a comment pamphlet in my hands and set me free. His gayness couldn't take my open sexuality.

Later, I called Mama to tell her about this poor man who had the waffle iron displayed near his Nike footwear mountain.

"I didn't know they still measured feet," she said. "After my mama died, my poor daddy wouldn't take us when we were little 'cause he couldn't handle all three of us in one store."

Left a widower with three daughters all under age ten, my Papa Roy was a creatively brilliant fellow. He got out the newspapers, and with a pen, carefully traced each of his daughter's feet. With sharp scissors and a steady hand, he cut the feet out as one would paper dolls.

"He carried those newspaper feet with him to the store and they laid them across the contraption and the salespeople measured them just like real feet," Mama said. "We never had a pair of shoes that didn't fit."

One more crazy relative shaking and threatening to topple the family tree, I thought, but couldn't say much because I realized Back-to-School shopping, the chore I dread more than Pap smears and DMV visits, would be coming up in a few days, just like the shoe freak said while trying to interest me in a waffle iron.

The past two trips had been nightmares. I wrote about the first experience in my previous book when my daughter, 3 years old at the time, screamed out the word "Asshole" when a big fat rednecky woman grabbed the last giant glue stick.

After that experience, I shiver and shake and am all but ready for a rush job to the ER, suffering runs of palpitations, panic attacks and even a collapse in the crowded and highly competitive glue stick bin.

I always dread late August when the mailman delivers the School Supplies list, educators usually giving us just twenty-four to forty-eight hours to round up the required goods prior to the first day of school.

Those without kids don't realize how dangerous this excursion can become, leading to a recipe for migraines, teeth gnashing, bloodletting, and all around evil and venom spewing.

You talk about mean? A store so crowded with mothers and their 2.5 children on sugar highs trying to be the one to get the last 10-cent, two-pocket folder? What we always seem to have in my small city is a two-day descent into retail indecency: The tax-free weekend, and back-to-school shopping. I'd rather suffer the revival of that torturous hair-removal device known as the Epilady, which my mother-in-law gleefully gave me one Christmas.

Here's what went down merely days after my run-in with the shoe freak. I called Mom and Dad, pretending to be missing them terribly, knowing full well I had the School Supplies list in my pocket and a plan to con Daddy into hitting the stores.

"I miss y'all so much. The kids cried last night because school is starting and they are literally pining for you both."

"You just bring them down tomorrow morning, hon," Mama said, adding she'd be fixing her famous spaghetti dinner (the kind that brings about Die Rear).

Early Saturday morning, I bribed the kids.

"Tell your granddaddy you'd be honored if he'd accompany you on a shopping trip for all that back-to-school stuff and I'll give you $5."

My son shook his head.

"Okay, then. Ten dollars."

"Deal."

Saturday, August 16: Super Save-Mart in Spartanburg, South Carolina. We give the job to my father and I am flat-out surprised at how happy he seems. Of course, he's never done this and had his feet rolled over and broken from cart stampedes or his scalp traumatized by bitchy women's hair-pulling over the last glue stick. Why, Dad hasn't been back-to-school shopping in his entire 70 years.

He entered the house like the proudest granddaddy alive, hauling his sack of goods like a fisherman with a full trotline, and saying he had a grand time fighting cursing women barking on cell phones and stealing all the good backpacks.

"We did it," he said, of his trip with my son. "I want you to know there were backpacks everywhere. Upchucked out into the floors. We got the best one. Everybody said it was the nicest. Even the lady shocking everyone with her cattle prod to break up the fights said so. I saw blood, people. Blood! It was crazy. Much worse than running out to the mall on Christmas Eve to find last-minute presents. I need some wine. Peg? Could you pour me a liter in my special glass?"

He was referring to the goldfish bowl we got him for his 70th birthday so he could tell his Baptist congregation he never had more than a glass or two of wine when partaking. Needless to say, each glass was really a bottle.

Later that very day, my mother, not to be outdone, suggested we take my daughter's list to the same store.

"I really don't think I can do this, Mama. Don't you remember what happened to me the last couple of times? Don't you remember Lindsey calling that white-trash woman an asshole and me having to say, 'I'll buy you a BASS POLE,' just to try to cover it up?"

"Come on," Mama said. "I'll take you to Stein Mart afterward and buy you something pretty." She knew she had me on that one. Therefore, off we went into shopping hell.

"What in heaven's name is that?" Mama asked, pointing into the cart where I'd heaved an item from the list.

"That's an antibacterial soap refill."

She couldn't stop laughing. "It must weigh 40 pounds. It's the size of a car tire. You can't take that to the teacher."

"Listen. She'll be thrilled to the bone. In grade school little kids need stuff like Kleenex for all their boogers and antibacterial soap for after they pick them."

They also need a certain mat to take naps on, which I've been unable to find, thus trip Number Three loomed.

Sunday, August 17: I am in a trance, trying not to panic while in the regular-sized Save-Mart in Asheville, North Carolina. "Where are those naptime mat thingamabobs all the kids have to have?" I asked a clerk who wore the same expression one dons after being chewed by a gang of filthy rats.

"Gone," he gasped.

"Will you be getting more soon?"

"No," he hissed, spit flying. "Never. Not in my lifetime."

Poor man. I can't really blame him for being short with me. All in all, the trip wasn't for naught. I knocked a lady out cold on aisle 5 after she pulled my hair and tried to steal my Crayola eight-pack of washable markers. I came home with two 20-cent glue sticks and a plastic pencil box, a pack of loose-leaf paper and most of the other items on the list.

All shopping was complete except for the mysterious contraption known as the Kindermat—nowhere to be found in my two-state search. Exhausted and in need of some tub time and aromatherapy, I called my daughter's Nana.

"I guess Lindsey can always use a towel," I said. "The stores said they were all gone and the shortage was near crisis level."

A moment of silence followed as Nana's brain processed this information. "Poor thing. She's not going to have a mat like all the other children to sleep on. What will she think and, more importantly, what will those teachers think?"

"They'll think her shoes look fabulous. We bought a darling pair the other day and if you need a waffle iron—"

"We can't send her without something decent to nap on."

"Listen, the list says a Kindermat OR a towel."

Nana began to sob. "She will be ruined for life. We'll find her something."

"I'm not going back out there. It's dangerous. I've got two bite marks, four bruises and will need a fresh tetanus shot. I did, however, manage to save roughly 77 cents per child."

*　*　*

The following year was even worse. I promised myself that no matter how cheap the Elmer's glue at Bargain Mart, I'd bypass that annual Back-to-School nightmare and shop for my kids' lists at one of the office supply chains.

Sure, I'd have to pay an extra dime for the glue, but chances were decent I'd still have two legs in working order once the trip was completed. I wouldn't end up black-and-blue, leg in a cast, cane at my side from the stampede of metal carts and Moms on a Mission crashing into us for the last 24-count Crayola box slashed to a quarter. And chances were fairly promising I'd finish up the list in three hours instead of four days.

It's not like we can memorize the list from previous years and figure the glue sticks are a given. Only the vat of booger and snot sanitizers could be counted on. That and the jumbo box of tissues along with the gallon jug of anti-Ebola liquid soap for all those germs that merge when one packs twenty-two kids in a classroom.

I stood grasping a cart in the middle of the store, frozen with fear, four lists in my buggy. True, I'm the mother of two, but this year I had two lists from each teacher, not counting the Wish List.

I couldn't blink or budge as the others politely murmured, "Excuse me," and went about their business as if I were a car with a dead battery in the middle of Interstate 240. No one was offering jumper cables, but no one tried to mow me down either since we were in a fairly expensive store instead of the cattle stampede at the super-bargain centers.

I was all but certain in this crowded but friendly store I'd also leave with most of the hairs on my head and the prospect of all teeth firmly planted in the gums. Last year, I read where in one state, a mother socked another mom in the mouth and four teeth went flying.

Then there was the year when my daughter cussed (as I mentioned earlier) and I'd left with half the supply list and a blood blister near my left ear. A mother wanting a three-ring notebook binder, the one I held in my clutches, claimed it was in her cart and I'd flat-out stolen it.

Her 5-year-old leaned over and yanked my hair with part of an ear, said a four-letter word and tried to decapitate me.

"Git outta our way!" the mother spat, revealing a pair of honest-to-goodness fangs and no front teeth whatsoever. "I need this here binder for kinny-garden."

This year as I stood trapped in fear but in a lovely office supply store, a friendly and smiling salesperson asked if I needed help. I nearly fainted. In all the years at the bargain marts, I'd had to chase down the help and corner them, cowering back in housewares because they just couldn't take it anymore, and who could blame them?

These lists seem to grow longer and more bizarre each year.

"May I help you find something?" the kind gentleman asked again, seeing I was semicomatose and speaking in tongues, not the kind in church but the kind when mothers have meltdowns.

"Mrrrrrphhhh. Mrrrrrrrphhhh, splatcha mola folda mon usted como loco," was all I could manage, handing over my lists.

"Follow me please, to aisle 11. Most of these items are stocked there with the exception of those things on the Wish List. You'll have to go to the grocery store or a pharmacy for those items." He scanned the list further. "Some of these items may be available only on the Black Market."

"Sì, señor, mola folda Crayola, Mrrrrrrrrphhhh."

Once I found the supplies, I thanked the man in my native language and moved onto the Wish Lists. I felt sorry for teachers who must fish greens from their own wallets for many of the supplies one would think the state could furnish.

I scanned the list one last time to see what was missing. Jumbo boxes of tissue: check. Jugs of soap: check. Band-Aids, Tootsie POPS, Bounty paper towels: check.

Coffee filters, Saran wrap, duct tape, boxes of animal crackers the size of Maytags: not yet.

"It won't be long," I said, during a phone call to Mama, "when the lists ask for Starbucks, Xanax, bath oils and aftershave. Maybe even a pack of Camels and some Yellow Tail wine."

"At least you only have to do this once a year," she said.

"Yes, that's right. Twice would do me in."

She made me a promise, fearing I'd end up in the cuckoo's nest again.

"Next time your children's feet grow, I'll take them to buy shoes," she said. "If I can't do that, I'll at least trace them on the newspaper and take those to the store. How's that?"

Perfect.

"And could you throw in a free waffle iron?"

Sister Sandy and the Family Jewels

Please, Lord, don't let the woman selling the Jesus pancake on eBay actually be related to me. Isn't it enough I have a crazy Aunt Betty?

I double-checked the item and felt my heart drop. There was no denying it. My younger sister by two years, who lives in Rich City, Georgia, and was married to a millionaire the first go-round, is running a small operation on eBay where she's selling off her jewels from the first husband. That's not the problem.

I don't think her second husband, a high school basketball coach, minds her hawking her prior mate's jewels and spending the cash on play pretties for him.

"I didn't used to be so eBay savvy," she said, a glass or two of wine loosening her tongue. "Oh, let's face it, I used to be rich. Saving money didn't matter much then. However, when I married a wonderful man whose riches lie in character not Wachovia, it was time to get creative. Why not start an Internet business? I thought to myself. Just like families gathered together around their radios in the 1950s, my family likes to gather around eBay. It's wholesome entertainment."

After a few days pondering how to raise start-up funds, Sandy realized she had a perfectly good Rolex watch that had been sitting in her jewelry box for years.

"It was a gift from my former husband, Daddy Warbucks,"

she said. "I would sell that on eBay and use the money to start our family's online business. I wanted a name that we could have fun with. People do have a sense of humor, don't they? That's why we settled on THC's Family Jewels: http://stores. ebay.com/THC-Family-Jewels. 'The THC stands for 'The Hidden Closet,' and 'Family Jewels' is to remind us of . . . Well, you know what it reminds folks of . . .

"The name has received almost unanimous support. I did have one lady cover her mouth as if in horror and say, 'I thought you were a Christian.' I just smiled and said, 'What Bible verse says that you have to lose your sense of humor in order to gain salvation? Don't you think Jesus ever joked?'

"We have had a blast coming up with catch phrases. We have actually used, 'Prices that won't make you turn left and cough,' and 'There's nothing more precious than the family jewels.' We stopped short of the suggestions, 'Take home a sackful,' and, 'Don't blow your wad elsewhere.' We do have some class, you know."

It wasn't long before the Family Jewels slipped in the Jesus pancake. Everything was hunky-dory until a couple of days when obviously her serotonin levels skyrocketed and she decided to branch out from the jewelry and add to her little store what she thought would be taken as a joke.

I was checking to see how well her aqua ring was selling when I stumbled upon her Jesus pancake and gave her a call.

"Have you lost your mind? What is this thing? And whose ugly teeth are those?"

"It's called 'The Jesus Pancake 2 . . . the Saga Continues,'" she said. "Those ugly choppers you see up close on the ad are Chad's, your precious nephew's. He needs braces, so I crammed the camera lens through his stretched lips and told bidders any money would go to his orthodontia fund."

"Does Mama know?" I asked, realizing this could be considered highly sacrilegious.

"It's a joke, Susan. I put a big disclaimer on the ad saying we love Jesus plenty and that the auction was just for fun. You know we can afford braces for Chad. He's the one who wrote

Jesus across the pancake with the maple syrup. It took us 100 pancakes to get it just right."

Sister Sandy, after collecting quite a few bids for her hot-cake, was booted off eBay for violating one or more of their rules. After reading her ad, I went online and was shocked to see so many breakfast items claiming to have the likeness of the Lord embedded in them, and even more stunned people were bidding on the phony merchandise.

Here's my take on all this craziness. If you really want to see Jesus, get thee heathen self into a church. You won't find the real thing hiding out in boxes of Aunt Jemima or Kellogg's. After careful research here's what I found these hoodwinking sellers are claiming:

Jesus On My Toast: "I grilled a couple of slices of toast this morning for breakfast. . . . I don't really have the heart to eat Our Savior so I've eBayed it. The toast comes in a clear, airtight plastic bag."

Someone sent this seller a comment: "That is not the real Jesus. My toaster makes better Jesuses than that."

Well, na, na, ne, boo, boo.

Here is another ad:

Miracle: "About three years ago, I put a simple, regular piece of sandwich bread in my toaster. When it came out, to my surprise, it looked like Jesus Christ . . . Do not miss this offer to have Jesus closer than ever before in your life." The starting bid for the stale bread was $100.

Another seller, claiming the "digital age is among us, praise the Lord, and aren't buyers fed up with the poor qualities of the deities on edibles?" was offering to emblazon any food item, including tortillas and pita bread, with the faces of religious figures. He reeled in dozens of bidding idiots.

Here's my all-time favorite . . .

* * *

Miracle Jesus Pancake: "This amazing pancake is in near mint condition with the exception of a bite mark from my 2-year-old son. It's also starting to shrivel up from dehydration."

Comment from a potential bidder: "What type of person draws on a pancake and then puts it on eBay to make a few bucks?"

Answer from seller: "What type of person searches eBay for miracle Jesus pancakes?

In My Sister's Former Life—
Where the Living Is Easy

The whole eBay stuff was strange because my sister had never once been the type to do anything but spend the money her first husband, David "The Wig Man," made. Back then, before she married David II, there was something about my lovely sister that sent me into fits of panic every time I scheduled a trip to see her.

I was jealous, consumed by the green of envy. I guess it was her petite perfection, the way I could stand next to her and feel like an Olympic shot-put champion. The way I could never spot the slightest ripple of bad eating on her perfectly buffed and tanned body. The way her nails looked as if they were done an hour earlier, and mine as if I'd spent the past forty years scrubbing pots with Brillo.

Her son, back in her rich-lady days, was turning 3 on Memorial Day weekend, and I was invited to her perfect house for his perfect party, complete with its *Star Wars* theme, all characters in full costume in the 90-degree Georgia heat and, if that wasn't enough, a carnival-size Moon Bouncer.

Normally, I have about half a cup of confidence. But when face-to-face with my younger sister by two years, especially during her hoity-toity days, I became awkward and huge, my clothes suddenly ill-fitting, flesh seeming to swell beneath them. I felt like a 2 AM Wal-Mart shopper in fleece.

I loved telling my friends about Sandy and Rich David and

their mansion and millions. Perfect Sandy who is also (most of the time) kindhearted and generous.

"She's got it all," I'd say to my friends, and they'd shake their heads and roll their eyes when I whipped out the pictures of her palace and her sunny-haired children. Sandy, standing in the foreground as if she'd never missed a night's sleep or eaten a cream-filled doughnut in her life. Sandy, who doesn't have to work and can spend her mornings drinking Mocha Lattes at Starbucks, followed by a two-hour toning at her spa, and later, shopping with friends or sipping margaritas after tennis matches at the country club.

"We live in two different worlds," I'd say, and my friends would nod as if they, too, had siblings who'd hopped off the path of their shared histories and into luxurious places some lives seem destined toward. Actually, my dear friend and fellow book club member Nancy Twigg has a sister who was the governor of Nebraska's wife for eight years before turning into a senator's wife when he went to Washington. She is well known in Nebraska for her tasteful renovations of the Governor's Mansion during her stay.

I tried to imagine my sister living in the Governor's Mansion for eight years and wondered how Nancy dealt with it. She told me her sister was pretty normal and lots of fun, even if she had been the first lady and a senator's wife for Lord knows how many more.

With my sister, back in her free-spending Platinum years, we had few similarities other than big ears (though hers were fixed) and children.

"She discovered she was pregnant while on a second honeymoon in Hawaii," I'd say at cocktail parties to my wine-sipping friends. "And I learned my news in the ladies' room of the West Asheville Kmart. I ran around and asked every stranger I saw, 'Is this test really positive? Are you sure you see two lines?' Most backed away as if I were showing them a rattlesnake. It never dawned on me I was cramming a peed-on stick in their faces."

*   *   *

I should have seen my sister's flight from common ground coming. She was a cheerleader whose light bones and agile body sent her flying and spinning down football fields, always the girl at the top of the pyramids. I was the one squatting at the bottom, the bent, broad-shouldered base whose job was to support such beauties, to lift all the Sandys up high so the world could pay them homage.

After college, Sandy chose a career in television and paid good money to have her ears sewn snugly to her skull, so that when broadcasting live during hurricanes, the gale-force winds wouldn't reveal our secret: mule ears minus proper cartilage, the starch of all decent ear sets.

I chose a career in which I could hide behind words, save my money and stand in the eye of storms without worrying about faulty ears.

Faced with these memories and the Memorial Day *Star Wars* birthday party vacation, faced with perfection in the elegant form of Mrs. Sandy Pitts (prior to her marriage to David II), I felt the panic broaden. To calm down I took action, first Cloroxing the news ink from my elbows until they turned white and crusty. Next, I shaved my legs and applied some dark, native-woman tanning gel that dried squiggly, like my kid's finger paintings. Thinking of Sandy's long, sculptured nails, I saved time and bit mine to near bone.

For good measure, I slathered on an alphahydroxy peel-off mask that ran into my eyebrows and ripped the right one in half. My only comfort was knowing that there's one in every family, a Mr. or Ms. Perfect. Someone with a 20-inch waist and ears not daunted by a sudden blast of wind.

It's not her fault perfection looms and blooms. It wasn't her fault that during the cushy years of Wig Man David, she lived in the kind of neighborhood where keeping up with the Joneses had surpassed a few choice dogwoods or a new Beemer in the triple garage.

In her gated burb of new money and semimansions, it seemed that landscaping was one of the most outward and obvious ways the neighbors competed. Sandy called one day back then to tell me the latest with her neighbors.

"What it is," she began, "is we live next door to this really rich widow woman. I bet you anything her landscaping costs more than her house."

Sometimes, it was too much talking to a sister who spent her days sipping lattes and wondering whether or not to fire her yard crew. Other days I was glad I was a corporate and domestic minion and had no excesses or frivolities, that my only yardman is the fellow I wed years ago.

"Once that old biddy moved in," my sister said, continuing on with the state of the widow's grounds, "I became painfully aware of how inadequate our lawn-care company was compared to the one she was using.

"I would watch her landscapers closely, and one day one of them came over to tell me I had a fungus in my grass and he didn't want it to spread over to his client's fine lawn. That's when I decided I had had it. I drank another cup of coffee, called my landscaper up and told her firmly we no longer needed her services."

"Was she upset?" I interrupted.

"No, but I did miss my annual poinsettia from her at Christmas."

The next day my sister up and *stole* her neighbor's yard help. She shared with him her visions and said if there was one thing she hated about wintertime it was that her Bermuda grass turned brown for months.

"Well, why don't you just plant some fescue?" I had said and she gasped in horror. No one, she said, dared plant that lower-class grass in her upscale neighborhood.

There had to be another way.

Thus entered the newly stolen yardman, who told her about the house down the street with grass greener than anything the human mind could envision, a product of his "environmentally safe" spray-painting services. For less than $500, Sandy could have her front yard and backyard shimmering like a fancy golf course in early June. After days of thinking the man might be nuts, she finally checked out his handiwork.

She stopped cold and held her breath. The sight before her

was spectacular, the answer to all her winter blues. She got out of her golf cart, mode of transportation for these types of neighborhoods, fell to her knees and all but wept.

A couple of days and hundreds of dollars later, her own yard sparkled like a flawless emerald and neighbors throughout the burb stopped to stare. They pulled over in their golf carts or Mercedes sedans. They squatted in her green Bermuda, sniffing and touching, amusing Sandy's 3-year-old son.

"Mama," he hollered. "We got some gawkers out here."

One morning as my sister was coming up the drive, her other next-door neighbor approached, grinning. "Damn, Sandy!" he said. "First, the light show you all had at Christmas. Now this? I left the house this morning and your grass was brown. I know rye doesn't grow that fast."

"Well, Stan," Sister Sandy said sweetly, "we choose to live in summer over here."

Another neighbor, a woman who shuns Sandy from all her social activities, was livid upon seeing summer arrive months early across the street and sprayed "WHORE" in hot pink across the newly painted grass.

"You tell her," Sandy said to the friend who'd reported the woman's ill remarks and crimes of graffiti, "that as soon as they come out with synthetic leaves for the trees, I'll get them, too."

Meanwhile, she's searching for a sign, something along the lines of, WET PAINT. KEEP OFF THE GRASS!"

When Wig Man David left her and Sandy fell from upper class to middle class but gained joy and a great husband in the process, she decided to have a grand yard sale featuring high-dollar items from the division of assets with the first David. These yard sale throwaways made my own furnishings look as if they'd been pulled from the Clampetts's cabin before their bubbling crude came up from the ground and made them roadkill-eatin' zillionaires.

One of Sandy's items that did not sell was a sofa. Only let's call it a sofer because in its present and festering condition, one simply can't say it properly. While the sofer had once been a glorious item in her living room, her two rambunctious sons had turned the couch into a shredded and stained abomination, and the cat's scratching and tee-teeing on it didn't add to its appeal.

Sister Sandy drove to Foam and Fabric to buy an iron-on patch kit to try to fix the holes in her sofer and keep the stuffing from popping out to no avail.

By the end of the day, not a soul offered a dime for that couch. People were avoiding it the way they did a purse I bought off eBay that smelled like a fish tank packed with soggy guinea pigs.

"We had to put up a sign and drag it to the road," Sandy said, laughing so hard she could barely get her words out. "David wrote FREE TO A GOOD HOME in black Sharpie and duct-taped it to the couch, then put it out for the garbage collectors."

Later that evening, they ran some errands and crossed their fingers someone would have snatched the sofer by the time they returned. They knew that their uptight, nouveau riche neighbors weren't going to be happy about having the beat-up couch putting a blight on their fairly fancy 'hood.

"We rounded the corner, and it was still there," Sandy said. An idea struck. Why not have a redneck party and mix up a batch of margaritas and invite the neighbors out to the sofer for a get-together?

"I had made the pitcher of 'ritas," she said, "and David and I sat on the couch by the roadside and waited for people to come. One neighbor showed up drinking a Big Check cola. It was hilarious."

That night everyone moved the couch into the neighborhood's decorative and lovely gazebo and continued with the festivities. But by the next afternoon, one of the new neighbors wasn't happy.

"Sandy," she said, wearing enough gold to rival a pawnshop display case and sipping Zinfandel bobbing with ice cubes. "Is that your couch in the gazebo?"

"Yes. They were supposed to pick it up yesterday."

"Well, I would certainly hope so. This type of activity is frowned upon here."

My sister isn't one to tolerate snoots. "Then smile, instead," she said. "Might make you look younger."

The next day someone finally loaded up the sofer and gave it a good home.

The neighbor returned with more to say. "I'm so glad they came and got it because I didn't know what I was going to have to say to you. What you did and then your harsh remarks aren't going to make for pleasant encounters between the two of us."

Sandy smiled sweetly, not wanting to tell this uppity woman that this neighborhood was like a housing project compared to her former mansion. "We're pretty new in the neighborhood and didn't know many people, but that old sofa brought us together with all sorts of folks we'd never met. They say friends are the gloves God wears when he touches us. I say a couch is the lasso he swings when roping us closer to our neighbors. If you're unhappy with this, stay indoors or complain to the property management company. Good luck there. I'm on the board."

The woman stalked off in her stilettos, spilling wine on her fairly green but unpainted grass.

The incident gave Sandy another crazy idea of hauling out her old Maytags so the neighbors across the street in the other development will come say howdy, maybe even bring a pie along to be more welcoming.

"I've been wanting to meet them for three years. If they won't bake me a pie, maybe I could make them a batch of pancakes and write Jesus across the top in maple syrup."

The Nuttiest Preschool Teacher
in the World

My sister is crazy just like I am. She also has the biggest heart and imagination of anyone I know. She's so much fun I can't stop laughing every time I'm around her, even though we are so different in many ways.

I'm the moderate Democrat my daddy nicknamed "Pinky Jane" after hearing Archie Bunker calling Gloria and Meathead that one night, referring to Jane Fonda's antics. Sister Sandy is the conservative Republican given to the occasional bout of proselytizing.

No matter, she's as twisted as I am. But even though we twist, it all ends up straight; we just have much more fun than a lot of stiffs afraid of tossing Drs. Spock, Sears, Brazelton, etc., down the drain and going with the flow.

Because my sister is also a good writer, and because I've had my period THREE times this month and a cyst on an ovary the size of a full-grown Yorkie, because I can't write another word without crying or cussing, this chapter will be one of those, "By Sandy Gambrell Edinger as told to Susan Gambrell Reinhardt."

I've always read those strange bylines and never knew what they meant, and still don't but here you have it: the story of my sister, the Preschool Assistant Extraordinaire.

For the past year or so, she's somehow gone from the lap of luxury (during her marriage to rich Wig Man David, or Daddy Warbucks), to the lap of the working world after marrying the wonderful and delightful Internet David. That's right, two Davids. Makes it easy on the family.

Her job is at a very ritzy and Christian preschool. She works with the 2- and 3-year-olds with a licensed teacher who has NEVER come across anything like my wild and unconventional sister and her way with the children.

In her own words, with a few of mine added, since this is one of those "as told to" stories, I'm going to let her have the page.

By Sandy Edinger, preschool assistance extraordinaire, as told to Susan Reinhardt, preschool fool, who now knows what those teachers were REALLY thinking as they peered in my child's lunch box.

Snack Time

It's always interesting to see what the mothers pack their little ones for snack time. We only have their little darlings for three short hours, but some mothers pack as if their child was going to a concentration camp. We always send the food not eaten home as a hint to mom that maybe she's packing too much. Next, we politely tell them that their child is not eating all of the smorgasbord she has so lovingly created. After that, their snack becomes fair game.

"Samantha's mom packed grapes, cheese, carrots, pretzels and goldfish. I'm eating the grapes. She's got juice anyway," I say.

"Get the pretzels for the snack drawer," chimes Sally, my coworker.

By the end of the year the snack drawer is full of junk food we have taken to feed the poor child whose horrible mother forgets to pack snacks. It's funny, too, to see just which kids get what for snack. We have a child who is extremely cute and chubby. Everyone thinks he looks just like a Cabbage Patch Doll. It is a problem for the parents because the majority of that cuteness comes from the rolls of fat that testify to his eating habits.

Oh, yeah, it's cute to see that chubby little cherub, but he is indeed overweight and it shows during gym time, not to mention diaper time. As a result of previous experiences with the plump and precious, we came up with a new practice: snack modification. Snack modification goes something like this:

"John brought sausage biscuits and Chips Ahoy! for snack with chocolate milk. What's in the snack drawer?"

"Hurl the biscuit. I'm getting pretzels for him. See if Lisa has extra fruit."

Circle Time

Circle time is when Sally teaches the curriculum and I practice crowd control. As one can imagine, getting a dozen 2- and 3-year-olds to sit still for more than two minutes can be a challenge. Having them sit without probing bodily orifices is even more daunting a task. This is where I developed a little curriculum of my own.

One day during Circle Time, and right after a particularly nasty round of bad colds had circulated throughout the class population, little fingers were working overtime in the nasal regions. After forcing about six hands down and sending several children to the tissue box, I noticed William, the prepster. Little Will's finger had completely disappeared into his nostril. Giant bulges were appearing on the side of his nose where he was working. For some reason I was fascinated by his work. Boldly, he dug deeper than any of the other kids dared go. Sally was distracted by my unusual calm and attention towards one child so she glanced in the direction of my gaze. She, too, was mesmerized.

We both watched the craftsman at work. The frantic digging seemed to take forever. And then suddenly there it was. On the tip of his tiny finger shone a prize-winning nasal creation.

That was my reality check. Grabbing him by the wrist so that this tantalizing morsel wouldn't make it into his mouth, I shouted, "He scored!!" as I whisked him to the tissue box.

That was the day I had had enough. My new curriculum was born: "Proper Picking."

In fact, the first lesson was held that day. When Will came back, I interrupted class. I had the children stand up and told them we were going to learn how to properly pick our noses. Did they not know that the number one cause of nosebleeds in young children was caused by digital trauma?

I said, "My goodness, you are all just a bunch of pickers, aren't you?"

And Little Savannah replied, "We are, aren't we, Mrs. Sandy?"

After teaching the children to grab a tissue before probing, we put the system into practice. Now we applaud "proper picking" each time we catch our children grabbing a tissue first.

"Hooray! Hooray! Carly is the proper picker of the DAY!"

Word of the Day

For some reason, Sally likes to teach the children a "three-dollar" Word of the Day. She always chooses words like "hilarious" or "imagination." Then she uses the word frequently throughout our day, having the children repeat the sentence. I like to mess her up some days by taking control of the task of coming up with the word of the day. Once, my Word of the Day was "rodent." Another time it was "bunion."

"We will be feasting on rodent stew tonight, children," she might say. "Rodents are the other white meat and can be found late at night or before dawn on most roadways."

Or, better still, she'll say: "There's nothing quite like a large bunion with which to scare off a potentially fine male suitor. Girls, remember proper foot care. Select the correct shoes and you shall be BUNION FREE!"

(Note from me, the real author . . . I'm afraid my sister's days at the preschool may be numbered.)

Preschool Penis Envy

In preschool there are scheduled potty breaks. State regulations require that we leave the door open so, on occasion, one child will wander in while another is doing his business. One day, Tony, a beautiful African American boy, was tinkling. Now, everyone has heard the saying about how African Americans have been blessed in the groin area. Let me say this before anyone who is extrasensitive gets their dander up. I'm not, by any stretch of the imagination, a racist.

All I'm saying is that we've all heard that wonderful rumor about the African American penis. You know you have. Now, I'm the one who usually handles potty time. I have seen all the boys go tinkle, and wieners of all shapes and sizes. I have two boys of my own, so seeing a penis is nothing new to me. However, on this particular day, Sally was doing potty duty. As Tony was going tinkle, little Joey wanders in and decides to take on half of the potty. Sally turns around to correct the situation just in time to hear Joey, mouth gaping and eyes wide, screaming, "Wow, that's a big, giant penis!"

As Sally rushes in, she catches a glimpse of Tony's prize region and her face contorts to the mirror image of little Joey's. Flustered, she yells "SANDY, you've gotta see Tony's penis. I, I, I've never seen anything like it. It's so much bigger than my son's was! I think it's the size of my husband's."

I had already seen Tony's penis so its magnitude was not news to me. However, I like to mess with Sally, so I casually walked over to the scene.

Tony was just standing there, typical grin on his face, adorable as ever. I said, "Tony, you've got it going on, don't ya, little man? You're packing some heat!"

He just smiled as he dried his little hands by the sink and said, "Mrs. Sandy, I packin' some heat!"

A Case of OAC

One of my major frustrations is when the industrious and talented main teacher, Sally, chooses what I call an overly ambitious craft. An OAC is a craft that is way above the fine-motor-skills capability for this age group. This means that it is actually she and I who end up doing most of the work for the children while the rest of the class plays at their centers or picks boogers.

I am always hinting to Sally by saying things like, "Sally, don't you think your need to use a hot glue gun, barbed wire, a circular saw and a reproduction of the electric chair for this project is a major indicator that this is really not for the twos and threes?"

The thought that we may be losing control can also occur on rainy days when outside playtime is canceled. Apparently this feeling is shared by all of the classes who exist together on the lower level of our school. The only time teachers seem to arrive early is when it is raining. The competition for time with the electric babysitter (TV set) is fierce. The glow box, as I like to call the television, is great for those rainy days or those days when you need to finish an OAC.

Since teachers have to sign out the only glow box we all share, it is not uncommon to see them running in the building a good fifteen minutes before their scheduled time. Sally has been known to watch the weather report at night and then drive over to school just to sign us up. You just have to just love her.

Potty Training

I am shocked at how long parents are waiting to potty train their kids nowadays. Last year I had our entire class off diapers by Christmas. This year has been a struggle. In particular, we have three boys who just don't want to cooperate. Since they are all well over 3 years old, this is immensely frustrating. I'm always on the lookout for the "dook stance."

The dook stance is named for dogs and how they wander off to find a special place, stretch up into that tall, humped-back pose, and with an intense facial grimace, strain to push out their load. When you see a dog in that position, you know what's coming. It's the same with a child. They wander away from the pack, stand up tall, sometimes holding on to a chair or table for stability's sake, and with little faces turning red from strain, squeeze out their payloads.

When Sally and I spy the dook stance, panic ensues. "Ahh-hhhhhhhhhh, Sandy, John's in the dook stance. Hurry!" I grab little Johnny and whisk him to the pot. Sometimes we make it; most times we do not. I lift Johnny up onto the changing table—holding on to him with one hand, leaning out the door for air from time to time—and change him, all the while complaining that I might as well be changing my husband who is 6 feet 4 inches and 250 pounds.

Whew. "It's okay, Johnny, but next time we need to feed the potty. The potty's hungry. Everyone has to feed the potty or it will starve to death and we'll have to use a festering outhouse, which is a hole in the ground with snakes and old doodies. You don't want to squat over a pit of vipers and someone else's doodies, do you?"

He never pooped in his Pull-Ups again.

Gym Time

Gym time is fun for both the children and the teachers. It's a great chance to relax, have fun and get even. It's also a time when the selfish ambitions of this age show most.

Sometimes, we let the kids have scooters to chase each other with. "I want the blue one." "Gimmee the yellow one." "I want the purple one like Savannah's."

This is as irritating to a teacher as fingernails raking the blackboard. I had to handle this situation early in the school year. How could I deal with this whining all year? I came up with a plan.

The next time it happened, I just looked at the first whiner and said, "You'll get what you get and you'll like it." Except I didn't really say it, I hissed it. He just stared at me, eyes wide-open, not knowing whether to laugh or cry. The next child dared to utter her color preference. She got the hiss as well.

And so it went, down the line. I hissed at most all of the kids that day. Then I gave each one a little giggle.

"You're so silly, Mrs. Sandy," they said.

Silly? Maybe, but my plan worked. At least I thought it did until I started hearing the kids at the Lego table hissing at one another, saying, "I have a bunion in my nose and the potty is hungry and a rodent is in the outhouse and Tony is packing heat."

I just wonder how long my adorable sister will last at the up-scale preschool. If they're smart, they'll double her pay and give her tenure.

In closing, I'd like to thank my sister for sharing her experiences. I realize that if you are a young mother reading this, you'd just LOVE to have Sister Sandy as your baby angel's preschool teacher!

She rocks. Plus, she's a Proper Picker.

They Call Him Flipper, She Calls Him Hubby

I know it's sometimes hard to find the right man.

But marrying a fish, I tell you, can't possibly be the answer, even if that fish is really a dolphin, which is technically a mammal.

A woman from London who couldn't seem to find a decent man, decided to up and marry a dolphin. I'd much rather be known as the crazy lady who runs over and gives her dog a serotonin reuptake inhibitor than one who takes up with a dolphin.

Well, bless his bottle-nosed heart. At least the woman landed herself a warm-blooded hubby and one who wouldn't make her cook hot meals at night or wear thongs for his viewing pleasure.

I imagine that when she met and married her darling dolphin, the phone call to her mother must have gone something like this:

Ring, Ring, Ring. Answering is the British mother of this rich, middle-aged daughter who's breathless with exciting news.

"Mums, how are you? It's me, your little Sharon, and I've finally found a husband who seems to truly fancy me."

"Well, darling, that's jolly good. You sure waited long enough. What's his bloody name, and what does he do for a living?"

"It's Cindy, but don't worry. He's a male and is 35 years old and perfect for me. I love him so much."

"Delightful, sweetheart, but what in God's name does this

chap do for a living? The last thing you brought in here had no job or a single prospect other than being a completely asinine sycophant."

"He's in the entertainment business and doing quite well," reported Sharon, the happy and blushing bride. "His aquatic skills are incomparable."

"Lovely, darling. Do be a dear and bring this young man to dinner, my love."

Pause. "But Mum, I can't. He lives in Israel at a resort and reef and has many shows left to perform."

"Surely he can take some time off for his beloved bride and motor on up to meet his new family, my dear."

Longer pause and a few deep inhalations. "Mother . . . I've . . . er . . . Well, it would appear as such that I've married a . . . um . . . Well, some call them dolphins."

Silence ensues, followed by the sound of gurgling, ice cubes rattling in a glass, and perhaps bourbon flowing like water.

"It's not like we're not both mammals, Mum."

I figure at that point her dear mum hit the floor and the phone went bouncing down the stairwell. This is what I imagined when I read about Sharon Tendler's telling of relatives about her nuptials last year with Cindy, her "boy-toy" dolphin she met fifteen years ago while vacationing in Israel.

Although the story of this rich Londoner marrying a dolphin sounds fishy, it's apparently true. The media was abuzz when Tendler took the plunge and exchanged vows with Cindy in the waters of the groom's home.

Not since the controversy about Tinky Winky and Sponge-Bob SquarePants being fay or gay has the press had such a rollicking good time with a story.

"At least it wasn't a same-sex marriage," quipped a coworker who'd had too much sugar one afternoon.

I Googled the woman's name, and tons of stories from reputable news sources popped up about her "marriage" to the dolphin who'd become the love of her life. The reports say that when she met Cindy the connection sparked and she began visiting him at the resort several times a year.

As for the ceremony, the bride wore a white dress to the dock at Dolphin Reef, becoming the first person in the world to wed a dolphin, shocking a huge crowd of spectators. She bent on one knee, her hair framed in a veil and pink flowers, and gave Cindy a kiss and a nice piece of mackerel.

The salty groom was waiting in the water after the ceremony, and friends tossed the happy bride into the pool to frolic with her new husband, their own version of a consummation.

Another sugared-up and naughty but hilarious coworker suggested Cindy's bottlenose might come in handy sometime.

"I'm the happiest girl on Earth," Tendler was quoted saying. "I made a dream come true, and I'm not a pervert. I really do love this dolphin."

According to the reports, the woman fell in love with this Flipper at first sight. She became the world's first person to "marry" a dolphin, though many of us doubt this union is legal.

This was the strangest story I'd come across since the one about a woman from Norway breast-feeding a litter of 17 orphaned pups, or the cat that dialed 911 for his unconscious owner.

I'll tell you a secret about how I discover this kind of news. Truth is, I sit right next to the entertainment editor who also writes the Beer Guy column and while slightly tipsy (a job requirement), he shows me these tidbits on the wire services. He has the kind of job where it is required he sample beers on company time, poor man.

The features staff sit in a section of the newsroom I call the Colon, since there are no windows, and it's a long and straight alleyway that ends in an exit door—the last flush before one leaves the building.

We were all punchy from a hard and long day and trying to look on the bright side of this latest piece of bizarre news, thinking of advantages to having a husband at sea, so to speak. Here are our top reasons why marrying a dolphin could have certain perks:

1. He doesn't require three squares a day served from a hot oven or a cold beer poured after a tough day chasing skirts. Or, in his case, chasing fish.

2. He won't leave the toilet seat up in the bathroom or his dirty socks on the floor.

3. He probably won't be flipping through any of the Victoria's Secret catalogs.

4. He won't go to bars.

5. His bottlenose will never go limp, thus eliminating the future need for Viagra or testosterone treatments.

6. The bride doesn't have to see her hubby but a few times a year.

7. He can't tell her that her butt's gotten bigger than a chest of drawers or that her boobs hang like laundry on a line.

8. He won't notice when she's gray and wrinkled and missing half her teeth.

9. He'll never watch ESPN or want to spend hours in front of the TV during the NCAA basketball tournaments.

10. If he cheats on her, chances are she'll never know.

Later in the week, after testing a series of new microbrews at a local tavern and sitting at his computer to review and write about these high-alcohol content beverages, the Beer Guy scanned the wire again and brought up another winner. He was laughing so hard I thought he'd have a myocardial infarction or whatever those who drink and eat and are too merry often have.

"Seems a woman in Iran had given birth to a frog," he said, slurring slightly. "I'm not kidding, Sue. It's right here in black and white. I'll shoot you an e-mail and you'll see." He opened up a bag of barbecue potato chips to absorb his microbeer buzz.

I read the story a few times, then went online to make sure it was true. About twenty different news sources carried the story including the BBC.

"It's probably the biggest birthing news since eight-baby Mandy," the Beer Guy said. "Remember her? That British woman who back in the 90s packed eight fetuses in her womb but lost them all?"

The frog birth was reported by the legitimate press and illegitimate press.

I didn't know whether to laugh about the absurdity of it all or cry for the poor woman who had survived labor and saw nothing for her efforts but a wet, gray frog surrounded in mud. I wondered if her husband had a video camera. Or if she even had a husband. Maybe she was just a desperate person making up the entire thing.

The BBC online quoted the Iranian newspaper *The Etemaad* as saying that the amphibian grew inside the woman's body, and that she probably picked up the larva while swimming in a dirty pool. Another news source said the gray frog was born alive and full term.

The paper never reported how much it weighed, or whether they put it in an incubator or slipped one of those cute little caps on its head—all questions I wanted to know. It did say that the woman had two healthy HUMAN children.

While the frog-child has yet to undergo genetic tests, *The Etemaad* says it sports quite a few human characteristics. If this is true, it's DEFINITELY the strangest story I've ever read. It reminded me of the woman in *My Big Fat Greek Wedding* who told the parents of her granddaughter's prospective groom that the lump on her neck was her former twin.

According to news reports, a clinical biology expert is quoted as saying: "The similarities (between frog and human) are in appearance, the shape of the fingers and the size and shape of the tongue." I thought frogs had, like, 24-inch tongues. If so, this frog-child got shortchanged getting a human tongue.

I learned from one newspaper that the woman had a sonogram that showed a cyst, and for six months she didn't have her monthly cycle. The cyst turned out to be the frog. I don't know if I buy any of it, but comedians and jokesters all over the country, including friends and colleagues in our Colon, had a field day with the topic.

One of the sweetest people in the newsroom had this to say:

"What's wrong with having a frog? I'd take it. It might be the only baby you ever have."

And she was right. Think of the many benefits of birthing a froglet. I'll name some:

1. There would be fewer flies in the house.

2. You wouldn't get stretch marks.

3. I doubt there'd be a need for an epidural or episiotomy.

4. You'd save a fortune on swim lessons.

5. He'd be the Olympic Gold medallist in the long jump.

6. You'd never again be the ugliest person in the room.

Now, here are the downsides of mothering a frog:

1. Decorating the nursery would be difficult, as an indoor pond might be costly and tadpole wallpaper is hard to come by.

2. Cuddling could cause warts.

3. The loud croaking could keep other family members up at night.

All in all, there were more bonuses in adding a frog to the family than in not. One thing is certain: I'm not swimming in any dirty lakes this summer.

Forget Muskrat Love

What used to be considered a great Friday or Saturday night for dateless girls with A-cup bras and no fake ID cards was making prank phone calls.

It was a pastime of my youth, a standard game at all-girl sleepovers prior to getting older and playing Spin the Bottle.

With caller ID, Star 69 and other gotcha features, those pranking days are extinct unless you don't mind going to prison or paying hefty fines.

A few years ago, to get the immature thrills of the Crank Call days, I discovered message boards, and even a chat room where I thought I could anonymously act ugly and never get caught. I realize this is juvenile and probably a definable psychiatric condition, but I swear it cured my blues about as well as chocolate, target shooting, shopping and fiendish eBay bidding.

It all started innocently enough and with good intentions, shortly after I'd found a message board devoted to a tropical island to which my husband and I were destined. We'd gotten a deal on an all-inclusive vacation package and I wanted to make sure I knew everything possible about the island, the hotel and its amenities. The more I read, the more convinced I became that the resort we'd chosen was a hangout for rowdy Spring Breakers, skanks, drunks, lechers and pervs.

This is when I decided to adopt an alter ego and transform

myself into the abominable Stinker Jenkins Brown, the bawdy cyberdrunk who liked prostitutes and corn "likker," and would strike every few days to scare potential college-age vacation customers from the destination we'd chosen.

I was afraid loud partygoers would overtake the place, and if I posed as Stinker Jenkins Brown coming to fester up the joint, maybe people would decide to go another week rather than the one we'd chosen, or panic and switch hotels. This is mean, I realize, and will buy you a coach class, one-way ticket to Hell if you asked my mama, but since it *was* Spring Break and most were just in the "Which Resort to Book" phase of the deal, I wanted to steer them elsewhere.

I figured the staff would thank me in the end because such a group of ne'er-do-wells would tear up the hotel and repairs could cost a fortune. It's much cheaper to have a hotel half-full of decent, law-abiding adults than having hundreds of Spring Breakers busting furniture, getting injured during drunk-capades and bringing about major lawsuits.

Thus Stinker Jenkins Brown, age 62 and right out of prison, hit the message board and told all excited posters he was headed to St. Paradise to stay in the White Sands Resort and Villas. He struck the boards with a whiskey'd bang, and the following are examples of his posts showcasing my more ludicrous behavioral flaws.

(I figure my immaturity is physically healthier than bulimia or meth-making, and financially sounder than a QVC or Home Shopping Network addiction. My mother, if she knew about Stinker Jenkins, would refuse to speak to me for at least four years. However, I came to love Stinker, and would release him every evening after supper and a few Michelobs in the months leading up to our first Caribbean vacation in fifteen years.)

"Howdy, people. My name's Stinker Jenkins Brown and I'm an old cuss from the hollers, fresh out of jail for a sex charge I didn't commit 'cause by God she begged fur it and had just turned 13. She had more of a mustache than I do. That

said and done, I need to escape and get really trashed and chase girls I'm not related to. I'm tired of my aunts and cousins. Hee har. So get ready folks. I'll be at the White Sands Resort and Villas on April 2, with four of my best 'Pen' friends, which in case you don't know, stands for penitentiary buds. I'm even getting my back waxed for the event and a new tattoo where the sun don't shine."

For a month leading up to this trip we'd saved for years to take, Stinker appeared almost daily on the board, answering others' posts with his hick wit and sarcasm. One poor man who kept posting irritating questions got the best of Stinker when he asked for the fourth time where on St. Paradise was the perfect place to take his new bride for a fabulous shrimp dinner.

Stinker doesn't cotton to men using the word "fabulous."

Here's what the man wrote—a man more obsessed with Shrimp than is Bubba from the movie *Forrest Gump:*

"I really want it to be special. She's my dream girl and loves shrimp and romance. I've never met a woman who loves shrimp this much so I want it to be the best money can buy. Please advise on fabulous shrimp. P.S. She even makes her own shrimp pancakes every Sunday morning."

Stinker Jenkins Brown had some mighty fine advice:

"Take that little piece of legal ass to Captain D's or Long John's," he wrote. "There ain't one on St. Paradise, but if you catch the ferry for about $20 a pop and then a bus for another $10 over to Cancun, you'll see both places on restaurant row. It's only an hour away and worth every damned penny. Both them restaurants have your deep fried and heavily battered shrimp plates for about $3.99 each or you can super-size for another 40 cents or so. I'll probably be there, too, as an added bonus for your dining pleasure."

The guy wrote back right away, typing out a single word:

"Dickhead."

Stinker also answered all questions on the board related to where to find good parties and easy women:

"You'uns jest need to meet me at the White Sands Resort and Villas. I'll have every hooker within a 10-mile radius by my side and gallons of corn likker. Come on down and party with good old Stinkeroo! I might even warsh my privates for the occasion."

A few weeks after the birth of Stinker I got kicked off the board, apparently by the site monitor who tracked my IP address and information. Incidentally, when we got to the resort, my meanness came back to haunt me (just as Mama said it would) and most of the hotel's clientele were drunk old men. Probably those who were waiting to party all night with Stinker Jenkins Brown and his Chain Gang.

That experience, unfortunately, didn't cure my message board banditing, and I'd strike here and there, as if I was 12 again with eight giggling girls on my green shag carpeting, half-tucked into sleeping bags and the pink Princess phone in the center of us, right next to the Southern Bell phone book listing everyone in LaGrange, Georgia, and surrounding areas.

The next time I needed information on a topic I knew where to go. Straight to the message boards. This particular incident concerned my new hamster, and I searched lovingly for the ideal board devoted solely to these adorable, precious-faced rodents. I'd bought a golden hamster at the mall, a starter pet for my children in the pre-dog years.

As soon as I got the beloved rat home, he began pooping so much his entire body turned wet and yucky, all the pine shavings in his cage sticking to his inside-out rectum. His fanny swelled and his brown eyes shrank. He could barely sip water and he smelled awful, an overpowering stench that permeated the entire house.

I checked out one of the various hamster discussion boards and read some of the posts, hoping for insight as to the types of ailments hamsters encountered and the solutions these kind people would offer. Here's what I found—a site that offered more entertainment than I could ever find on cable TV:

> **Help Me I'm Sorta Dumb** wrote: *My friend's hamster had some of the symptoms of what I think might be a stroke or even a demon. And now I have a couple of questions. After she was done playing with him, she went to put him back in his cage and the hamster would twist around, flopping his body and his head around like an evil spirit had overtaken him. He tried to hang like a bat but was foaming and growling. He bared his big bottom teeth and green stuff frothed down his chin. What could this possibly mean?*

A concerned hammy owner—**God Loves Hammies, too** from Ohio—answered the question and offered wisdom:

> *You must get him into church immediately. Make sure he's on various prayer lists. I had one do the same thing, took it to the vet, and they said, "All you can do at this stage is pray."*

Good Lord. These posts about hamster disorders and behaviors caused me to wonder two things: Were these people for real or just zealots and perverts with fetishes? Could such a small pet possibly become inflicted with so many maladies, both of the physical and mental variety?

Then there was **Newly Widowed** from South Dakota, who wrote:

> *My cute lovely golden hammy is dead. Last night he was sleeping like a baby, and when I examined him this morning, I go and see that he had something stuck in his abdomen, and at*

first I think maybe it's one of them 'outie' type belly buttons, so I tried pulling on the crusty tip but it only hurt him. He yelped and had real tears on his face. This morning he was dead. I guess he's in a better place.

"This must be a joke site," I said to myself, as I figured it was now safe to type in my own concerns about my new pet's blistered and soaking-wet fanny. My husband entered the room, hearing me talking to myself and noticed the screen where a bunch of dancing hamster icons decorated the page.

"What is that? My God! Are you on a hamster Web site?" he asked.

"No, I'm on a 'How to Poison Your Husband and Not Get Caught' discussion board."

"Get a life!" he muttered and trudged to bed because it was 2 AM and his wife was talking about teddy bear hamster troubles instead of wearing a teddy from Victoria's Secret and getting friendly on the Sealy.

While waiting on someone to reply to my post, I read a few more, because the truth is, the board was hilarious and much more engaging than my mattress at this stage of the marital game.

This headline, from a concerned hammy parent, caught my attention immediately: HE AIN'T GOT NO EYES!

I recently received a hamster that was born with no eyes. I was wondering if that would affect his ability to breed with a normal female hamster.

My fingers itched. I felt a prank coming on and just couldn't help it. Oh, if only I was a normal woman who could go to the mall, buy some Estée Lauder and get this out of my system, but NO! I was 12 years old again, my head in pink sponge curlers, my girlfriends giggling all around as I opened the phone book to the Italian restaurant section to order a Sheep's Ear Pizza or to Eckerd Drugs so I could pretend to be Chinese, trying my best to ask for sanitary napkins.

"You haffa fagina Band-Aid, mistah?"

My fingers, shaking slightly, hit the computer keys as if numbers on the Princess phone of my youth while I answered HE AIN'T GOT NO EYES!

"Actually, it could help matters if your hammy "ain't got no eyes," Love is blind, as they say, and a frisky hammy, like a frisky hubby, needeth no eyes as long as they have a pointing stick, if you get my drift."

Not yet tired and enjoying these reads, I continued the message chatting and posting.

LAZY HAMSTER!!!!!
"My hamster is so lazy. She's never up early in the morning or late at night. Why is she so sleepy when she sleeps 24 hours a day? And how can I stop her from being lazy?"

Well, that's a no-brainer.

"Get her a husband," I typed. "She'll never have another moment's peace or rest."

After about an hour of this No-Life nonsense, I finally received a couple of replies to my post. The others said I needed to take my darling hamster to a vet immediately and that the condition was one called WET TAIL and completely and utterly fatal within days. By the time I had discovered this message board and wealth of help, it was too late. The vet put my poor hammy to sleep and I sat there and cried like a baby even though I'd only had it five days.

I soon bought another that lived two years and died from tumors that erupted on his sides, exploding goiters I treated with Neosporin and love. I'd take him out for walks and feed him forbidden foods, knowing he had cancer and I needed to give him joy in his last days. Often I'd slip Motrin and mild tranquilizers in his water bottle and he seemed at peace and even smiled slightly on several occasions.

The next hamster, Hammy III, died of a heart attack. I'm certain of it because of her position in the aquarium. I came home from work and she was lying on her side, one paw clutching her tiny rodent heart and the other reaching out as if to dial 911. Her face registered chest pains and her eyes bugged out.

We buried her in tinfoil and a shoebox, just like we did with Hammy I and Hammy II. The message board and kind supporters said, *"We feel your pain and are here for you."*

They understood what the common man didn't—and that was how fetching and attaching a hamster could be, these tiny teddy bears of the heart.

It's a comforting thought to know that when I graduate to a guinea pig, there is also a message board for those angels of the rodent world.

Doggy Liposuction and Humpathons

A wonderful coworker came into the office the other morning quite distraught about her dog. We know people love their pets as if they were children—some more—giving the kids the Alpo and the dog the blackened tuna with the raspberry ginger sauce.

"What's the matter, Melissa?" I asked, noticing she wasn't her typical smiling self. She's never been one of those irritatingly chipper coworkers who change personalities when their Lexapro kicks in, but she's always pleasant.

"It's my dog," she said, and sat at her desk, slowly turning on her computer to begin another day in the Features department. "She's had major surgery."

I took a bite of my 65 percent dark cocoa candy bar, a must for a journalist on deadline when the boss won't let you have a pint of Wild Turkey. "Is she OK, hon?"

"Her bottom will be sore for a while, but much more comfortable. It was getting so large she couldn't even walk."

I thought I'd heard incorrectly. Was she saying her dog had a superfat ass that needed surgery? Or did she mean perhaps a St. Bernard had tried to hump the dog and got stuck?

I tried to imagine what sort of ailment the animal could have had. "She's home, right?" I was asking questions trying to ease into my real question: "What in the world happened to that dog?"

"She's getting better, and the pain meds are helping. Poor Stella."

All right, enough, damn it. I'm asking.

"Hon, what happened to Stella?—if you don't mind talking about it."

She looked up from her computer. "No, I'm all right. She had some liposuction and they used lots of stitches."

I about dropped my chocolate bar and would have but it had cost $3. She couldn't have possibly said her dog had lipo. Could she?

"Liposuction. You mean that procedure where they jab giant suction tubes in you and crank up a slurping machine?"

"Uh-huh."

"Why and on what area would your dog need lipo, sugar?"

By now, several coworkers were listening and a smile crept on Melissa's face.

"Her vulva," Melissa said. "It just kept getting larger and larger every day."

Well, heaven forbid. I'd never heard anything like this in all my twenty-five years writing for the paper and believe me, I've endured some real crazies calling up with wild stories. An elderly man swore that a gorilla tried to climb into the passenger side of his restored DeSoto automobile one morning. "I could tell he loved my car and wanted to drive it," the man said. "Call my neighbors, I've got proof." I'm quite certain his neighbors were the men behind bars right next to him.

Melissa, though, is a sane and rational woman, making me wonder why she entered into journalism in the first place.

"Did I hear you correctly? Did you say your dog had surgery on its vulva?" I tried to remember what a vulva was, knowing it was some part belonging to the possum.

She nodded and I couldn't help it. I started laughing. Then she began to laugh, and the entire department, with the exception of a dullard, laughed, too. Turns out one day that doggy's possum began to swell and never stopped, soon becoming so large it was frightening to others and debilitating to the dog.

One isn't used to seeing dogs with big old vaginas like the butts on baboons.

I was like a 13-year-old boy in sex-ed class, unable to control my laughter. Poor dog. Poor old pooch with a giant puss!

Melissa is a good sport and didn't mind revealing all the uplifting details concerning how her beautiful dog, Stella, one she rescued from death, began developing GDVS—Giant Dog Vagina Syndrome. Each day her canine's vulva continued growing until soon it was dragging the ground like a long wedding-gown train.

She took Stella to the vet. Well, let me tell you something. That dog got the royal treatment. You've heard of the latest surgery Dr. Rey on 90210 does? Puss-beautification procedures? Women going in because they don't like how their Coochie Snorchers look after having had kids? Well, this dog got the works and then some!

"They performed liposuction of the vulva and cut parts of it out," Melissa said, as poker-faced as if reporting a news story on air. I wondered why she didn't burst out laughing. I also used to wonder how those people talking about Kotex and FDS didn't crack up on the commercials, too.

"Stella looks and feels so much better."

I checked and Stella's vet confirmed that the dog had a nip and a tuck. You may think that's strange but lots of people, especially Hollywood and socialite types, send their animals in for plastic surgery procedures to make them better-looking. I'm not making this up. Google it and you'll see.

According to an article at www.msnbc.com, facelifts, tummy tucks, nose jobs, breast reductions, testicular implants and cosmetic dentistry aren't just for rich humans beings. Some of the procedures, as in precious Stella's case, are necessary, while others are simply the choices of vain owners.

In Hollywood, there's actually a doc they call "Veterinarian to the Stars." The most popular surgeries involving pets include reconstructive operations, vets say, but occasionally a dog owner isn't happy about sagging teats or ugly fannies.

Let's say, for instance, the dog's eyelids drooped to the point he couldn't see his pan-fried grouper encrusted with almonds and a lemon butter sauce? Or her tummy got so big it scraped the ground when she tried to walk across a room.

Some dog breeds truly have conditions that lend themselves to plastic surgeries such as full facelifts (think basset hounds) eyelifts, rhinoplasty and tummy tucks, vets say. The cost is usually about $1,000 a pop.

Which leads me to the question I plan to ask Stella's vet who has yet to return my follow-up calls and it's been six months:

"Could you perhaps do a tummy tuck on me if you are able to do one on a dog? I'm not much bigger than a Great Dane."

Think of the money we'd all save by not paying the Dr. Reys of the world $9,000 for the job. I could pay Stella's vet and come out looking like Halle Berry for a fraction of that price.

Here's what one vet said, ignoring me when I decided to ask *him* for a tummy tuck.

"The most common areas for our plastic surgery expertise concern an animal's skin folds, particularly around the eyes, lips, tail and vaginal areas."

"That's wonderful. I'll take it all, except for the vaginal area. My belief is, 'If I don't HAVE to see it, why bother fixing it?'"

This doctor did not laugh.

I also learned that chin lifts are common in dogs to curb excessive drooling, which would be really good for drunken golfers in Myrtle Beach who hit the titty bars at night. And dental work can be performed on dogs. Think of all those breeds with underbites.

One vet said he performed a root canal on a ferret. And many say braces are fairly common. My opinion is that if a vet would go to that much trouble, why can't he toss a few willing Human Case Studies into the mix and see how the results come out?

In the end, Stella's vulva returned to near normal, with the exception of a vagina that moved higher and can now be seen by the naked eye just below her tail where her anus used to be.

I'm not sure where the anus is. Maybe somewhere along her spine?

The point of all this is that pets are expensive and can cause more chaos than a bunch of children running loose.

My former dog Putt-Putt—the one we bought from the two-fannied lady, a woman with a big hanging front ass and not much of a back butt—had wrecked two cars, chewed through $500 worth of plantation shutters, gnawed the cushions out of all the family's shoes and amputated every Barbie my daughter owns.

This was about when Stuart decided to get the Pomeranian, especially since Putt-Putt hated his guts and bit him every chance she got. Prior to our Pom's being weaned and ready, I had Putt-Putt spayed and found her a loving home.

Why people endure what pets do is beyond me. We love them so much, at least the good owners do, we spend our last dimes on their vet bills. And I can attest to doggy vet bills costing more than it did for me to have both my children combined. I kid you not.

On a recent afternoon, close to quitting time at my workplace, members of WAG—Whining About Grossness—an informal dog owner's support group, met up in the office hallway near the watercooler. We are several members strong and feel the great need to purge any and all disasters and destructive behaviors of our dogs.

One of the members was concerned because her dog, Wesley, a mix of various fine breeds, won't stop staring at her when she sits at the table.

"He doesn't even blink," she said. "It's the weirdest thing."

"He's waiting for food," I said.

"No, he's got food."

"Table food," I said. "They'll sit hours waiting for a single canned green bean. They hate their dog food. They'd rather eat rutabagas than a hefty mess of kibbles."

"Mine still eats poop," another member said.

"Well, at least that saves you on dog food bills," someone offered.

"To be so sweet, dogs can sure be nasty," I said, and told them about the elegant luncheon I'd attended last fall, the women all dressed up and making polite conversation, when suddenly the hostess's pedigreed pet got "The Fever" and engaged in an X-rated session with a giant throw pillow.

"Conversation ceased," I said, "and the women froze in horror, clutching their delicate wineglasses, wondering whether to guzzle booze or enjoy the show."

"Maybe they were getting some lessons to take home to their Viagra'd men," the wittiest of our WAG bunch suggested.

"That's why you should have animals spayed and neutered," a more practical WAGGER suggested.

"That doesn't stop their urges," I said. "They're like randy old men. They'll run all over town making condolence calls. They still have the basic package. I mean, do all women with hysterectomies or men with vasectomies cease having urges? You do the math."

Everyone I know who owns a dog has a memory jammed with expensive anecdotes.

My sister's Chihuahua swallowed a baby-bottle nipple and had to have $900 worth of surgery. I considered myself lucky that our Putt-Putt, after eating Barbie's hands and feet and a chunk of my husband's leg, will simply throw it all up on the carpet.

For the animal extremists who are offended by these tales, I'd like to point out that we love our furry demolition derby, the latest member of our family, the Pomeranian we named Zipper because he zips all over the house.

We give our pride and joy two squares a day, vet care and, recently, had him neutered, trying to keep the population down as well as save on those embarrassing moments when the pooch takes great interest in a visitor's leg. I will say it didn't work and he humps his stuffed monkey every chance he can.

After little Zipper's pubic alterations, my then 4-year-old who's now 8, saw the vet's handiwork and decided the dog was now neither male nor female but a mixture of both.

"Will he have to go to the bathroom twice as much now?" she asked, big eyes shining in wonder. All I could do, all any dog owner can do, is laugh. Otherwise we'd go insane.

My latest incident with Zipper ended up causing a riot among a few readers who decided, once again, I must be the most evil and neglectful pet owner born on this planet.

It all happened when I ran over him, just a wee tad.

My poor, poor dog. First, the good news: he's alive.

Now the bad: he has no business being that way. Not after THREE brushes with death in a single day. It was all my fault, and I admitted as much to the PETA people. I even told them to look up my name in their files and see I was once a member and contributor and LOVE animals.

It was simply one of those wild days when I was on the phone half the morning, working from my home office and enduring the type of conversation that leaves a girl rattled. Five minutes after hanging up, I backed out of the driveway and noticed the postman near the mailbox. I proceeded to the STOP sign and felt a slight *thump-thump* followed by an atmosphere-splitting noise.

Jumping from the car, I raced to the middle of the road where Zipper, my black Pomeranian, yelped and yowled from the asphalt, his hindquarters unmoving.

Pomeranians are known for their histrionics. They will act as if they are dying if someone so much as tries to clip their little toenails. Divas, they are.

The mailman stopped inserting letters. "Did I run over him?" I asked.

He nodded. I leaned over Zipper, who was by now moving both legs and trying to smile. That's another thing about Pomeranians. They smile, honestly. I scooped him up gently and rushed him to the animal hospital where I cried and cried, just like I did after putting one of my hamsters to sleep. The dog panted and tried to squirm from my lap to investigate the premises, as dogs are wont to do.

They called my name from the front counter. "Mrs. Reinhardt?"

"I, uh, ran over my dog." The staff and those in the waiting area gasped. "I only ran over him a tad."

They took him back to an exam room immediately, and the vet, a nice young man, said nothing appeared broken but ordered X-rays to make sure and to increase my total bill by several hundred dollars.

Later that afternoon, my family picked up Zipper and called to report he was bruised but doing well. Lucky, considering. When I got home from work, I figured the dog was sore and I'd give him his pain pills.

"Where's Zipper's medicine?" I asked, wanting to make up for my having run over him a wee tad by getting him stoned on some doggy narcotics.

"Right on the counter," a voice from upstairs yelled.

I picked up a large bottle, quickly scanning the label. Bupropion. Hmm. Sounds like an opiate derivative to me. This is going to be one happy dog. I opened the bottle. Lord, what a huge pill—purple, too, like the kind I'd imagine Barney (the irritating TV dinosaur whose voice gives me hives and seizures) would take.

For some strange reason, this pill looked familiar. I chopped it up and mixed it with some cheese. The dog gave me a weird look and ate the medicated snack, especially after I opened his maw, which he had clamped tighter than a clam shell, and stuffed the pill down his throat.

And then, like a hammer over the head, it hit me. Oh, no. No, please, no. Don't let this be true. "God help us all and don't let this be what I think it is. Please. I'm begging, God. I'll do good deeds for the rest of the month and won't snarl or say a mean thing about anyone. I'll visit shut-ins and make casseroles for old people. Well, maybe not. But I'll at least cook something besides Tuna Helper for my family. I'll buy the Heavenly Ham for my mother-in-law on Easter and not the cheap free one at the grocery store."

I checked the bottle again. It had MY name on it. Bupropion. SHIT!!!! I knew now what it was: the generic formula for Wellbutrin. Oh, heavens, I'd given my dog an antidepressant often prescribed for people who want to quit smoking. Since I don't smoke, I take it as a de-groucher. It's supposed to make me more pleasant, but Mama says it isn't working and I'm grumpier than ever. Like she has room to talk, being a nearly 70-year-old woman still getting her period along with PMS.

This couldn't be good. A tiny dog cannot possibly survive 100 milligrams of Wellbutrin. I dialed four animal hospitals and a personal friend who's a vet.

"You WHAT?"

"I gave the dog a Wellbutrin by mistake."

"How much does he weigh?"

"About 12 pounds."

"You need to pour hydrogen peroxide down his throat until that pill comes up."

"Won't that kill him?" I squealed.

"No, but that pill will."

I called the neighbors across the street, the Parhams. Dr. John Parham is a physician at the Veteran's Administration Medical Center, and I was sure he'd know what to do. In my right mind I would possess better reasoning . . . maybe. On second thought, my calling Dr. Parham was similar in nature to a pregnant woman calling a dentist to check her cervix.

The dear man sent his sweet wife and daughter over with the peroxide and a dropper. We wrangled Zipper who was wilder than any rodeo animal and tried like the dickens to get the peroxide down him. We may have poured too much.

I kept waiting for him to throw up and thus his life spared. Nothing. An hour passed. Nothing. Another hour, nothing. He walked the wood floors as if drunk and hit the furniture and would lie down and paw the air. I called the vet again.

"It's too late now. If he hasn't died yet, maybe he won't. Keep watching him and give us a call if anything changes."

In the end, my dog survived. But all I could think of was how I nearly killed him three times (if you include pouring peroxide down his throat) within an eight-hour period.

Then a thought hit, the kind that always makes the guilty feel better. Rationalization. Maybe the Wellbutrin helped Zipper feel less depressed about getting a tad run over.

And maybe, just maybe, he'll never take up smoking.

Ten Toddlers and Girls Gone Wild

As Lindsey grew older, reaching the normal childhood milestones, I soon learned she had inherited my temperament (not a great thing) and curiosity.

I'll never forget when she was about a year old, and we were at the Chick-fil-A counter ordering our food. Lindsey was in her stroller and had a bird's-eye view of the counter's underbelly. As I considered my chicken options, my daughter grew so quiet I almost forgot she was there.

Rule No. 1 of parenting: When a child is quiet, NEVER, EVER relax. Those are the times something big is up.

I looked down at this precious bundle of cherubic joy. Then my mouth dropped along with two bags of food.

This stage in parenting is known as Motherly Mortification. My freshly scrubbed child had the brightest bluest lips I'd ever seen in my life. Electric Blue is what I'd call it if I was hired to choose Crayola names.

I reached into her chomping neon mouth and she was smacking on a piece of bright blue, preowned bubble gum, compliments of the fine selection left by unmannerly past diners. Apparently, she'd discovered quite the mother lode beneath one of the restaurant's tables, which were eye level with her stroller.

I nearly died wondering who'd chewed the gum first, imagining a mouth with oozing boils and festering pustules. I yanked a baby wipe from the container in my bag and stuffed it into Lindsey's mouth, cleaning like crazy as other frenzied parents stood nearby watching in utter fascination and probably thinking: "Who is this nut job sticking Huggies ass wipes in her daughter's mouth?"

After that, I decided that whatever she stuck in her mouth from the ground couldn't do as much damage. That's when the five-second rule came into play. If it hits the floor and you swoop it up within five seconds, it's good to gobble.

I figured this was much better than sucking carpet, which is exactly what a toddler did at my house during the year I joined a neighborhood babysitting co-op—translation: the one year I nearly pulled out every hair on my beady little head.

The couple in charge, adorable preppies, required a background check on both me and my husband. This was not cheap, my dearies.

When first asked to submit a police report to my own neighbors, I balked and decided I wasn't going to cooperate. I was quite ashamed, having had a checkered past and quite the record. The whole burb would know I had a DWI back in the 80s and a few speeding tickets, along with a second-degree trespassing for one of those college protest things. Not to mention they would find out I took down a telephone pole with my Subaru one evening in 1989. And that I drove with an expired license and tag back in '95 and protested a proposed rock quarry in college and landed in jail.

I always thought that after seven years, the slate was wiped clean. But it wasn't. Every little crime was there in black and white. In the end I paid the $60 bucks for the report, and as I handed over my tarnished record I turned six shades of red.

I prayed they wouldn't read it too closely—And they must not have because—the next Saturday night the doorbell rang and the babies and tots arrived. Moms and dads had big plans and I had big fears.

All in all, though, I thought, it went fairly well. To keep them entertained I popped in *Raising Arizona*, and popped corn, too. How was I to know what that movie was about?

My turn rolled around twice during that year.

Frankly, I'm surprised the parents even brought them after what happened last time. Then I realized it was close to Christmas and they were desperate to get in some last minute shopping, hobnobbing and eggnogging. They figured I had a pulse and respirations so I had to be a better sitter than their yellow labs were.

The doorbell began ringing.

"Hi there. Can you say hi to Ms. Reinhardt?" my dear friend Norm Lizarralde asked his two cherubs. Both boys, cute as speckled pups, tore out of their parents' arms and headed for the raw cookie dough in the kitchen.

"We won't be gone long," they said, and smiled, thrusting diaper bags and cell phone numbers into my hands. "Just be sure not to show them *Raising Arizona* again," Norm said, laughing.

"Yes . . . well . . . er . . . right. Sorry, Norm. I didn't realize it was PG-13. Tonight we're watching *Bad Santa*, with Billy Bob Thornton, but don't you worry, it doesn't even have a rating."

His face lost color.

"Just kidding. You and Julie go have some fun. We'll be fine. I passed the background check, remember? Hey, I was young and foolish," I said. "I'm not a pedophile. That ought to score some major points." Oops. Wrong subject.

Half an hour later my house was rocking with the Ten Toddlers and their squeals.

My son heard the raucous and scurried downstairs.

"I'll give you $5 an hour to help me out here," I said.

"No way. Ten plus extra if some are really awful."

I was desperate, "OK. Mr. Extortion."

Boy, tell a 13-year-old to pitch in during Romper Room Gone Wild is like asking him to tell a girl her hair is beautiful or actually dance at a school dance instead of standing around the snack bar and ordering M&M's and Sierra Mist.

He jumped right into his role as Toddler Teen Patrol. "Listen up, kids," he shouted. "I need you to all calm down and shut up."

"You can't tell them to shut up. They're babies."

All was going OK until I noticed one of the children wouldn't stop "nursing" the carpet downstairs. I realized it was old, but I never knew it could offer such sustenance. I tried everything possible to pry the neighbor's toddler from the fibers, but every time I attempted moving him, he screamed and kicked those mad baby feet.

"That one boy won't stop gnawing on the rug, Mom."

"Tell the others not to step on him. I guess that must be the spot where you spilled your hot chocolate last week."

I put on some G-rated movies and soothing music, but the Ten Toddlers were much more interested in jumping from one sofa to the other and faking various injuries.

Eventually it was almost time for them to head home and no one was hurt and the carpet sucker had fallen asleep in the wet spot he created. I was certain they'd give good reports to their parents.

"Mith Whinhart ith thow nithe," they'd say. "She gave uth cookies."

As the parents came to pick them up, I smiled like a much nicer and younger Martha Stewart. "Oh," I said. "It was such fun. They were all precious." Lies. White lies. The kind that don't land you in hell, according to Mama.

The carpet muncher's mom took her baby in her arms and stared for a long time at his face. "What's that gray fur sticking out of your brother's teeth?" I heard the mom ask her little girl as they headed out the door.

I ducked into the kitchen and pretended to round up diaper bags.

Two months later, I resigned from the Neighborhood Co-op Babysitting Club. I think a lot of parents are quite relieved. I know I am.

This whole experience prepared me for the wildest party I'd seen in years: my daughter's "Friendship Party." They might call this episode of first-grader fun the "Little Girls Gone Wild."

The sound was like walking into a gymnasium full of cheer-leaders. At best. At worst, it was like falling into a stall crammed with squealing little pigs. And at times, it became a tangle of wildcats fighting at sundown.

My little girl, a first-grader, took it upon her social-butterflying self to invite a group of girls to what she designated a Friendship Party. It wasn't her birthday, or anything special, she simply up and decided her mama wouldn't mind a bit. That I owed her this for being a mother who had to schlep it out in the corporate world for medical and dental coverage and couldn't be a room parent.

She bounced home from school announcing who she'd asked to come on Saturday.

"I don't know their parents and they don't know me," I said. "They may think we're pedophiles or psychos."

"It's OK," she said, and named the girls who had already said they could attend.

I knew what was next: I would spend an hour on the phone calling mothers and daddies who didn't know me from a stray dog, trying to convince them it was fine and we'd love to have their daughters over for what was now a Pizza and Pedicure Party. My daughter had gotten a bubbling Dr. Scholl's foot massager from Santa, high on the list of all nursing home residents.

On Saturday, the angels showed up in their sweet clothes and delighted yelps of joy upon seeing each other. They hugged and carried on as if they were grown women who hadn't laid eyes on one another in at least two days. You know how women can be. Well, I learned on Saturday that little girls are exactly like grown women. EXACTLY!

One minute they'd be having a grand old time tying the chairs with jump ropes and dragging them around the road like limp dogs, and the next minute someone would run up to me tattling.

"Bunny and Tricia Marie had two minutes with the skates and the scooter and I haven't had a single turn all day. I hate them both!"

"Well, tell them I'll have to pull their ears off if they don't share."

The child's eyes widened and she grinned at the thought of it.

"Mrs. Reinhardt says if you don't give me the bike or scooter, you won't have ears for very long."

And the girls shrieked and I was certain the neighbors were on the verge of calling the cops because of the "Girls Gone Wild" party at my house in the otherwise low-key burbs.

After a frenzy of mayhem in the yard, I gulped a bit of prayer and PMS tea and hauled them all to the neighborhood park. As soon as they saw the creek, they went flying. I tried to stop them.

"Don't get in that festering swamp!" I yelled. "We've found 10-foot cobras snaking around and hissing foam, and there is also a group of Great Thorny Fanged Turtles that shoot out hot purple poison." It didn't stop them. "The Rabid Water Possums are especially vicious."

All to no avail, until one girl fell in, got her pants wet and muddy and a new game was born. This one is sure to wipe my name off the PTO ballet box.

One by one they ripped off their pants and ran around the park in tops and undies.

"Your mamas are going to be mad," I said, rounding up britches and chasing the girls who were now rolling around in the sand in their undies that said SATURDAY across the waistband.

My mother, a revived Baptist, later said, "That's awful, Susan."

And I felt as judged as if I had been hurled before the good Lord. I guess the experience taught me the old adage is true: girls are made of sugar AND spice. And I loved every minute. Even if the PTO scraps me from the fall lineup.

Parenting Tips You Must Never Tell the Pediatrician!

I knew at a young age I was the product of weirdoes and would thus become one, too. I figured this out shortly after carrying the boot for a month.

The boot was one of my daddy's unusual punishments, among the many.

Back in the day, my day, you got spanked and/or grounded. We had no Xboxes to confiscate or Game Boys to hide. It was a flyswatter at the hands of Mama, a stinging disciplinary weapon she kept atop the fridge.

Sometimes when we were wretchedly naughty, which was an AWFUL lot, she'd whip out her flyswatter and smack our legs. Often, the remnants of Georgia flies the size of young chipmunks would coat our legs along with the webbed pattern of the plastic swatter.

I hated when she came at us with the flyswatter. I much preferred my daddy's wacky punishments.

For instance, he was so worried his daughters would end up really fat with huge asses, thus reducing our chances of marrying a man with a job and decent income, he'd make us walk up and down our ski-slope steep driveway to burn calories.

"You did what? Made an F?"

"I got a high F. Highest F in the class."

Mama would reach for the flyswatter.

"No, Peggy, I'll deal with this. Susan, you go walk up and

down the driveway until sweat pours from your face. It'll trim that butt and teach you a lesson that studying comes before dates, and that a small ass is what most men prefer. I don't know of any man who wants a women in need of a WIDE LOAD banner across her fanny."

The boot was an interesting punishment. Here's how it came to pass that I carted a nasty work boot to school for a month: I was/am one of those ADD (attention deficit disorder) people who loses everything not bolted or duct-taped to my body. Books, purses, money . . . anything loose and unanchored, I'm guaranteed to misplace for eternity.

Such was the case with my blue suede coat with the mystery fur collar. You've heard of mystery meat. Well, we argue to this day what kind of animal gave its life for that coat's collar.

One afternoon I came home from junior high school without the blue suede belt to the coat. My dad was livid. He went out and found a mud-caked, ugly old boot somewhere along the highway, probably the roadside where my fur collar originated, and ordered I carry the monstrosity to school—JUNIOR HIGH! of all places—every day for an entire month.

"No, Daddy. People already think I'm the weirdest girl at school. What will they think now?" I was screaming and crying.

"They will think you're one of a kind, honey."

"I don't want to be one of a kind. That's why they all HATE me now. I'm an outcast. This boot just sealed any doubts one or two may have had lingering, that I might be OK and not a complete freak."

This punishment did not, nor did many in our home, fit the crime. Why not just burn the rest of the coat, donate the roadkill collar, give the whole thing to Goodwill, then force me to sell magazines and knickknacks door to door to earn money for a new one?

"I'll even rake leaves," I begged. My daddy knew I hated this worse than anything else on Earth. What kind of father makes his daughter cart a filthy boot off to school where impressions and fitting in are the most important of all junior high curricula?

"You forget to bring that boot home," he warned, "and I'll give you something much more embarrassing to keep up with."

What could be more embarrassing? Dirty underwear? A box of Kotex?

"You will carry this to school for thirty mornings and bring it home in tip-top shape for the next thirty afternoons. Never will the shoe be left in a school locker for you to hide away the reason for carrying it in the first place. You understand?"

I was 12 or 13 and mad as hell. Even though I went to an all-girls middle school, they could be crueler than the boys who were bussed over for one hour a day for band. Hence the reason so many girls played instruments who otherwise wouldn't have given a clarinet the time of day.

"Not band, Daddy. Don't make me take that thing to band."

"From the bus to band. From band to lunch. From lunch to all your classrooms! If I hear it's had a cushy break in your dark locker, I'll increase its time at Westside Junior High by a month. You hear?"

From the corner of my eye, I saw Sandy, my younger sister who always managed to escape trouble and Daddy's oddball punishments, smirking. Smirkers are evil. I hate smirkers.

She watched closely, and whatever sin I'd committed to deserve boots, groundings, the occasional lash of the thin leather belt or fly-caked swatter, she avoided. Sneaky little thing, she was. Much worse than I, just better able to hide things.

"We just bought you that coat," Mama said, "and you've ruined it already."

"It wasn't cheap," Daddy added. "Had that thick mink collar. Fur cost same as diamonds."

Mama chimed in. "What good's a decent coat when you lose the belt? You can't replace a baby blue suede belt, honey."

"Would have been better to have lost the mink collar," my father said. "I could have run out in the road and cleaned up one of the raccoons or squirrels and Mama could have gotten out her Singer and sewed that sucker right on there for you, but no. You have to go and lose the belt."

"I'm sorry about the belt," I said. "I don't know where it went. I had it and then I went to get it out of my locker and it was gone. I'm pretty sure someone must have stolen it."

He poured a bourbon and water, shook it around while the ice clinked and that sharply sweet smell of potent liquor rose up and stung my nose. "That's right," he said, swallowing his first sip of mellowness for the evening. "Everybody in the whole entire universe is dying for a blue suede belt. Who the hell wants a mink—"

"It's raccoon," Mama corrected.

"Raccoon . . . mink . . . muskrat . . . squirrel . . . baby monkey . . . badger . . . family of moles . . . That's not the point. Anyone would have taken the coat and not just the belt. Susan lost it. Pure and simple. And she's going to learn she can't keep losing stuff. Nothing she owns has its parts. You know she has had four Social Studies books this year. I've paid more money on Social Studies books filled with Communist thoughts than I have on rib eyes for the grill. She's got to learn, Peg."

"But why that boot? Where did you get that thing?"

He turned the mud-caked giant's boot in his two hands. "I was down at West Point Lake near where they're building all those fancy new homes and there it was, right along the shoulder of the road next to a muffler. I was going to get the muffler and let her take it, but it was rusted and I wasn't sure she was up-to-date on her tetanus shot. Kid's gonna take it to school and let's see if that doesn't cure her lack of respect for her own property. She'll stop forgetting things. You'll see."

Mama opened the refrigerator and poured a Schlitz in a glass. She wasn't the kind to drink from the can unless extremely stressed. "I think it's weird, Sam. Why don't you just put her on restrictions?"

Daddy jumped up from the brown couch and set his drink on the coffee table, spilling some onto the wood. "What kind of lessons do restrictions teach? We put her on restrictions when she caught all those grasshoppers and laid them out in the Moseleys's bed and tucked the sheets in tight. Remember? Mel pulled back his covers and nearly had a second heart attack. Restrictions didn't do her a bit of good. The boot is something she'll never forget. Ever."

He was right.

Even so, my coats, to this day, are still missing belts. Only now, no one makes me carry a boot. Payback will come, however, and the man upstairs delivered two children unto my womb who lose everything, too.

And like my father, my parenting style can be considered somewhat unconventional. Because my sister and I were raised by weirdo parents, albeit good ones, we became weirdo moms. We are the kind of moms who make our children cringe when seeing our behavior.

For example, I pop in a Boston or Foghat CD and think nothing of an all-out boogie while driving and they sit in the backseat screaming for me to stop. I embarrass them, thinking I'm such a cool mom, but one who disciplines, too.

I mostly spare the rod and pack up toys. I have one tip that works quite well, called "Reverse Santa." When the kids enter a Satan's spawn phase, I put on a fuzzy red and white Santa hat and grab a big pillowcase and sing, *"You didn't watch out, you always cried, and always shouted, I'm telling you why, Santa Claus is returning to town. He knows when you've been lying. He knows when you've been bad. He knows when you don't mind and shout and the chores are never done."*

At this point I round up their toys and favorite electronics and stuff them in the pillowcase, grinning like a Grinch with half a dozen evil uteruses and eight menacing ovaries. They look at me as if I'm insane, which I am, and I cart off my bulging sack and hide it. The biggest problem at my age is I forget where I've put the sack once the punishment is over.

Another one of my potentially psychotherapy-inducing tactics is when they are acting out repeatedly and saying how much they dislike me and want another mom (not often, but on occasion). I tell them, "Fine. I'm calling the Department of Social Services where they have a large list of foster mothers that live in Tiny Tina's Midget Trailer Park and smoke three cartons of unfiltered Camels a day and drive El Caminos with bald tires and overflowing ashtrays. I'm sure you don't mind sharing a bed with six other foster children with head lice, and eating beans and fatback every night. They also spank a lot—pick-a-switch style—and have no toys to speak of." I realize this is a mean stereotype and most foster moms are unselfish, wonderful people. OK. That's it for political correctness.

I had to stop doing the Foster Mom routine when Lindsey cried for thirty minutes and I felt like the worst mother on EARTH. That is, until I learned from my sister, a couple of friends and the fine members of one of the best PTAs in the world, the means *they'll* resort to when at wits' end.

These tips would make Drs. Spock and Brazelton seize on the dining room floor and sputter, arms and legs thrashing.

First, here are some stories from my crazy sister, mother of two young boys.

It's the Cat's Fault

When Chad was little, I needed to be able to pass gaseous emissions in front of him without having to leave the room. I told him that girls did not pass gas, it was just a boy thing, and that I was sorry, but it was the cat's little problem. "Must be that rich food. I'll switch her and YOU to Price Busters cat food."

It was not until he was 6 years old that he realized our cat didn't have a gastrointestinal problem, and that girls, indeed, did fart.

All in the Blended Family

When making the decision to marry for a second time, one must understand that it isn't just two people, it is two families hitching up. Dave was a basketball coach when we decided to get married and it was during basketball season so there was no time for a honeymoon. We got married on a Thursday night and had to be at a game on Friday.

Since the kids were in the wedding and were used to being home with just me, we all slept in the same bed on our wedding night, after having the reception at the local family sports bar. Things get a little more realistic the second time around.

(As her big sister, my take on this was they did it in the church bathroom right before the ceremony. Shhhh.)

Ammunition Acquisition

Force yourself to learn to play at least ONE of their video games. They think it's cool, but more importantly, their friends do. They will always tell your child how lucky he is to have a mom who will play video games with him. This is great ammunition when you hear, "But Mike's mom is letting him do it." You can simply say, "Does Mike's mom play Xbox? Can she shoot an air rifle like I can? I don't see her at the Target Range blowing holes in paper men with .38 Specials."

Just Let 'Em Be Boys

If you have boys, let them discuss bodily functions on road trips. For goodness sakes, they want to. They think about them all the time, and Jesus says if you think about it, it is the same as if you have actually done it. So let them spew as much potty talk as they want and the mystery will perhaps (but doubtfully) lose its magic. You are simply living in denial if you don't think they do it with their friends. Besides, it makes for great family fun and bonding.

We play the Potty Game on long trips. One person starts a story with a sentence beginning, "Once upon a time . . ." Then the next person gets to add one sentence and so on. We did have to make a rule that the game had to go around to everyone at least twice before bodily functions were added because it would end up something like this: "Once upon a time there was a large white elephant." Next person: "The elephant felt lonely because he was the only white one." Next person:

"Then he learned to roll around in poop so the other elephants couldn't tell he was white."

Once my then 11-year-old and I played a game where we had to come up with as many ways as possible of saying a person has to go number two. The one who couldn't come up with something would lose. We came up with the standards like, "laying cable," "dropping a load," and "pinching a loaf."

Plenty of people had to come up with road-trip activities such as these before the invention of video games and DVD players. Come on down off that high horse and try it. Have some fun with your kids. There is one rule of caution. It is important that you tell them that they are to keep this type of activity within the family.

Go ahead and put the video games up and go home for a good bodily functions discussion with your kids. Make memories to last a lifetime. You don't even need a MasterCard to do it.

That's it for now from my sister. Now here's what members of the PTA at my daughter's school, a multiple-award-winning Governor's School of Excellence, revealed on the subject of unconventional parenting. Lord, I love these women.

The Haw Creek Valley PTA

"I am totally unconventional," says our beautiful blonde PTA president and mother of two boys. "Like, I don't make Justin wear shoes to gymnastics because he just has to take them off when he gets there, and I let the boys watch most any movie . . . and I answer things vaguely. When they were younger, a steamy sex scene came on and they were like, 'What is that???!!' and I told them I just didn't know myself, we'd have to look it up on the Internet tomorrow.

"We also run around in our jammies all day on Saturday unless we have to go somewhere. Every now and then we eat brownies for breakfast because they are made with milk."

Don't y'all just love this woman? Here's more from her:

"We have a rabbit that runs around our house like a cat," she said. "I never worried about bottles, potty training and thumb sucking. I just ignored them and they eventually went away! Once, Brendan took to wanting to cut off all of his clothes so they were shorter around his wrists and pant legs, and for about six months I kept cutting up all his clothes for him until he snapped out of it."

Mercy, she's the kind of mother who defines laid back. She's my new hero. I thought surely she had to be on Thorazine, but dang, she's drug free.

Next up is another one of our PTA's finest. And she's not even Southern, so you can't blame us for being the craziest women in America.

"Hmm . . . I have many," she said of unconventional tips, "but right off the top of my head I'd have to say that the way I used to terrify my daughter into eating her vegetables would be borderline unacceptable. I told Bailey that if she didn't eat them, I would have to take her to the doctor, where he would have to administer vegetable extract injections. Then my husband would call our number with his cell phone and I'd have a 'conversation' with Dr. Fuller, saying things like, 'Well, I don't know . . . She's eaten a couple carrots . . . Not enough? I'll try, Doctor . . . Okay, there she goes, she's eating some more . . . I think we'll be okay this week . . . Thanks, Dr. Fuller.'"

Our former PTA president, another delightful woman, had a wonderful two-day punishment for her son during a time he kept refusing to listen to her.

"He was constantly arguing with me, so we decided that we would go two days without talking to each other except in an emergency, or when absolutely necessary. After a day of me holding up my hand and saying, 'Don't talk to me,' he was quite anxious to talk to me again."

Here's another from this cool mom:

"When my son refused to clean his room repeatedly, and argued about it constantly, I gave him a two-day warning, and at the end of that two days, I took everything that was left on the floor and drove to Goodwill. It was hard for me to put new toys that he had just gotten for his birthday in a bag to get rid of, but it was quite effective.

"At one point, I decided I would pick up everything my son left around the house, put it in a box, and sell it back to him with money he had to earn doing other chores. Another time I told him if he didn't calm down and stop losing his temper, I was going to call the police and tell them I had a violent child and needed their assistance.

"When I actually picked up the phone and started dialing, he immediately started to do better.

"Another time when my son got extremely argumentative, disrespectful and was even mocking me, I decided to take a break, told him I was going to go somewhere where I wasn't treated abusively and left him with his grandfather for a day and a half without telling him where I was going or calling him. While it was not as relaxing as it would have been had I planned a minivacation, it gave him time to realize that he really did like me as a mother after all."

Even doctors have resorted to the atypical when it comes to their offspring.

One PTA mom said, "I had both my kids at the doctor's office the other day and they were acting like problem kids. The doctor was telling me that her trick was that when her kids misbehaved toward each other, like fighting and saying, 'I hate you' or 'He won't stop poking me,' she would make them walk all the way around her neighborhood cul-de-sac holding hands."

Here's one of my favorites from a mom I can relate to for sure:

"I'm co-grade parent in Mrs. Snelson's. Deanne and I were chatting at the school last week, and I morphed off into my creative (aka crazy) parenting stories.

"Funny how today's catch phrase can really be nothing more than yesterday's required survival skills! I myself am still going through the parenting process; making it up as I go along. I'm definitely better the second time around, as I don't have as many stories to tell.

"See, I have two daughters: 22 years of age, and 11 years of age. I figured if the oldest didn't die during the first decade she was here, it was time to try it again. So we did. Poor Sam. That's my oldest. She really had it hard growing up. I am a firm believer in the old school of 'I'm not telling you again.' So I didn't. Garbage didn't get taken out? I can handle it. I just double-bag it and place it gently on her bed. Same with the silverware that always manages to stay in the sink and never makes it to the dish drainer.

"I only say something once. Survival of the fittest, and even though she is more physically fit than I, I have old age and humor on MY side! My father always told us that the best revenge was living long enough to see your grandchildren embarrass your children. Damn him, but he was right. I get even, though. Once we were driving down the main street in our little southeast Florida town, and Sam was ignoring me, or something along those lines. When she gets like that, I don't get mad, I get even! I roll down the windows and start talking very loudly. No big deal for most, but I like to tease her by doing my tirades with a fake Puerto Rican/Guatemalan accent. 'Chew jus gots to see my new chews! They so CUTE. Let me 'splain it like dis: I be stylin'!' Of course, I pick the best time, like when one of her friends is in the car next to us at the red light. I'm evil. My father would be so proud.

"Another time Sam made the mistake of complaining that her father and I were boring. Boring? Me? Heck, I was almost old enough for Woodstock...I have more rock concerts under my belt than belt notches! Boring, indeed. So, after the shock of being called boring wore off, her father and I decided to show her just how unboring we were. We chose our weapons carefully. Okay, they weren't weapons so much as pots and pans. And a strainer. Yes, our new hats shone brightly in the midday sun, blazing away for all to see. Jim sported a lovely copper soup pot with a long sleek handle of black, while I could be seen walking the red carpet in a brand-new metal strainer, tag still stuck to the side.

"We took our wonderfully horrified daughter all around

town. Through Farm Stores, a well-known drive-thru convenience store speckled throughout Florida. We stopped for gas at our local station. Heck, we even went into Minors Market!

"I don't think Samantha could have slipped any lower in her seat belt without strangling herself. We arrived at our final destination of my sister Claire's house, where our daughter ran off to cry and complain to my niece. My nephews, on the other hand, thought we were better than sliced bread and promptly grabbed pans of their own, hollering, 'Mom, can we go with Aunt Carye and Uncle Jim to ride around with pots on our heads?' My sister never batted an eye; she remembers all too well the funny things our own parents did to us as we were growing up.

"We survived. They will, too."

The British Are Coming!

It's not just Americans resorting to bizarre and unusual parenting styles. Stephen Herbert, an English chap, is our delightful new neighbor along with his rather normal and lovely wife and two spirited and charming children. Translation: children like my own that they can throw down and who make you (at times) want to jump from a plane without a parachute or, better yet, leave for Tahiti for a week or two.

Herbert, perhaps unbeknownst to his dear, precious wife, enjoys telling his children bedtime stories. Not ordinary fairy-tales most moms and dads coo to their cherubs in the late evenings, but stories ranging from horrifying to fascinating and all related to world events—both past and current.

Good Lord, these kids are just 4 and 6 years old. They barely understand Blue's Clues, and the delightful Mr. Herbert is telling them about Stalin and Hitler, Roosevelt, Nixon and others.

"It's important to educate your children about historical figures," he said in his adorable British accent, "so I integrate them into fairy tales. If Anna's been bad and stroppy she gets

Adolf Hitler—what his life was like and that sort of thing. She doesn't particularly like the story at all because everyone dies at the end.

"On the flip side, if she's good, she gets a decent character from history such as Mohammed Ali. If she's halfway a pain in the ass, she'll get someone boring. I tell her about George Washington, who is seriously dull, or some other such figure.

"The other thing which is good for when they misbehave in the car, is when it's cold and they are screaming in the backseat, then you simply open the windows where they are since you're up front with the heater. When they shut up, I close the windows."

The tricky part, Herbert said, is when one child is good and one bad. "It's hard alternating windows and air flow."

As for good old-fashioned discipline, Herbert is nothing like the British Supernanny, Jo Frost. "I swear at them," he said, laughing. (He's truly one of the best fathers I know, but also has a warped side that makes him one of our favorite neighbors.) "The other threat is to kill off their favorite cartoon characters, Max and Ruby, the two rabbits. They're the most annoying, even more so than Barney, so when the kids are misbehaving I tell them I'm going to run over Max and Ruby."

For instance, Herbert might say, "I saw a car accident tonight and it was Max and Ruby, so I put the car in REVERSE and ran over them again to make sure they were dead."

The children are so used to their dad's parenting style, they just laugh.

"With Thomas," he said of his youngest, "it's harder. I tell him if he keeps crying so loud, the monsters will hear him and get him during the night. He's gotten used to it and doesn't believe me anymore."

If you're upset at Stephen Herbert's parenting skills, too bad.

"Those who moan," he said, "are those who don't have children."

Amen, my British brother.

In order to end this on a loving note, my e-bud Ben Baker, member of www.southernhumorists.com, a group of superfunny and talented writers, summed up parenthood in a poignant way:

Last month my child was born.
Last week my child was in elementary school.
Yesterday I did the same thing I did today.
Today, I hugged my child and said, "Forgive me for not being a better parent."
Today, I said, "Excuse me" to my child and picked him up and carried him with me.
Today, I asked my child what he did in school, what he had for lunch and what they did at recess.
Today, I struggled with word problems in math homework with my child.
Today, I stomped through a mud puddle with my child in my office shoes.
Today, I ate lunch with my child at school.
Today, I went fishing with my child.
Today, I sat with my child at his bed and told him a story until he was asleep.
Today, my child told me I was a hero and I can do anything.
Today, I was a step closer to being a real parent.

The South Be-Otch Exercise Plan

The family beach trip is coming up in three short weeks, but my body left town years ago.

What's a woman to do when her figure—which would have looked pretty darn perky during Kappa Alpha Beach Weekend '82—shifts and sags some twenty-five years later?

Oh, exercise, they all say. Just work out. Well, been there, done that, and the arms still swing like a vine full of chimps. Not all the barbells in the world can cure Triceps Genetic Anomaly No. 14. Gym classes and discus hurling may bring a respite during adolescence, but those with this troublesome defect must soon face the facts: the sacks will return in full waddling force.

Here's the key: Always keep them folded across the chest, which by the way, hides Pectoralis Disorder No. 85, a condition most often associated with a need for Wonderbras, wads of Kleenex and duct tape. With the arms and chest covered, what's a poolside 'potamus to do about her bigger, lower half, that arse that on some women (even me during times of continuous grazing and stress) is large enough for gorilla bedding?

I checked over swimsuits from the nineteenth century, consisting of smocks and stockings and bloomers big enough to hide the Igloo and foldout chair. The dictum of the day being no skin allowed, unless one counts ankles and elbows. Nothing like contemplating the old swim dress to infect a woman's fragile mood.

Please, don't even mention the thongs. Those are for sluts if worn in public or, in my case, that most unfortunate accidental choosing prior to the birth of my second child, when in a panic I raced in pain to the hospital wearing a red thong underneath my Mee-Maw robe.

Those ridiculous fanny flossers may be de rigueur in Rio, but bring them to Myrtle Beach and you've got a South Atlantic Crack Epidemic.

Here's the bottom line: Without Bardot's body or strands of impeccable DNA, without lab-rat metabolisms and teen-boy thighs, a woman is waging full-fledged beachfront fashion combat.

If only exercise had worked, but for me, it did not. I just got fatter, thinking I had full rights to gobble two Whoppers instead of one since I'd kickboxed for forty-five minutes. I'm sure all the pumped and proud endorphin addicts will tout the 30-mile-uphill jog as a day of bliss, but a cellulite-free heart isn't what I'm trying to wedge into a bikini.

I've tried Thighmasters, fat-blasters, Tae Bo, boxing, step classes and weight training and NOTHING has fixed the Triceps Genetic Anomaly No. 14. I will acquiesce and admit rigorous exercise does lead to weight loss, which, in finely toned individuals is a good thing. In women my age, it is another.

The point is, I've never seen a fat woman with loose skin. These fluffy females are quite firm, even if on the large side. Extra weight may be bad on the ticker, but listen up. It'll sure fill out some loose skin and, in case you haven't noticed, these plumpstresses have flawless and unlined faces. That right there is enough proof to make me want to sit on my ass and do nothing.

Here's an Irrational Beauty Tip for those headed for the shores and don't have time or interest in a toning routine: Buy a giant tube of Deep Dark Tanning Lotion. It will make you look buff and cover spider veins.

If you get depressed, just remember, even the likes of Cher will one day have to face the facts. That the beat may go on, but youth eventually sinks like a sunset over the Pacific.

Until the trends change—and the normal-weight Dove Soap

models are a good start—we women and men will continue to fret over what we weigh and how we look in swimsuits.

No matter what men say they prefer—and we all know men who say they like women with meat on their bones—this whole weight thing still has people flapping and squawking about how fat they are.

I won't divulge names, but a fairly well-known nappy dresser, who preens and takes as much pride in his appearance as a peacock in full display, bemoaned the appearance of a third chin the other day.

"Guess you'll have to buy more razors," I said. He didn't appreciate the joke. He was also upset about a new roll of fat that had formed near the base of his skull.

"I'm going to have a big fat face, that kind where you can't really see the person's features because they get all lost in the flesh."

"Quit being dramatic," I said. "It's shallow. Be glad you have a few chins and a head."

But I had no room to talk. "At least you didn't birth a second stomach," I said. "I'm the only mammal besides the cow and giraffe who has two."

My new stomach gradually debuted, but made its grandest entrance one morning while I tried to zip up my Hefty Girl jeans. Metal teeth flew like bullets from my pants.

When you've spawned a new stomach, it's World O' Elastic and Stretch Poly for you from then on out. Maybe a bit of fleece thrown in for variety. Fleece is good for hiding extra stomachs.

When I finally broke down on January 2 and weighed, the bathroom scales set a home record. I heard cries from within the strained dial as it continued climbing to new heights.

Desperate and nearly defeated, I recalibrated, pushing the dial back a couple of pounds. The next day, I weighed again, hoping to be 2 pounds lighter. Instead, I weighed the same, upping the grand postholiday total to nearly 10 pounds—the equivalent of a small piglet or a fully operational second stomach. I named the new organ The Unwanted Mass, TUM for short, and have vowed to remove it by April 15—Tax Day deadline.

I vowed to do the dreaded task: exercise. I knew the first step toward losing weight is just that—a step. Lots of them. Walking until the rubber smokes from the sneakers and sweat drips from each of one's chins.

Some people join gyms. I've been a member of at least half a dozen over the years, the latest of which I attended only seven times in 2005. I used these excuses: It's too far from home. There's never any parking unless your car will climb trees. They oversold. Men lurk and some even have erections while bench pressing, which makes me want to vomit. Women walk around naked, no matter how rhinoish their hides. They don't shave their regions and carry on conversations with others, their possums in full view and in need of a weedeater.

The next year I broke down and joined a new gym where no menfolk were allowed. Heaving hunks were a plentiful sight at the Old Gym. They might be a nice distraction, but more than a few would hog the good equipment and ogle the young Single-Stomach girls. This made the Dual-Stomach women feel blue and likely to consume KFC and hit the DQ. They'd also leave their sweat and stench on the benches, forgetting to spray and wipe, same as when they don't lower the seat lid on a toilet and piss has flown everywhere. I'm not speaking about all men. I'm sure if you're a man reading this, you are ultraclean and conscientious, and never have a hard-on while on the StairMaster.

With the new all-women's gym, I'd gone every day for a week, dutifully putting in time and effort. So imagine the shock when the following Sunday morning I reweighed, expecting to see fewer digits on the scales and instead another pound flashed. Where is the justice in this?

Depressed and angry, I opened a can of Pillsbury Cinnamon Rolls and slathered on the icing. Each pastry had 400 calories. I ate two. One for each stomach.

Since regular heart-pumping weight training exercises didn't seem to light a fire in my brain or heart, I decided to join the hip and serene and try yoga, figuring never judge something until you try it. And not just once. Try it at least six times before adopting an opinion.

When I told Mama and Daddy I was going to do some yoga, they said, "Does this mean you're going to become a Scientologist next?" They must think yoga and Scientology are for celebrities and freaks.

I said nothing, but a few days later had my sixth yoga class, and I have to admit, I don't fit in. Something about the mascara and plastic-banana hair clip and the Wal-Mart bag that housed my sneakers and socks all added up to yoga no-no's.

When my husband, Tidy Stu, called the other day and said, "Should I meet you with the kids at aerobics?" I answered, "No, I'll be going to the yoga class." I felt so Zen and trendy saying the word "yoga." I imagined Gwyneth and Cher and Madonna, all yogaing their way into radiant litheness.

"Yoga?" he screamed.

"What's wrong with it?"

"It's so . . . so . . . granola. That's what everyone does every morning at the LEAF Festival."

He was talking about a massive festival in Black Mountain, North Carolina, where the shower-free crowd camps and plays drums and talks about peace and love, guzzling soy or wheat beer by day and puffing reefer by night.

After these six sessions of Flow Yoga, I can honestly say, yes, it is earthy. But often that's exactly what a harried working woman needs. Forget tight fannies and six-pack abs. At this point, I'd settle for a two-pack. Yoga class is the one place I can go and not have to worry if my breath reeks of onion or garlic. The collective and ultradeep inhalations of the Downward-Facing Dog crowd are redolent of root and herb glory. The aroma is one swimming in pungent BO and patchouli and the occasional release of gases.

One man in the class would NOT stop farting because, as he later told the teacher, "It's my body's NATURAL way of releasing toxins."

Yoga class is also the one place I can go and not fret that I haven't shaved in three days. Most participants haven't seen a razor since the Daisy first hit the market in the 70s. Yogamites are by and large a natural lot, a tranquil group who live in harmony with the world. Bless their chaturanga'd hearts.

Several of the participants, when not moaning and farting, would tie bandannas around their bountiful manes of dreadlocks, these Mufasas of the yoga world.

For those who aren't familiar with this ancient practice of strengthening and stretching, yoga classes typically begin with lots of shut-eye and breathing. Much of the focus centers on quieting the mind and stimulating the inner organs toward better functioning.

It is a far cry from the thundering, pounding, stomping and stepping in those power classes where people wear makeup and tend to shave.

Truthfully, during yoga classes, I felt like I didn't belong, like an imposter among all the lotus posing and humming. My mind raced. I looked around the room. Chests rose and fell with deep, healing breaths. Eyes closed. It was a wonderful workout for those who can sit still and shut up, but I'm a fidgeter, and as we finished, the lovely instructor turned off the lights and stealthily crept around the room, massaging the random head. When she got to mine, I let out a squawk, unaware that she was anywhere near.

For some twisted reason, I kept peeping to see if she'd rub a Mufasa's head, which isn't good for inner peace, but I just couldn't help myself. At the end of the session when the lights flicked back on, I spotted my charming friend Heather. Heather is an Earth Mama on the outside but a country bumpkin by birth.

"Hey, girl," I said, disturbing the peace. "I thought for a moment I was the only redneck in here." A hairy woman laughed beatifically.

"No," Heather said, misting like a dewy Earth Goddess. "I'm here. I brought my mama one day. I was scared to death she was going to show up in her favorite lime green tube top and come before the dentist got her new teeth put in."

Over the summer, busy with a freelance writing project, I decided to see what would happen to the body if one tossed exercise aside including yoga.

Sugahs, it's not pretty. I became a garden overgrown, sprouting bumps and gourds, a compost pile of flesh where puckers and dents dominated the terrain. One day my daughter decided to point out all my figure flaws. Well, if that's not enough to get a woman off her whoopsie daisy, what is?

In the end, I had to face the truth, should such be mined to its full depths. I did NOT want to exercise in public. Or anywhere else, for that matter. Apparently, I'm not the only woman who starts up exercise plans and ditches them quicker than they do boyfriends in El Caminos.

I was in Wal-Mart with Mama the other day when she ran into one of her oldest friends.

"How in the world are ya doin', hon?" Mama asked.

"I'm OK, I guess. Just been swelling a lot, got The Bloat, you know. I sure hate puffing up. Makes me mean."

I know all about the evils of The Bloat, which tends to appear shortly after Halloween and clings throughout the winter, meaning none of my clothes fit except those nasty elastic garments.

I don't know any men who contract The Bloat. They just swell and stay blown up for good, unless the wife restricts caloric intake and carts His Heftiness off to Weight Watchers or the YMCA.

Whenever The Bloat wedges its water-retaining claws beneath my skin, you can bet the witch-switch is flipped. Nobody's nice under such conditions. Nobody.

There is good news, though, and I'm here to bring it on.

A headline appeared on Mama's computer screen that said, "SURPRISE! SOME BODY FAT IS A GOOD THING."

According to an article, not all body fat is created equal. Here's the deal, people. Fat in the tummy is deadly and increases one's chances of a big old myocardial infarction, also known as a heart attack. Yet we precious pork lassies who are somehow able to "channel" the fat into the arms, thighs, hips and buttocks are not only less likely to croak, but more likely to live longer than our Twiggy counterparts.

Research published in *Circulation*, a journal published by the American Heart Association, says full-figured gals are less likely to have plaque-clogged arteries than are women whose weight is concentrated in the abdominal area.

When the fat is spread all around, something researchers call peripheral fat, this may even have a protective effect. The news, however, is not a free ticket to the pig trough. Reason being, we cannot direct our bodies to ship fat to certain locations and avoid others.

I say this new information opens the market wide for anyone claiming to be a professional Fat Channeler, those who can either spook or coax the fat toward arm pouches and inner-thigh swags, or who can tell us how to prevent our fried foods from puddling in our midsections.

A Fat Channeler or Fat Whisperer could make a fortune on those of us who don't have the luxury of peripheral fat but have tummies like Buddha's. Wouldn't it be nice to hire a Fat Channeler? I'll bet Oprah has one. Or is getting one for Christmas.

Just as I was about to truly give up all exercise efforts for good, I read about a new strategy. Tone up at the office. No gym involved, no naked people, erections, sweaty machinery or changing of clothes.

The article said go to work dressed as one normally would, and use different parts of the environment and furnishings as posts in which to get firm and healthy.

I chose the weekly editors' meeting for a start, because the chairs have armrests.

Dip. Press. Dip. Press. Just another awkward moment at my workplace.

"What's wrong with you?" a coworker asked, taking me by surprise. "Are you trying to have a close personal relationship with that chair's cushion?"

Ceasing all motion, I caught my breath. "I . . . er . . . This is . . . um . . . good for toning the upper body, the triceps, if you suffer from Triceps Genetic Anomaly 14."

She shook her head, tapped her pencil and went about her business, probably thinking what she always does: "that's one strange chick."

It's all the fault of the two people who anonymously keep sending me subscriptions to *Reader's Digest* and *Prevention* magazine. Every month these magazines feature diets and exercise tips, and lately they've gotten downright bizarre. Used to be a person could pick up a mag and rest assured that the best way to get fit is to buy some good tennis shoes and break a decent sweat.

But the editors of these publications have caught on. They know we're lazy. They know many of us don't have an hour every day to hit the gym and huff our way into aerobic health.

Headlines in recent issues of magazines ran along these latest trends: THE NEW WAY TO LOSE WEIGHT—50 HABITS OF "NATURALLY THIN" PEOPLE. It was too tempting to pass up.

This is where the office dips and presses came into play along with the afternoon meeting fiasco. Everyone was gathered around the big table discussing important stories to be written. I was thinking about the 50 Habits of "Naturally Thin" People and decided that this was the ideal occasion to place my hands against the armchair and go for some triceps dips.

Dip. Press. Dip. Press.

My editor looked up from her important papers. "Is something wrong with that chair? I've noticed you're doing quite a bit of bobbing, Susan."

"Oh. Well. That's just one of the secrets of 'naturally thin' people I was trying out."

She quickly snorted and turned to another reporter, trying to forget I was in the room, which is pretty normal regardless of what I'm doing.

While they talked business, I was thinking about the other exercises a person is supposed to do while in her office to blast away flapping, untoned muscles. Here's how one goes about it, according to the story:

"While you're at your desk chair, pretend you're going to sit but don't! Stop and come back up without using your arms."

Imagine that. And they say to repeat this ten to twenty times. I'm sure my colleagues would just as soon see Richard Simmons in a pair of short-shorts and fake tan (we really did see him one time) than witness a coworker squatting at his or her desk.

Or how about this tip from the magazine on fitting in firm time while on the road, actually driving behind the wheel? Fun as it is to catch someone picking a booger in traffic, this little exercise is guaranteed to screech a few tires and turn some heads.

It's called, "Tone in Traffic." What one does is squeeze one's derriere each time one taps the brake. I'm not sure about others, but if I clenched my butt while tapping a brake, I'm sure the car in front of me would end up in the junkyard.

Some fannies were meant to stay flabby. Mine is one of them.

Hair It Is

Saints preserve us. When it comes to hair, just as with any subject, everybody has an opinion. Usually, those with the least on their noggins yelp loudest when a woman does the unthinkable: takes a pair of razor-sharp shears to her tangle of weeds and decides, "The Time Has Come."

Here's the deal. It's just hair. I'm lucky to have any at all. I swannee, there are men on this planet who'd just as soon see a toothless babe in a nursing home sporting Britney Spears's trashy tresses, even on a face that looks like a swatch of wadded-up linen.

Do men not care how old we are? Is long hair just as important to most of these creatures as are football, three squares a day and four to six humps a week? I mean, come on, fellows. Flowing horse manes may be lovely, but sometimes a girl over 40 just needs a change. Give us a break. It's the smile that counts. The insides, not the outsides. Right?

I guess not. Men's preferences are even mandated in how much possum (va-hee-nah) fur a woman should have. I think they call it the Band-Aid strip, but I'm not going south with this story, I'm staying north of the border.

It all began two nights ago, when my wild Aunt Betty called screaming into our answering machine to hurry and call her back. Her voice had either a coating of martini madness driving the vocals or something tremendously wretched had occurred.

I was hoping her bladder hadn't fallen out again from her insistence at age 70 to continue jumping up and down on a trampoline and cutting flying air splits for the church fashion shows.

See, she has no uterus, so Mama was partly right when she said parts can fly out of the va-genie when the Ute is removed and so forth. Aunt Betty may be wild, but plenty of my kin are hanging by slender threads on that unpredictable borderline vine of sanity. When I finally got through to her, she had one thing to holler.

"John and I were online tonight, and Lord have mercy . . . Hold on while I fan myself." She began heaving and making noises, and I heard ice cubes rattling before she composed herself to return to the phone. It reminded me of the time she called to say her husband had taken out a nursing-home insurance policy on her and she was so furious she didn't cook for a week. When the poor nursing-home insurance rep came to their house one evening—a meek-looking fellow who appeared in need of some Ensure and a good enema—Aunt Betty decided, as usual, to go for the SHOCK value.

"Well, hey there, sugar," she said to this poor, scrawny, anemic man. "I understand my dumb-ass husband has called you into my fine living room to take out a nursing-home policy on me."

"Ma'am, we call them long-term health care—"

"I will not be placed in a home. I see what my husband is up to and he hasn't eaten or had marital favors in a week, and it could go on longer if we don't straighten this mess out right here and now before *The Bold and the Beautiful* comes on and I have to shoo you on out of here."

He swallowed from nerves, and his Adam's apple, the fattest part on him, bobbed like Big Bird's beak pecking to escape his neck.

"If you haven't noticed by now, I resemble Ann-Margret, the movie star. I may be of a certain age, but I sure don't look it, now, do I?"

What could he say? Truth is, Aunt Betty really is sexy and

has a vaVoom figure including a set of natural double or triple Ds.

He cleared his throat and rubbed at his armpits and pretended not to sneak a sniff, then said, "It's not how you look, for that matter, it's for protection and your own good later in life when things aren't exactly—"

"Listen up. You've said your piece, and my asshole husband has said his. Now hear and see mine." With that, my dear, sweet aunt pranced over to this pitiful fellow who at 50ish probably lives at home with his mother and watches the *Wheel* at night during supper. She proceeded to do a number on him as only Aunt Betty can do to men.

She shook and rolled, undulating her hips, and shimmied within inches of his reddening face. She jiggled her huge tits at him and said, "Do these look ready for the home to YOU?"

He emitted a strangled-sounding squeak, like a bird asphyxiated by a boa. Needless to say, she managed to banish the nursing-home idea from her husband's mind, and when and if the time comes, she'll move in with one of her kinfolks. Probably her cute son-in-law.

When she called me that night all in hysterics, I had no idea what had happened to bring about such a frenzy of distress. I wondered if the nursing-home issue had returned so I called her back in a hurry, figuring something of a husband-in-the-doghouse nature had occurred. Either that or someone had keeled over. This phone call must be pretty serious from the tone of her screech.

"Hon," she began in a wobbling soprano, "we couldn't even read your column we were so shocked by your . . . your . . . Oh, God help us all!"

"My what? You were shocked by my what, Aunt Betty?"

"Who do you think you are? Oprah freakin' Winfrey?"

"What????"

"Your hair. What in God's sweet name have you gone and done to it?"

I couldn't believe my ears. Hair? "What are you talking about, Aunt Betty?"

"Honey, are you in trouble with your hormones? I mean, we all get crazy after 40 but what the hell have you done to yourself? You look just like Oprah."

What? This phone call was about my hair! I loved Oprah's fluffy, chickadee, duck-feather hairdo. I wanted some Oprah hair and a stylist gave it to me.

"You can't just go around looking like Oprah, Susan."

"And why not?"

"Because you're white."

"Only on the outside. I have a chocolate center." It's best to deal with Aunt Betty the way she deals with others. I would go to the mat with her on this issue.

"I cut my hair. Big deal. It feels good and I've gotten so many compliments and a free subscription to *O* magazine, featuring Oprah on each and every cover."

More silence, followed by the clink of ice and the gurgle of Aunt Betty's gin and vermouth mixing within her second or third martini. After a few sips, she spoke. "Compliments? From who? The blind? You were so beautiful BEFORE. Why? Just why, my sweet niece, would you make yourself look ugly on purpose?"

It had been a hellishly rough week of defending my new hairdo to readers of my local column. They don't want change. That's why Dear Abby never got an updated look. It's why Erma Bombeck kept her same picture, and I know that for a fact because her very own daughter told me during a writers' conference. Not that I'm anywhere near Abby and Erma's league, but for a local columnist, people don't want the switcheroo hairdo.

"Well?" Aunt Betty asked. "What the hell prompted you to go and do a thing like that for?"

"I had to cut it. Lice and stuff," I lied. "After Stuart discovered a vole and four volettes or whatever their spawn's called using the back of my head as their nesting grounds and source of nutrition, we decided the day had dawned. Time for the hedge clippers."

I couldn't stop yammering. "Four women also called and

left messages saying my short Oprah hair made me look younger."

She snorted and harrumphed. "You know your Aunt Betty loves you, but you are going to need a new picture. This one is unacceptable."

"I'm not getting one. Stuart and I like to laugh at this one. We have a sense of humor. If you don't stop talking about my hair I'm calling the salesman from 'The Home,' if you get my drift. I love ya, Aunt Betty, but it's my head."

I hung up and called Mama. "Your big sister is having a conniption over my hair, saying I'm trying to look like Oprah and it is a big mistake because I'm white."

"Who cares what color you are? Oprah is beautiful. Count your blessings."

What I've counted instead is the number of evil e-mails readers have sent. Why, you'd think I was part of that castration ring down in the western part of our state. The readers were livid and as opinionated and outraged about my hair change as if discussing abortion, politics or religion.

It's just hair, people. Hair!!!! A few have all but poured gasoline on my head and flicked their Bics when it comes to this new picture. No one likes it but dear and precious older ladies and fellows with cataracts. I've even had a death threat. It's a shame when a professional writer's hair becomes more important than what she is trying to convey in print. Why can't they just look past the hairdo and read about the goat that gave birth to triplets against all odds? Why can't they find interest in the 112-year-old who had her first pedicure and a lengthy French kiss during Bingo night? These are important events, much more so than a new hairdo is.

Think about it. There are children with cancer needing cures and financial help. Abused women in need of safe shelters and people with all sorts of horrible problems and afflictions, and here people are worried over a dumb little hairdo.

But that's how it goes. People have called and cussed me

out, screamed that they can no longer read my words until I cover up—as one precious reader put it—"that electrocuted groundhog atop your head."

The icing on the bitter cake arrived via the United States Postal Service from a man who lives in one of those supposedly "peaceful" mountain communities where they chant and enjoy sun salutations and soynuts.

I am printing a portion of his letter, to let you know that after reading his threats, I removed my photo from the column and used an assortment of photographic aliases, such as the Britney Spears mug, and those of Catherine Zeta-Jones, Julia Roberts and other beauties. It was a fun week, but finally the editors made me go back to my ugly old picture.

In all fairness, the letter writer issuing death threats had a few nice things to say about my work before he started in with his word machete, hatcheting his way through a girl's heart and hairdo.

"I'm 64," he wrote, "and have a bachelor's degree in journalism, advertising and twenty-five years as a commercial photographer. My reason for writing is that I hate your new photograph."

Well, darlin', you aren't alone. Call my Aunt Betty, if you want.

"The old one was much better, and the current one makes you look older and somewhat evil. Your photographer and hairdresser both need to be taken out behind some remote barn and quietly put to death."

Whoa. Those are some strong thoughts on something as minor as a hairdo.

"Your picture looks like a happy prison photograph," he continued. "I wouldn't be so critical if I didn't have some professional advice. So here goes:

"Hairdo: Get yourself a 'boy cut.' Ditch the pointy head and cut about five inches off the side flips. Curl the remaining hair forward softly, around your maxillary muscles, and comb your top hair into soft bangs.

"Makeup: Starting with your base foundation shade, let's call it plus or minus 1 or 2. Eyeshadow—plus 2. Bridge of nose—minus 2. Nasal wings—minus 1."

I had no idea what a nasal wing was, but, glory be to Vidal Sassoon, this man seemed to know a lot about the human body. It's good to know I have nasal wings in case I fall out of a building one day and forget my parachute.

He went on to add more of his professional advice:

"You need slightly more dramatic lighting. A 3:1 contrast ratio would be good. Tell your photo editor to ditch the shoulder fade. Next photo shoot (which I hope will be soon), chin up about 15 degrees; turn your head 20 degrees to your right, but look directly into the lens. Think about a puppy or a slab of prime rib."

I suspect this man needs a hobby. But if he cares to take a new picture, I'll let him have a go. As long as he leaves his guns at home.

His name, by the way, is Dick.

"Your name suits you," I e-mailed him back, certain my editors would fire me.

After Dick had his say, a woman I'll call Eunice had hers in what I've come to call Nasty-grams, those e-mails that all but shoot flames. I decided after reading her missive I'd e-mail her right back, even if it meant my editor would march my ass up to HR—HUMAN RESOURCES—that scary place where no one in corporate America cares to go. There is a rumor that once you go to HR, you're never seen again without a set of cardboard boxes with which to remove a year's worth of service and slavery.

Dear Eunice:

Hi there. I just received your sweet letter and have taken your suggestion to heart. And scalp. It is always refreshing when a woman reads a note letting her know that her hair is an abomination to world peace and aesthetics.

Here's the line from Eunice I especially enjoyed:

May I suggest you get yourself to the hairdresser for
a really good haircut and up-to-date hairstyle? You're
uglier than a four-headed pig.

My fingers began typing faster than Mozart could work his
ivories.

Well, here's to looking at you, dear Eunice. You were
quick to point out that I'm not a teenager anymore, and
I couldn't agree with you more. My abdominal overhang
tells me every morning that the days of low-rise jeans
and crop tops have ended.
In addition, another hats off to your astute obser-
vation of my age. Due to your penned assessment,
here's my new photo and trendy hairstyle. (This was
the day we ran the Heather Locklear photo instead of
mine.)
Bless you, woman, for bringing the matter to my attention.

And to the sixty or seventy others who had an opinion on
my new hairdo, here are half a dozen good reasons why some
women, including me, don't get to the salon as often as others
wish they would, plus why some 35-and-ups continue to wear
their hair long:

1. We have children, a job, a house to clean, a dog that tin-
   kles on the floor and a husband who needs attention to
   his jibblybob.

2. Time is of the essence and money is tighter than a tubby
   man's wedding band.

3. Long hair is especially good when a woman—of any
   age—has a set of ears that rival the pair on Anna Nicole

Smith's dearly departed husband. Ever see the flappers on that poor man? They rose from his jawline to the top of his head. Looked like a pair of Magic Johnson's loafers.

4. Long hair provides excellent cover for midlife acne. It also makes comfortable bedding for an assortment of insects that otherwise might be homeless and vulnerable to the elements.

5. Some of us are afraid of the shrink-wrap look, avoiding as long as possible the two prominent 'dos of midlife: the cropped-head poodle fur and the brown helmets.

6. Long hair, particularly when teeming with live insects, is a good detractor for other physical flaws such as a hefty ass or thighs the size of a baby Sequoia.

In closing, I'd like to add a few suggestions for those who need hobbies besides critiquing the hairdos or physical appearances of others:

1. Donate time to a children's or battered women's shelter.

2. Deliver a few Meals on Wheels. Preferably on foot or by burrow.

3. Give blood at the local Red Cross. Lots and lots of it. All of it, if possible.

4. Go out and clean the communities and highways, hook up with some inmates and tell THEM what you think of their hair and see how long you have a heartbeat.

5. Visit a local nursing home and ask the staff how you can be of utmost assistance. Perhaps, by donating your own hair or a kidney, cornea or lung, or scooping out the crud in the bedpans, you'll have a new attitude.

I know that sounds mean. But you just don't mess with a woman's hair. It's in the Bible, or should be. Proverbs 121, Verse 55: "He or She who is fool enough to ridicule another's follicles, shall arise with nothing on his or her head but scabies."

The Gambrells in Europe:
A Four-Act Comedy

Spain

Every year, sometimes twice if the price is right, my parents pack up and go to Europe. They feel they've earned it, especially after raising two daughters who nearly did them in with their romances and bust-ups and wild, heathen ways.

We all wondered if they'd keep their appointment with Spain and the French Riviera scheduled just two months after the 9/11 attacks, when a lot of people were afraid to fly, but Mama and Daddy said if the Lord was ready to take them, so be it.

They also go to altar call more frequently than most, and I accused them of doing this so they could finally stretch their legs, but Mama says it's because she feels the presence of the Lord urging her forward.

"Sometimes our young preacher looks so pitiful, Susan, when he begs for the sinners to come down and no one answers his pleas," Mama said, explaining her constant trips down the aisle to redemption. "After singing the same stanza over and over, your daddy and I just go on down. I guess people think we lead double lives we're at that altar so much. Probably think I'm a floozy on the side."

The other night she called to tell me that the Spain trip was definitely a go, but that Daddy was having fits about her packing job.

"I know the trip is two months away, but I went ahead and started getting things together, Susan. It's no different than that friend of yours who cooks her Thanksgiving turkey and dressing in January and freezes the thing for ten months. I don't think he's over that time we went to England. He's never let me forget it."

England was Mama's first trip abroad. She was going for a week and packed four large bags (this was before airlines had a limit) and stuffed them with curling irons, jewelry, shoes and enough clothes for the four seasons including any variation in between. She also worried about the food over there, thinking her system would just lock up, sort of like an engine does when low on oil, unless she packed an assortment of dried fruits like raisins and prunes, along with KitKats, her favorite candy bar that she swears no one ever has when she really needs one. Like when I was giving birth and she brought her own 10-pack into the delivery room.

My father on the other hand, packs like Mr. Bean, the super-geek from the British TV show by the same name. He carries only one small bag, the kind you can place overhead in the plane. Inside are one pair of drawers, maybe two, a pair of pants, a single shoe for each foot, and a couple of hankies. Who needs more?

"There's always a sink and soap," he said, "and I can turn my drawers inside out. Lots of times I don't even get tinkle on them so there's no point in carrying around a whole bunch unless you got bladder problems and my prostate's fine."

He takes it to the extreme, but not as far as my friend Tracy's husband used to go. He was a true Englishman, and whenever they traveled, he took only clothes with holes or tears, or those destined for the Goodwill.

"That way he doesn't have to bring anything back," Tracy said. "He throws them in the garbage can or hangs them on someone's door and runs away. I was so embarrassed one night while dining at the Captain's table and I looked over and Elliott had giant moth holes in his wool suit and ink stains on his tie."

Daddy was almost that bad. Last Sunday as he sat in church and tried to focus on holiness and the narrow road to the Pearly gates, he just couldn't help himself. Instead of seeing disciples and Jesus, he kept thinking of his upcoming seventeen-day riverboat cruise, and in his head he visualized with a shudder the sights witnessed the previous day: Mama rushing around the house, cramming everything but the toaster and two cats into her multiple suitcase sets.

And that was for a three-day business trip. How in the world would he guide her as she packed for this lengthy upcoming excursion? As he pondered this, the choir lifted its voices unto the Lord and my dad lifted his eyes unto his church bulletin and began writing notes in the blank spots, as if he was a schoolboy with too much to say and in the wrong place to say it.

The contents of those church scrawlings were enough to set my mom's burners on high.

She whipped out her kitty-cat stationery that night and wrote me a letter, explaining her predicament about how hard it is to travel with Daddy.

Writing small enough to fit an entire incident on two pages, she said in her letter:

> *Your dad and I are at it again. You know we're planning another trip to Europe, which takes more than the six or eight minutes he's willing to give it. "Well I was enjoying the choir singing Sunday morning and he leans over with a note that says, "Check me out, Peg. See this getup? What I have on is what I'm packing for the cruise. I will wear this same outfit for both of the dressy nights."*
>
> *Well, How Great Thou Art, I wanted to tell him. Must be nice being a man who hardly ever pees and who can wear the same outfits day in and day out. Must be nice being a man and having nobody pay much attention to your clothes unless you aren't wearing any. No need for hot rollers, Estée Lauder, or*

six pairs of shoes. No use for wrinkle creams and Retin-A and a box of bran flakes in case they clog up our colons with all that European cheese.

Oh, but isn't he always happy when after his stomach bloats he notices I've packed raisins and prunes? You don't hear him complaining then that the luggage was over the weight limit and he had to pay fifty extra bucks. You'd think he'd be thanking me, but no. Not your daddy. He decides via his church bulletin to tell me about his upcoming packing intentions because he knew I couldn't talk back at church. Then he turned to me and whispered a bit too loud for my taste, "Peg, all tourists ever need are two wind suits! That's all you need when you travel," he writes.

I informed him we were traveling in June and I didn't intend to wear warm-ups or wind suits. The name doesn't fit. Anyway, I don't like to hear that rustling sound they make and they are for fat and frumpy women who've let themselves go to pot. They're for women who can't button or zip regular clothes. Can't you just imagine the noise we would both make on our walking tours if we wore those ugly old whistley wind suits?

Mama wrote that she sat quietly in church trying to sing, but all she could think about was what my father had said about packing and his attire. She spent the next few days giving it some deep thought.

"We will be gone seventeen days," she informed him. "I plan to take 8½ outfits. I will wear 8 of them twice. Then, on the two dressy nights I will wear half an outfit."

He didn't say another word.

Once arriving in Spain, their vacation got off to a rocky start after a bunch of old codgers set the tone by saving seats at every turn. Mama thought that mess ended in junior high, but apparently it rekindles during the golden years.

She looked around and was beginning to wonder as men doled out their 12-inch pill organizers and women clutched walkers and Kleenex tissues. She was thinking that this was some sort of last-fling trip the frail and dying had booked, and walked over to an enormous picture window and wondered, "When will the fun begin?"

My dad found it fast. Gazing out the window, he pointed and nudged, trying to get my mom to look. His eyes had honed in on the topless bathing beauties all around the pool.

"Peg, there's tits galore down there, come here and look."

"Sam, I'm a good Baptist woman and don't care to see poolside hussies greasing up their milking machines. You didn't tell me the beach and pool would be topless. Is this why you wanted to come? So you could have a teat feast? Is that why the vacation was so cheap because we're staying in a brothel?" She continued and Daddy couldn't get a word in edgewise. "Why, all the people in this hotel are in their seventies. I bet the hotel paid those girls to sit out there and make all the poor widowers forget their dead wives. I'll bet their dead wives are rolling around in their little coffins wishing they could come back and sock it to their horny old husbands daring to look at these harlots out here. I hope you're not planning on actually going swimming in that pool. You might catch mange or worse . . . maybe those things Susan talks about . . . What does she call them? Crotch crickets. That's it. I'm sure there's not enough chlorine in the world to sanitize that bunch of—"

"Come on and look, Peg," Dad said. "Don't be such a prude all the time. The Lord didn't mean for Christians to be stiff old bores. Get over here now." He yanked Mama to the window and there they were, glistening like greasy hot dogs on a grill.

She caught her breath. "With this kind of operation going on in here, I doubt anybody will want to tour the cathedrals and the historic Great Mosque of Córdoba, don't you reckon?"

"Nothing like seeing a bit of God's glory before checking out his churches," Dad said, grinning and drinking red wine.

"Close those drapes, Sam, I mean it. How did we end up on this upper floor right above these prostitutes? We've got a world out there God has decorated! Beautiful, high mountains with the Mediterranean Sea at their feet. We don't need this pool filth going on below us, so I want you to call the management now and tell them we didn't pay hard-earned American dollars to see a peep show."

Daddy grinned and drank. He knew that once she swallowed her horse pill of hormones she'd settle down. He had the decency to close the drapes and join his wife at the table as they discussed the activities that lay ahead. They decided to return to the hotel lobby to see if anyone had shown up worth talking to, someone besides grouches and seat savers.

To my mother's utter joy, a blessing arrived in the form of a spitfire from Cape Fear, North Carolina. This little lady had a penchant for multiple husbands and glasses of beer.

Her name was Mary Elizabeth, and by her side was husband Number Three, Frank.

"I've never had a divorce," she said. "I just loved them all to death. After the second one died, I said, 'No more.' But Frank came along, and he was so hard to resist. We had so much in common. We both play golf, we both love God, and we both like to get all beered up and have fun."

Mama was instantly drawn to this 78-year-old charmer who talked with her entire body, muscles in sync and motion with every word from her mouth. She seemed to have a permanent smile, and her eyes flickered in tears of mirth and booze. Mama knew she'd met a true friend in Mary Elizabeth when the conversation at dinner turned to her favorite subject: funeral preparations and death.

"Well now, Mary Elizabeth," my mother said, "I'll tell you, I really was afraid to fly and just knew that our plane would be hijacked and we would be killed. Sam said we shouldn't let those terrorists scare us, so we decided not to cancel and to be brave. I did prepare, though, just in case I didn't survive." She explained how she'd gathered up a stack of Post-it notes and a pen and sneaked from chair to cabinet, from dish to diamond, tagging items with names so everyone would know who got what in the event of an untimely demise.

"I put them where Sam couldn't see them because he would

laugh at me," Mama told her new best friend. "I told my oldest that if we died, to make sure my flowers were red to match the flag on her dad's coffin. I mean, if our caskets are beside each other, pink flowers would clash with the red, white and blue flag on his casket."

Mary Elizabeth smiled and sipped her second or third beer. "I did all of that, too. I put names on all my furniture. My kids know about my wishes, too. I'm to be buried in a teddy."

"A teddy?" My mother thought she meant a stuffed bear.

"I got three teddies," said this woman nearing 80.

Her husband just sat there nonplussed, as if accustomed to his wife's wild escapades and notions. My mother, realizing a teddy was skimpy lingerie, soared into sheer heaven, having met someone else with whom to discuss "arrangements."

"Mary Elizabeth," Mom said, "are you going to wear a teddy underneath your funeral dress?"

"The teddy," she said, "will be the only thing I have on."

"Do what?"

"That's it. At least I didn't pick the crotchless kind Frank prefers. My teddy is lime green and I'm having an open casket."

After that trip ended, I was hoping their European travels were over and their jetsetting thirsts had been quenched, but I was wrong. They signed up again a year later and returned with more wild stories.

Germany and Austria

My mama finally returned from her three-week riverboat ride through Europe, but not without fatigue and a hint of too much pampering in her voice.

She sighed and grouched up while talking on the phone one night, compliments of jet lag and the full-service life she's more accustomed to giving than getting. I was happy she had enjoyed such an indulgent trip and that she wasn't too terribly busy to send postcards, some of which I'll never throw away.

Postcards from the edge

Here is one she sent my 2-year-old daughter, featuring a huge yellow duck on the front.

Dear Lindsey:
Mama Peg and Sampy are in Austria today. We are having a wonderful time. The ship is beautiful and everyone is old. The lounge looks like a nursing home with a bar. Lots of wheelchairs and canes. One woman's hair has not moved since we've been here. We love you.
Mama Peg and Sampy.

Next came the postcard from Germany.

Hi! We love this trip. The ship, food, and people are wonderful. Lots of old codgers aboard. Our room is great. We have a large wide window and the scenery is outstanding. We toured this monastery before leaving the Danube that has 365 windows, one for each day of the year. We love you.

Then came the final correspondence, a real doozy from Bamberg:

Hi! We still love our trip. They keep us so busy. Not much time to write cards. There is a lady on this boat who thinks she KNOWS EVERYTHING! She loves to complain and fuss. I call her "Mad Dog." One man came to high tea in a bathrobe and bare feet. He did remember to insert his teeth, but only after I told him I couldn't eat pancakes while staring at his big black hole.
Your dad enjoyed his birthday on the boat. They all sang "Happy Birthday" to him and gave him a cake with a firecracker for a candle.
As for the lady whose hair hasn't moved, she let me take a picture of it today.
Miss You, Mama.

I called my mother to further investigate her obsession with the woman whose hair was like a mannequin's and never so much as let loose a single wisp.

"It was the most beautiful French twist," Mama exclaimed as if critiquing fine art. "She said she'd gone to her hairdresser and said, 'Fix my hair so that it won't budge for nineteen days.' I kept waiting for her hair to collapse. Each day I looked it over for signs of defeat, but it just stayed put. I told her I wanted to be there with my camera when it came apart.

"It never did fall, but by the end of the cruise, it had started catching debris. Little fuzzballs were hanging off the back. I guess she couldn't see them because there weren't any in front where she could pick those out."

I formed a mental picture of a woman's hair like a spider-web, sticky and sturdy, a variety of items trapped in her Aqua Net.

"Were there gum wrappers back there, too?" I asked mother, who was still tired, still spoiled and snappish.

"I told you what was back there. Fuzzballs. And maybe a few specks of lint."

France

The next year, when they signed up with the same tour company to do a riverboat through France, I knew Mama would again get a fixation. She chose as her target of interest a man named Paul, whom she kept calling Bill, which I'll explain later.

"One day I was walking on a tour and all of a sudden a man whisked in front of me and fell down to his knees," Mama said, a thick pack of photos from the trip in her plastic Louvre bag. "His name was Paul, but we'll just call him Bill because that's what I called all the men, since from behind, with their gray hair and their blue jackets and khakis, they all looked like a man I'd met named Bill earlier in the cruise."

"She called everybody Bill," Dad said, accustomed to his

wife's quirks. "Anytime we ran into someone she'd smile and say, 'Hi there, Bill.'"

Anyway, Paul (Bill) was down on his knees in front of my mother picking up empty Marlboro cigarette packs.

"He brought them up," Mama said, "and would proclaim: 'I have to pick these up. It's a sheer necessity.'"

"Why's that?" I asked her.

"Because, Susan, and he said this to everyone listening: 'The first wife takes it all. Just up and takes it all. That woman over there is my second wife. Now I pick up empty cans and Marlboro packs.'"

My mother thought he was telling a whopper. How could he afford this trip if he was some kind of nickel-this-and-dime-that kind of man? Soon as he got his words out he called over to his wife to verify his habit of getting trash.

"He summoned this absolutely beautiful woman up to him," Mama said. "She was striking, with this silver hair and blue eyes. He brings her on over and says, 'Look at this fine jacket Joyce's wearing. I got it with these Marlboro coupons.'"

"Well, I just love it," Mama said. "It's just perfect for the French Riviera."

"She's got the pants at home to match," he said proudly as he scanned the countryside. "What I'd like you to do while we're here in France is help me. I'm trying to save enough to buy the rubber raft, so I'll train you how to spot them."

"Spot what?" Mama asked.

"The spent Marlboro packs. Once you get them, I'll show you how to cut the coupons off the back."

My mother was intrigued. She could not believe this Country Club type with the glamorous wife was hunting crinkled cig packets and soda cans.

While they viewed the Eiffel Tower, he viewed the ground below.

"By the time I have you trained, you can go back to the USA and start collecting and mailing them to us," he said. "I really do want that rubber raft."

One night at dinner, everyone dressed for the Captain's

table and the two couples sat together. As a side note, I'll explain. Kooks tend to migrate toward one another. No further explanation needed.

My father, after sipping several native wines, dared ask how Paul (Bill) had met such a lovely woman as Joyce. Paul sat up taller and said in a voice meant for everyone in earshot to hear: "We met at a rape and sodomy trial."

My parents continued to eat. These are people accustomed to craziness. "Well," my daddy said to Joyce, the wine and wit pinkening his cheeks, "I hope he was found not guilty."

By then the sweet, glamorous wife in the Marlboro jacket spoke up. "Oh, no," she said. "We were on the jury. He asked me to lunch during the recess. I should have known what I was getting into because all he did while we were out was look down at the ground and pick up old cigarette packages and sticky cans."

Paul (Bill) said the Marlboro people would call him periodically, to see how he was enjoying his smokes. He'd tell them how wonderful they were, though he'd never smoked a cigarette in his life.

For the remainder of the trip, as my mother continued calling all the men Bill and my father bandaged his fatigue with wine, the geriatric Marlboro man kept his nose to the ground.

"He picked the whole time," Mama said, showing me pictures of him and his lovely second wife. "One night I was down the gangplank, the ramp or whatever that thing coming you off the boat, and I heard a swish and looked to see a spent pack of Marlboros right in front of me. I did down to pick it up and heard someone laughing. I ed over to the side and Paul was right there, sort of hiding. d thrown them at me as part of the training."

"I just wanted to make sure you knew to pick them up," he said. "I'll teach you how to cut them later on."

My mother stood there smiling.

"First wives," he said again. "They get it all."

Holland

Last year Mom and Dad decided to hit Amsterdam on another seventeen-day riverboat cruise. If she thought the tits in
Spain were shocking, that was nothing compared to what she
would soon see in the Red Light District.

As much as she feared hussies, this was the smuttiest place
on earth, and I couldn't help but laugh out loud thinking how
my mom, The Hussy-Prevention Specialist, would, of all people, soon be in Amsterdam's Red Light District. For all I knew,
Daddy probably told her it was an area of art and lots of beautiful lights like the kind put up at Christmas.

She and my father, a randy Baptist who doesn't mind the
occasional brush with a hussy, were on the fourteenth day of
their European cruise when the ship drew closer to decadence.
All the fine people on the boat were in the lounge, propped up
by wheelchairs, canes and wineglasses. The tour director
bounded forth with great exuberance and announced:

"Tonight, we will sail all night, out of Germany and into
Holland. We will be in Amsterdam when you wake up."

The guide rattled tamely about the wooden shoe shop
they'd visit, then said, "And later, we'll have something a little
different in store. We will be touring the Red Light District."

At that point, men sprung from their wheelchairs, jumping
up and down in thunderous claps and whoops.

"Now listen, folks," the tour guide said, trying to hush the
excited men, one whose cane and composure had become un-
hinged. "Don't bother to attend unless you are physically fit
and can keep up with the group. Also, the bicycles will run
over you. I repeat, they WILL run over you. And absolutely
no cameras. These women have day jobs, and they don't want
their bosses seeing pictures spread everywhere."

The next day, shortly before 6 PM, the lounge was abuzz
with passengers awaiting the Mother of All Hussy Tours.

"Something was missing," Mama noticed, scanning the
room. "All the medical aids. No walkers, no canes. These ail-
ing and immobile people who'd been slow as snails all week

had come alive, mostly the men who hobbled to the front of the line."

Once there, they descended farther and farther into the recesses of hedonism. "It was an alley with a canal running down the middle of the street," Mama said, describing the district. "Buildings on both sides housed the girls, and all had huge, wide picture windows like stores. The women compete trying to entice you to come in. They had on underwear, no nudity."

My father saw something out of the corner of his eye. He whispered into Mama's ear.

"Are you thirsty?" he asked.

"Yes. Matter of fact I'm parched."

"There's a water fountain over there," he said, pointing to a man's thingamabob spewing water.

Mama gasped and Daddy roared. She decided to remain in a state of thirst.

Up until that point, Mama said she hadn't worried too much about the working girls' plate glass come-ons.

"No decent man would want them," the Great Hussy Eradicator said. "I actually heard some of the men say, 'No Way!' That is, until we got to the Window Washer. Oh, no, this girl was knockout gorgeous. She was standing in her window looking all innocent in her white lace underwear."

As Miss Lace O' Matic saw the tour group approaching—men who looked more like deacons than customers, women who looked more like missionaries than madams—she cranked up her show.

"She starts spraying that window all over with her Windex," Mama said. "The group was now gazing in at her." There was a dead silence. Mama wondered where the woman's paper towels might be hiding.

"No need for them," she said. "Why, that girl stepped up to her foaming window and dried it with her bra and the back of her panties. I've never seen such motion and shimmying. Can you imagine that?"

As Mom and Dad were walking back to the cruise ship, Dad reached for her hand and pulled her in close. He knew she'd had Hussy Overload. He knew it was all too much for his sweet bride.

"Tomorrow," Mama said, "I'm hoping for a cathedral. You've seen your T&A and now I need to see sweet Jesus and Mary."

How can a decent man argue with that?

Career Day Including a Skull in a Stomach

One of my literary heroes is Laurie Notaro, a former Gannett columnist turned best-selling author who admitted in one of her delightful books she was almost a flop during Career Day at one of the area schools.

As a columnist and writer, lots of schools have asked me to join in Career Day, that chance for elementary- and middle-school students to see that there are jobs out there besides wearing paper hats and spreading mustard and mayo or cooking up some meth in a singlewide in the hills.

A bunch of so-called respectable types with careers that come with major props (a big draw with the kids) are always setting up their fancy booths and gadgets at these things, but what does a writer have? Well, we have pencils, newspapers, paper clips, sticky notes, laptops, cameras and other office staples no child in his or her right mind would jam a booth to get their grubby hands on.

If the writer is on friendly terms with the Prize Patrol Promotions employee at the office, she might be able to snag a few water bottles, litter bags, small footballs and whatnots with the newspaper logo imprinted upon them.

I BEGGED the prize lady at my office for some giveaways but she flat-out ignored me, bless her heart, the precious evil thing. I told her if she couldn't even cough up a few pens, I'd be a huge flop at Career Day, but I think this may have caused her great glee. That darling and adorable woman who gave zilch to pass along to greedy kids is no longer with the company. The fact that all those potential prizes probably went home in her trunk matters not.

A woman must rise above such things. While I may not have material goods to attract children and teens to my booth, I had a big mouth and a mind full of wild and mostly true stories. Embellishments aren't just for outfits and window treatments.

If only I hadn't said that the poor prize-patrol woman had that unfortunate mole hair resembling that of the pubic area, and if only someone hadn't overheard me and told her, then maybe she would have sprung for some nice prizes like the foam-rubber footballs she joyfully handed over to a male columnist when he did a Career Day gig.

As it was, I had nothing but a booth and some charm, though at 7 AM it's hard to rouse up a grin and energy discussing my job. This is where great, whopping fibs come into the picture.

Don't get me wrong. In Career Days past, I played it straight and showed the bored-to-tears kids the newspaper and all its sections and explained how one could get a job as a journalist covering all sorts of exciting things others would never have a chance to cover.

"Like what?" asked a boy not too embarrassed to pick his nose and flat-out eat a booger.

"Well, like going to the city council meetings and hearing about new fire codes. Or maybe learning before anyone else how the city is planning to annex a portion of Allendale Road so as to increase the tax base."

They walked away frowning, disgusted and prizeless. They found the military booth and got to hold bombs and weapons. They discovered the firefighters and grabbed their big old hoses and were even allowed to douse small, contained fires!

Even the health care workers had goods: a blood pressure machine, guaranteed to amputate small arms, along with free rubber hearts. The athlete's booth had a freakin' climbing wall that took hours to rig up in the gym.

I just sat there alone at my booth drinking coffee and pretending to be awake.

I had taken along one of my Laurie Notaro collections and reread her Career Day story when she was all but upstaged by a little dog that had replaced her column spot for a day, and her experiences with the various PROPSTERS who lured in little kids with their fancy getups and giveaways.

And so there I sat in my son's middle-school gymnasium, reading passages of Laurie's nearly failed Career Day story. With her permission and blessings, here's a portion of her text:

"Here I was," she wrote, "a guest speaker at a middle school and I hadn't brought one single prop. Not one. I hadn't even pulled into the parking lot, and already I was a miserable failure."

At least, she reasoned, someone thought she had a career.

Which is what I tried to tell myself as I agreed to sit in the gym for five hours while seven-hundred kids armed with the same nine questions tried to pretend they gave a flying rat's ass about my job.

I mean, come on. Who wants to know about being a newspaper columnist, both of which Laurie and I were/are? Only she has several *New York Times* best-selling books, and I don't.

That aside, I knew from reading her Career Day story I needed props and prizes, and that the kids wouldn't come near me if they didn't get so much as a free paper clip, which I managed to pilfer from the supply closet.

Laurie learned this the hard way. As she entered the school, she was dismayed by all the props and extras the others had brought. The pilot—all gussied up—toted a globe. A racecar driver had the gumption to haul in a massive trailer, car and accessories. A woman doing facials gave out glitter and samples. A baker doled out freshly made cupcakes, and a veterinarian appeared with a batch of puppies at his booth.

As the day progressed, the questions flew for Laurie.

"How much do you make?" they all wanted to know.

"Less than half of any male columnist," Laurie said.

"Which is what?" the kids continued.

"Um, gosh, I don't know," she fumbled. "More than selling your plasma, how's that?"

I knew if Laurie Notaro could survive Career Day unscathed, I could give it a go as well.

The promotions department's assistant somehow found a giant banner and fifty foam-rubber footballs. I was so euphoric I wanted to invite her to dinner.

The big dilemma was trying to figure out how to stretch fifty footballs into seven-hundred—the number of students who would come thundering through the gym from 7:45 AM until noon.

I walked in with my banner and footballs and set up shop. Then I looked around at the props. Mercy! How could my blue banner compete with the gadget that shot flames—real fire? Or the booth where hammering and construction were under way?

The real sinker was my booth's placement—directly across from the military man's, who would raise his many guns in demonstration and rip off a few thunderous rounds.

Naturally, that's where all the middle-schoolers migrated. I don't blame them. I wanted to handle the gun, too. I could think of myriad uses for that weapon, but instead, sat there and waited for the clumps of kids who'd heard I had a few footballs hidden under my table. They'd ask the obligatory questions as their little eyes searched for where I'd stashed the loot.

"What helped you most in your current career while you were in junior high?" they all asked, my favorite question.

"Well, I'd say it was being teased about having buck teeth and giant horse ears that helped me most in my current career. It gave me compassion for others."

They walked away stunned. A lucky few carried foam-rubber footballs. The others stuck up their noses and harrumphed.

My favorite part of the day was when a student fresh from Yugoslavia or the Ukraine, a beautiful girl who knew about twelve words of English, scanned my newspaper, trying to figure out what exactly I did for a living. Her eyes fell upon the ad for Murphy beds.

"You a Murphy bed?" she asked.

I smiled. "Yes. I sure am. I love being a Murphy bed and promise it's a great career." I gave her my last football and waved good-bye with a huge smile.

The day ended and I was as crumpled inside as out. I told myself NO MORE CAREER DAYS EVER!

That lasted a year or two until one day a teacher friend buttered my ass up good and I agreed to drive twenty miles to her little elementary school in the country and talk to many different classes of fourth- and fifth-graders who'd rotate from room to room to learn about different careers.

I sat my big butt in a rocker and waited on the little pretties to come in so I could regale them with tales of the fabulous life of newspaper writing. No more boring old stories of land-use disputes and arguments over the new site for the Super Wal-Mart. Since I didn't have a single freebie to give, I'd have to use what I knew best: humor and tall tales. Plus, a few naughty business cards promoting my PG-13-rated book I'm sure their parents would later love.

It was a day of no props but lots of shocks. I had an arsenal of wild stories and was ready to fire. Maybe I'd tell them about the groundhog I saw cooking in someone's Crock-Pot. Or perhaps the severed hand in the bucket a coroner once forced me to view.

The first class came in and took their seats, expectant looks on their faces as they searched my rocker for signs of goody bags and prizes. At first, while my teacher friend was in the room observing, wearing her fine churchy clothes and sweet Junior League–like manners, I remained well behaved.

"This is Mrs. Reinhardt who writes for the paper and she's going to tell you all you need to know about this exciting career, and you may ask her questions later."

I started off boring and normal, minding my manners. As soon as the teacher felt comfortable enough to leave her charges and head down to the break room for coffee and danish, I switched gears faster than a NASCAR driver does.

"What's your favorite story?" most of them would ask.

"Well, now. Funny you should ask." A zillion went through my head: The one about the psycho who squirted semen through a straw at ladies shopping at various stores around town, getting it all in their hair and on their clothing. Or I could tell them about the sicko castration ring going on in the more western part of the county. But even I knew better than to say these things.

Why not, though, tell them about the man who had half his head in his stomach?

I had just met this wonderful gentleman who had grown a chunk of his skull in his stomach for medical purposes and I knew the kids would be overjoyed to hear about Jake and his unusual medical procedure.

"His name," I said as if telling a scary story, "is Jake Boosinger and he loved playing golf better than anything else in this whole wide world."

In order to play his best Tiger Woods–like game, he would need a hip replacement. I explained to the kids who wanted to know what that was and I said it's when they slice you open and blood runs down the floor and doctors take out the old bone and put in a fake one, but it's OK because you can walk better later.

Oh, I had them enraptured, and kept checking the door to make sure the teacher hadn't come back.

"This Jake man," I said, "all of a sudden had a massive stroke and—"

"What's a stroke?" about five of them asked.

How would I explain? "It's when your brain blows up, pretty much," I said, capturing their attention, all eyes wider than a spooked cow's.

"Anyway, children, Jake wasn't ready to die. There was only one way on this planet to save his life."

They waited on their haunches, leaning in for the answers.

"What? What? What?" they chanted.

"This may sound strange but his brain swelled and swelled and kept right on swelling just like that girl in *Willy Wonka & the Chocolate Factory*—you know, that blueberry girl?" They all nodded. "If something radical and major wasn't done, his would have exploded, you see, shot straight out of his skull like a cannon ball.

"The surgeon had a wonderful idea and told the family it was a long shot. They said, 'We can remove part of his skull and plant it in his abdomen—'"

"What's an abdomen?" half a dozen asked.

"A stomach, you stupid idiot," answered a boy in the front row.

"They planted half his skull inside his stomach so it could attach to the vital blood vessels and tissues—those are things you need to keep body parts going—so that part of his head wouldn't die, you see."

They all raised their hands as if they needed to pee in their pants from the excitement.

"We'll take questions in a minute," I said, checking the door again for the teacher, knowing this would get me kicked out of Career Day in a heartbeat.

"They used to put the skulls in the refrigerators during these cases, but it works better to bury them in the tummy, doctors have discovered. It's the same surgery that saved Roy Horn's life."

Eyes narrowed. "Whose life?"

"Roy Horn's. The famous magician and tiger trainer from Las Vegas who had his skull removed after that tiger got hold of him during a show."

Oh, they were loving this. Yes, who needed prizes or a climbing wall? Who needed gunfire or puppies? That's for Career Day sissies.

"How long would he have to have his head down there near his dick?" the nasty little boy up front asked, and others snickered.

"What's a dick?" a few of the more innocent and properly raised children asked.

"Go home and ask your mothers. Tell them this little boy said it aloud in class and that will resolve the matter.

"Now, back to the story. Once the man's brain healed, they were able to replace the skull bone. But, you see, for a while he only had half a head. There was a giant dent where the other half went missing, but they covered it with a minitarp or something of that nature."

You should have seen the dropped jaws and staring.

"This is a big fat lie," the mean, nasty-mouthed boy said. "You're a lying bitch."

Hands flew up. "What's a bitch?" several chanted.

"Go home and ask your mother. Tell her this same boy that said 'dick' also used the word 'bitch.'" I stared down this hellion child with my meanest look. "At least I don't say bad words and, yes, the story is true. It's in the paper this week. I doubt you can read anything but filth and maybe your daddy's *Penthouse*s."

"What's a *Penthouse*?" more children asked.

I was about to give up and tried to stay on course. "The operation is called a hemicraniectomy. Write that down for extra credit," I said. "The doctors asked the family what they wanted to do and Jake's daughter thought for just a split second and said, 'Scrub up,' and then Jake said, 'Go ahead and cut off the top of my head.'"

I told them how the doctors took off 80 percent of the right side of Jake's skull and created a skin flap in his abdomen to place the bone just beneath.

"Did he die? What happened? Where is he now?" The questions flew like a just-opened cage of butterflies.

"Nobody really knew if he'd survive the surgery," I said with a great rise and fall of the voice, like a musical concert. "But four hours later he woke up. His family was scared his wonderful wit and personality would be gone.

"But old Jake opened up his eyes and took two fingers and tapped them on his head."

Ah, what a bunch of spellbound children. And no teacher to stop me from rattling on.

"Abby Normal," he said. I knew the kids wouldn't get the reference to the movie *Young Frankenstein*, but they laughed anyway.

Sometimes in hospitals dogs come in to visit patients, I told them. Well, crazy old Jake told the nurses, "If you see a dog running out of here with a skull in his mouth, you better find him 'cause he's likely to bury it and won't remember later where he put it. When they took out the staples from my head, I told them doctors, 'Well now, how can I get any good radio stations if all my hardware is gone?'"

More laughter. I was a hit. A propless wonder.

"You guys want to know the kicker?"

Yeah, Yeah, Yeah! they all shouted.

"When the trick-or-treaters came around to the nursing home for Halloween, everyone wanted to knock on Jake's door to see the man with the skull in his stomach.

"Jake played it up big. He lifted his shirt and showed the kids the hard, round spot where a chunk of his head was prominently visible. He told them he'd prefer they knock on his skull than his door and he'd give them some candy."

"How is he now?" one sweet child wanted to know.

"He's great. He's just hoping the hair will grow back on the bald part of his head. They put the skull back in place but there's no hair. He told the nurses he was hoping to get some of it to grow back, kind of like a Chia Pet, you see."

"I saw a Chia Dick on the Internet," the evil, trashy boy said.

I scanned the room and saw no sign of the teacher. I walked up to his face, got half an inch from his eyeballs and said, "Because of your foul mouth, I'm quite certain that one day, you'll have your own head festering somewhere in your gullet. You better shut that foul little mouth of yours up or next time I come here, I'm going to staple it or seal it permanently with my boiling-hot glue gun. Got that?"

He said nothing.

Career Day was over. I handed out my naughty bookmarks and they wanted my autograph. My giftless, prizeless talk was a hit. Funny thing is, I never heard back from the teacher or got any thank-you notes from the classes. Then, a few years later, perhaps her memory failing, that same sweet teacher invited me to come back.

All I could think of was that the poor woman must be really desperate. Or maybe the firemen and blood-pressure cuffers couldn't make it.

For Sale on eBay: My Husband

My husband, Tidy Stu, has taken a hiatus from cleaning. He still alphabetizes and sizes the canned goods, Campbell's on one side, Progresso on the other and so on and so forth; however, things are changing.

And this time I didn't have to drug him or poison his tea with a nice dose of Lexapro or Zoloft. He willingly gave up the Tilex and scrub brush that were as much a part of his wardrobe as T-shirts and baggy jeans were. Part of it had to do with being middle-aged and his back going out on him. Funny how men's backs can suddenly blow and they still have the power to seek contortionist's activity on the Sealy Extra Firms.

The other reason he up and quit cleaning is the Internet, which, for all its worth, is nothing but seduction at the fingertips.

Tidy's gotten himself all cozy with the computer, like a lot of men out there who stay frozen to a screen. Mouse potatoes are what my writer friend calls them. Porn Poachers, says another cynical woman whose husband ran off with a hussy he "met" in one of the chat rooms, and he a preacher no less!

Tidy Stu has not, thank the good and generous Lord, been going to FindObedientwives.com. or ComeSeeMyBigUns. com. Instead, he's taken a fancy to playing Internet checkers, and he sits for hours at the screen yipping and verbally assaulting his opponents.

"Ah, you big, dumb shit not seeing that easy move. Get ready to say good-bye, you puny-peckered checker boy!"

"Please, Stuart. We have children with big ears. They hear every word you say. Remember when Lindsey was only three and called two people 'assholes,' then told those two old men, 'I'm gonna bust yo ass,' after you let her watch that Eddie Murphy movie seven times? Please, careful what you say in front of them."

I pictured 12-year-old kids somewhere in the world, being stomped by Tidy Stu, the reigning King of Internet Checkers, his filthy mouth floating from our screen doors on summer months and rising up the hill to the house where the Prayer People have godly and decent meetings every single night of the week, not just on Sundays and Wednesdays like Baptists. They line their cars along the street, night and day, for the sake of living a pure and decent life, and I'd hate to think they hear streams of "Fuck you, Checker Pecker!" echoing from our front door and right into the center of their prayer circles.

One night as Stu sat at the computer cussing his opponents, I offered to prepare him a nice meal with a boudoir bonus if he'd skip Internet checkers. Since this addiction began, he has not budged for hours except to pee and open up a box of Cheez-It crackers or pour a bowl of Lucky Charms.

"Hon, don't you think you'd like a nice, home-cooked supper and something a little extra later on after the kids are asleep?"

"Extra? We're down to twice a season and dropping. I'm almost desperate enough to find the dog rather fetching," he said, not turning his head or blinking an eye. He held that mouse for dear life and clicked all over the checkerboard-patterned computer screen.

"Ah, what a big, fat asshole," he said, turning to face me. "I whipped him and, look, he's quitting. What a limp wimp."

This habit of my husband's could mean another round of medications in his tea, only he won't take beverages I serve anymore after discovering the Zoloft incident a couple of years ago when I was trying to lower his libido and cleaning obsessions by offering him a delicious serotonin reuptake-inhibiting elixir.

I'm often eating lunches with Ma Ferguson, my precious friend whose marriage ceremony I had to finish when her reverend's colostomy bag exploded and he handed me the Bible, while someone called 911.

Ma and I get together regularly and complain about not being loved enough, not nearly as adored as we deserve and treated worse than our dogs that at least get watered, fed and petted daily.

"What's wrong?" she asked. "You look beat. Do you need a Darvocet?"

"This is how I always look," I said. "Aged and . . . well . . ."

"Well, what?" Ma asked. "You can tell me. Is it work? Are they still trying to make you cover all those Lions Club pancake breakfasts? Is that one woman still always threatening you're next to be fired?"

I let my head fall back, as if I had no neck. "Yeah, but there's nothing I can do about her. My new mantra is this: 'If one door closes and slams the shit out of your big toe, another will open and offer you a pedicure.' That's why I don't care what she does to me anymore. What's dental insurance? A medical plan? A 401(k), retirement and a pension plan compared to the freedom of government cheese and WIC?"

"They don't give out government cheese anymore," Ma said. "And WIC is only for women who are pregnant."

I threw my loose head to my knees and wouldn't look up.

"What's wrong, honey? I haven't seen you like this since you thought Stuart was cheating with that woman who ate her baby's placenta."

"Oh, mercy. No. Nothing like that," I said, and started laughing until the tears pooled. "She took that placenta to the apothecary and had him make vitamin tablets and cooked the rest for her husband in the freakin' Crock-Pot. This is nothing like that. It's just that Stuart has a bit of a problem that's cutting into his time cleaning, earning a living and even using the bathroom. It wouldn't surprise me if he bought a catheter and some Depends."

Ma Ferguson, right before she bursts into laughter, always wears a mask of concern that's sheer as a bride's veil. Any minute she'll fall over in fits of hysterics.

"He's got an addiction, Ma."

"Oh, honey, I'm so sorry. We can do an intervention or call—"

"No, it's not drugs. It's . . . it's . . ." I couldn't stop laughing. "Don't you laugh, OK?"

She pulled me up from the floor and onto her brown leather sofa. "You know I would never laugh at a serious problem."

Before I could get the words out I couldn't stop laughing long enough to tell her the story. I fell from the couch again and rolled around on the floor, grabbing my stomach and bottom in case I peed or my uterus fell out. After a good five long minutes of whooping it up, I finally grew composed enough to tell the story. Meanwhile, I looked up to see Ma sprinkling holy water around the room and could feel drops wetting me like tears. She must have thought the Devil had entered my soul.

"Hon, he's got him a big problem," I said.

And Ma Ferguson patted my shoulders, then held one hand, the other working the sign of the cross.

"It's OK. Tell me. We can go in the laundry room and pray afterward and you'll feel so much better."

I pictured all her Virgin Marys and Jesuses next to the washer/dryer units and started laughing all over again. "Ma, it's not like that. He's addicted to playing checkers online and cussing out his opponents, and he can't stop, not even for sex, so you know it's a disorder.

"He goes on there for hours, yelling at the people he plays with and types in the meanest things to them. He calls them the Sons of Bitches and Shitheads of the Checkers World. He told one poor kid who was beating him, 'Until your pecker hits the three-inch mark don't even join in when you see my name on the game.' It's awful, really."

The sound of Stu's addiction when said aloud was so crazy we both doubled over howling. "He doesn't even beg for the booger anymore," I said, referring to his vulgar sex advances and pet name for my underused and cobwebbed possum.

She fanned herself with a Burger King bag. "That's a shame. Internet checkers. I never knew there was such a thing. Where does he find people to play?"

"Apparently there's a whole subculture of nerds, intellects, drunks or plain old unhappily married men and adolescents who sit around a checkerboard hollering at their computer screens and cussing each other out for kicks."

Ma Ferguson couldn't catch her breath. She was in hysterics, fanning and falling over, eyes all watery and wobbling.

"It could be worse," she said, snorting and coughing up what sounded like esophagus parts.

"Yeah, I guess he could be hooking up with those lonely, desperate women who are out there waiting to wreck marriages with their red lace teddies and lies. At least he's doing something in full view of everyone."

"It beats his obsession with the canned goods and pasta boxes being in order from smallest to tallest, right?"

"He still does that. This checkers thing . . . You know, he's really good at it, too. He goes to the expert level and socks it to 'em."

Ma fetched a bag of chips and two O'Douls. "You know you have to be smart to play checkers," she said, wiping streaks of mascara from her face. "You must be so proud."

I gave this some thought. She couldn't possibly be serious, but you never knew with her because she said things that Jesus would say when overcome with her religion, which she practices daily and is never stingy with the holy water and knick-knacks, though her husband, Pa Ferguson, often complains about her spending $60 a week on "those damned glass religious candles the Mexicans can't live without."

"In my viewpoint," I said, "checkers are like *Wheel of For-*

tune and chess is like *Jeopardy!* Even the dummies like the *Wheel* and can win SUVs and Hawaiian vacations, but only smart people can get the answers right on *Jeopardy!* I never play it or watch it because it just confirms what I've always suspected."

She crunched her Lay's and sipped her fake beer. "What's that, honey?"

"That I've always belonged in Special Needs classes."

Ma Ferguson told me not to worry and that this checkers addiction was just a passing fancy. One man's obsession with his Porsche or secretary is another man's Internet checkers.

"Just think how easily entertained he'll be in the nursing home," Ma said. "When you get ready to put him in, he'll be the best little resident. All neat and clean and alphabetizing the kitchen pantry, maybe even jumping for joy on Checkers Night."

"Yeah. I guess so. While the other geezers are pulling out their wilted pork swords and doing a number on them, Stu will be in the activity room playing checkers."

"That's true. You oughta feel blessed, really," she said, patting me again. "I know people who go from room to room in those rest homes and try to hump anything that breathes, whether they know them or not. It's sad and I know they aren't in their right minds, but must have memories of doing the old nasty 'cause there they go, pushing their wheelchairs up to beds and cracking bones just to climb in with some drooling stranger."

We fell down laughing all over again, and Ma closed her eyes, probably asking God for forgiveness, that dear woman.

I gave this some thought, and she was right, as usual. I'd heard about my great-great-grandmother at 94 boinking the bootlegger still young enough to have the birth cheese on him.

"I realize this is just a phase with Stu. It'll pass and something else will take its place."

Ma held my hand. "Everything comes to an end," she said. "Pa Ferguson stopped selling those paintings over the Internet and he got out of that pyramid thing he swore would make him a millionaire in ninety days."

Mercy, was she ever right. Tidy did, indeed, move on from checkers, but it was like Mama's promises of drug progression: first beer, then liquor, then pot, then hard drugs, then prostitution, then death . . ."

Stu's next addiction is one shared by millions: eBay. Nearly everything we currently own has of late arrived FedEx. The doorbell is always ringing at my house.

"Ma'am, your husband has another package. Sign, please."

"That's the fourth one today," I said, lugging in what must have been the third trumpet he'd won from eBay. He hunches at the computer when there are seconds left to bid and his fingers itch to be the top bidder as he pounces and types in his offer and typically wins and then starts up the cussfests he used to have during Internet checkers.

"You big dummy. Don't you know how to bid, you old mother . . ."

My son was listening. He's an adolescent testing us and nearly killing us with his back talk.

"Mother's only half a word," he said, laughing and walking away.

I got so tired of this addiction that I did what most wives do when they can't beat them. I joined him.

I created my own eBay account to see what all I'd been missing. Oh, what a land of pure glory, people. Within two days of scanning and searching for everything from hot buys on Groovy Girls to recreational vehicles, even old school buses, I was hooked.

Heed this warning from the novice and newest eBay addict: if you don't know how to bid, don't do it. The first couple of times I bid on something, I felt that giddy rush of a boozer in Vegas, rolling lucky sevens.

I'd won a Groovy Girls bed for my daughter's toy collection, saving all of 50 cents, but once shipping was figured in, I'd lost $4.95. Seems once a person wins a bid, her hands get hot and the fever strikes. I was now beginning to understand my husband's addiction as I sat at the keyboard and clicked in a bid for a microdermabrasion cloth, guaranteed to reduce all signs of aging and make me as pretty as Christie Brinkley or Angelina Jolie.

For $9.95 I could have poreless, flawless skin. Three days later, the FedEx man brought my prize to the door and I began scrubbing away, polishing age spots with the magic blue facial rag.

When that thrill ended, I decided to go for the chemical peels. At a reputable doctor's office, such peels can run between $100 and $500. But on eBay, I could buy enough acids to melt the skin off a rhino's hide for about $19.95. That was the equivalent of some twenty peels, worth thousands of dollars. One must be careful it's of a certain chemical grade or severe damage could occur, such as loss of entire face, blindness, death and dismemberment.

I won the bid, and a vial of acid arrived in the mail, complete with gloves, gauze pads, cotton swabs and WARNINGS! I washed my face and applied the acid, hollering and fanning my flaming cheeks.

A few days later my skin looked 100 years old. Within five days the old hag skin began to peel and slough off, and I was never sure where a piece of cheek or nose might land.

At the monthly meeting of the Read It or Not, Here We Come book club, I noticed a part of my smile had fallen in my lap along with a section of forehead.

"Watch your plate, Jocelyn," I said. "Seems the chin is next to go."

In the end, the peel worked fine, and my skin looked refreshed as promised. I do not recommend this for rational people. It's risky, and for about a week you'll scare small children and grown-ups who'll whisper, "Don't go near that woman unless you want your skin to rot, too."

A few days later I needed another fix, and I typed in my eBay password and bid on what was called "The Rolling Toaster," a 1973 Winnebago that resembled a toaster from the 1950s. When my husband learned of this, particularly the horror that my bid was winning, he disconnected the account.

"Why in the world would you bid on a broken-down RV called a 'Rolling Toaster'? Are you insane?"

"Probably."

"I don't get it? An RV?"

"I thought we might have some fun driving it across country. I thought it would be a hoot to own something called a 'Rolling Toaster.'"

"That piece of shit wouldn't make it five miles. Listen here. You are an unfit eBay abuser," he said. "Who in their right mind would buy an old Winnebago that doesn't even run?"

"The ad said it's in great shape."

"One sharp turn and that thing would be rolling for sure. Right off a cliff. Your eBay days are over. If you try to sign up again, I'm calling your mother."

He's always threatening to call my mother. I'm sick, sick, sick of that old trick. I've learned to call her first.

"Stu's fixin' to call you and tattle on me."

"I don't want to hear it," she says, and hangs up.

While my eBay days were temporarily over, his addiction continued to grow. Each day more of the fix was needed and sought, chased as if it was the elixir of life.

We own a violin with bad strings, a trumpet with missing pieces, a saxophone, a piano, a host of musical replacement parts, a laptop computer and nearly anything you can name without a heartbeat.

Usually, he gets good deals and decent products. But the last straw was the evening, cold sober, he bought a car sight unseen on eBay, and I was dumb enough to go along with it since I never got my Rolling Toaster. He sat glued to the computer for three days, waiting like a buzzard for the auction to expire so he could sink his MasterCard into a used luxury SUV. We'd owned one of these models before, and it had been a great car I'd bought from an Amish family who weren't supposed to be caught in such things.

I heard a loud whooping. "We won the bid!" he yawped.

"We always win the bid," I said gloomily as Eeyore. "Tell me we didn't get that car."

"It's nice. Look at these pictures. The guy selling it is a licensed dealer and has all positive feedback on his deals." I looked at the car. Yes, it seemed flawless for its age, but even so, I got on the phone with the seller. "This thing, was it pulled from the junkyard and fixed up like one of those poor, unfortunate women on that show *Extreme Makeover*?"

"No, it's a Jersey car."

"Was it in a flood, blizzard or other natural disaster?"

"No. It's a great car. My best friend owned it."

"Did he smoke?

Long pause. "No."

"Did he enjoy Taco Bell or McDonald's meals in this—"

Tidy Stu snatched the phone. Some husbands simply have to have the last word. This "nonsmoker's" car arrived from the Jersey Shore smelling like a giant ashtray and with a dozen major parts missing and hubcaps so rusted they appeared to have been salvaged from a major fire.

I dropped to my knees when I saw the movers unloading it. I was so shocked no tears fell, no sounds could squeak from my tightened vocal cords.

I pulled myself up and surveyed the vehicle.

"Oh, my goodness, toss me in the river alive!" I said. "The antenna's broken off, there's no CD player in the box, the seats are ripped, the bumper's half-torn away, the tires are balder than a Chinese Crested. And . . . Oh, gosh, I need a Valium IV drip! Would ya look at that? A hubcab's gone AWOL, and a chunk of leather and fabric have been chewed out of the side door panel. Check out the paint job. Some primate's painted the dings with Wite-Out or fingernail polish. Someone take me away!"

Just to have everything wrong righted was going to run close to $2,000.

"It's got a great engine," he said, lifting the hood with pride.

"Getting this car," I said to my beloved, "was like finding out your wife has a strong heart, hence your engine comments, but has no teeth, cirrhosis of the liver, one lung and a bum gallbladder."

This is the point at which I decided I'd have the FINAL word, a silent missive guaranteed to work much better than

Zoloft or oleander and would keep me out of an orange jump-suit or lying atop gurneys while anti-death-penalty activists chanted, "No More State-Supported Murder" and lit candles on my behalf.

This is why I decided it was time to put my husband up for sale on eBay. Drastic means call for drastic measures, as any woman married for more than five or six years will attest.

My ad read as follows:

For sale in fairly mint condition: a man who can turn mildew into sparkle, who can take a junk room and whip it into organized wonder within the day.

This prize of a guy takes two showers daily, and is great with kids and dogs, especially grooming them with unusual hairdos. He can also play the saxophone like Branford Marsalis and is not addicted to porn, but instead checkers on the Internet.

The bid starts at $50,000. Four days and six hours left on the clock. Reserve is $100,000. Free shipping in his own Lexus bought from the Jersey Shore or the junkyard.

The only problem with my eBay ad is I fear my husband will bid on himself.

If you bid right now, I'll throw in a free set of luggage bought on eBay and in great condition if you don't mind suit-cases with broken zippers and latches that don't shut.